A PRIEST AND THI

A PRIEST AND THE PARANORMAL

by

J. Dover Wellman

1988
CHURCHMAN PUBLISHING LIMITED

© Copyright J. Dover Wellman 1988
A Priest and the Paranormal
by
J. Dover Wellman
was first published in Great Britain in 1988
by
CHURCHMAN PUBLISHING LIMITED
117 Broomfield Avenue
Worthing
West Sussex
BN14 7SF

Publisher: E. Peter Smith

and distributed to the book trade
by
BAILEY BOOK DISTRIBUTION LIMITED
Warner House
Wear Bay Road
Folkstone
Kent
CT19 6PH

ISBN 1 85093 090 2
All Rights Reserved Worldwide

Printed and bound in Great Britain by
Biddles Limited, Guildford and King's Lynn

To

Dorothy, my wife

CONTENTS

Foreword   xi

An Introduction: The Soul and Its Faculties   xiv

PART ONE   Case Histories

1	Perils of the Ouija	3
2	A Case of Black Magic	10
3	A Case of Possession	17
4	Four Young People and a Dog	28
5	Three Addicts Receive a Blessing	37
6	A Haunting Exorcised	44
7	Disquiet from a Demon?	50
8	Funerals and Experience	55
9	A Case of Obsession	60
10	A Case of Transcendental Meditation	65
11	A Haunted Self	71
12	The Approach of Death	77
13	Two Cases of Harmful Hypnosis	83
14	A Poltergeist	91
15	Confidence Restored and a Guided Journey	97
16	When Words Fail	102
17	Angels of Childhood	110
18	Angelic Rescue	119
19	Air Raids and Phenomena	122
20	Witness to Angels	132
21	At Death's Portal	138
22	Animals	142

PART TWO   Essays on the Paranormal

 1 Release of the Spirit-Soul   151
 2 Worship — The Vehicle of E.S.P.   156
 3 The Aura — In Life and in Death   165
 4 The Aura and Mood   172
 5 Spiritual Healing   175
 6 Further Thoughts on Healing   178
 7 Miracles   182
 8 The New Creation   186
 9 The Seance   189
10 Revelation of the Beyond   196
11 Some Thoughts on the After Life   202
12 Hypnosis   209
13 Mysticism   216
14 A Speculation   222
15 The Nature of Angels   224
16 The Angels and Ourselves   228
17 The Ascension of Jesus Christ   233
18 The Great Commandment   236

FOREWORD

"At the name of Jesus *every* knee shall bow." These words of St. Paul, often lustily sung in churches as a hymn, state the Christian's conviction of the supremacy of his faith over all others.

He cannot, if he be true to the lordship of Christ, dilute his faith with the idea that other world religions are superior, or even equal, to his own in their tenets, practices or worship.

Christianity is the religion beyond compare and its prayerful hope is that *all* people shall come to recognise Jesus Christ as the *full* light of the world, the complete disclosure of God's loving relationship to man.

It is disturbing, therefore, that many desert Christianity with the excuse that Eastern religions, for example, offer them a more spiritual experience. It is even sadder when some who are unattached to any church engage in the occultism of bizarre cults which proliferate today. Although often dressed up in pseudo-scientific terms and modern idiom these are usually based on old pagan beliefs having nonsensical rituals which fascinate the impressionable.

The fault could lie in the failure of the orthodox Churches (who have become more and more engrossed in political, social and economic matters) to commend in a sufficiently persuasive and intelligent manner their spiritual doctrines and to provide an adequate teaching on mysticism. Without mysticism there can be no Christianity, or indeed any other religion.

I hope this book may encourage seekers after spiritual experience and enlightenment to turn only to the soundness of the Christian Faith. Moreover, to trust in the orthodox Churches because they provide balance of mind and spirit to safeguard from the serious psychological harm which is all too possible for those, especially the more sensitive and imaginative, who delve unprotected into the occult.

Selected from many others, the case histories I record in the beginning of the book may underline for all believers the glory of faith in Jesus Christ. In order to shed further light upon them the closing Essays have been included.

It has been my purpose not to use 'theological' terms to express Christian beliefs and doctrines. This may be at the risk of some tedium to those who are acquainted with them through regular churchgoing but will assist, I think, those who are not.

There is a word of caution. Psychical experiences can be very fascinating. Some are certainly stimulating and often sublime for those in whose lives they occur.

However, they should never be regarded as the all important aspect of human life. Nor should their recipients think of themselves as 'special' people who are particularly favoured by God above their fellows.

Those who get over absorbed in the occult risk becoming cranky and boring! they may even do real harm to themselves — and also to those whom they seek to impress by their particular form of psychic interest.

The fact is that we must live in *this* world and accept the reality of all the limitations it imposes regarding matter and the five senses.

We should, therefore, recognise God at work in the ordinary events, and the continuing mundane routines and processes of our lives, as much as in the unique upliftment and illumination of those psychic experiences and revelations which may be vouchsafed to us. (And bear in mind many folk *do not have them*).

In short, if we cannot see God in the ordinary as well as in the extraordinary we shall remain spiritually incomplete (not to say immature) no matter how exciting or rewarding the psychic aspect of our lives may be.

It is all a question of balance!

I acknowledge, as I did in *A Priest's Psychic Diary*,* my continuing debt to Abbot Weisinger for the brilliant illumination he provides in the body-soul/spirit-soul concept in his book: 'Occult Phenomena in the Light of Theology'.

---

* *A Priest's Psychic Diary,* published in 1977 by S.P.C.K. at £1.95. Copies may be obtained from the author.

I realise how my own faith has been deepened and refreshed by those who have sought my counsel and prayers. No words can fully express my thankfulness to them. I am grateful beyond measure to my congregation for its own prayerful support, and to my wife, Dorothy, for years of understanding love and helpfulness during my ministry. Often she and I have shared the surprise and elevation of psychic experiences. Nor must I forget my very good friend John Symonds, authors and playwright, who ever urged me to take up the pen and, in his words, "get something down on paper." My thanks are due to my former secretary, Mary Naylor Smith, M.B.E. for patiently typing and re-typing my script over a long period, and to my niece Pamela Collier for the final typed copy.

I would add my thanks for the influence of long conversation with my great friend the late Reverend Frank W. Moyle, a former Rector of Allesley, Coventry.

Emmanuel Vicarage   J. Dover Wellman
Lyncroft Gardens
Hampstead
London NW6

AN INTRODUCTION: THE SOUL AND ITS FACULTIES

We observe that human nature consists of a body and a life-force (or soul). Analysis of the body shows that it contains elements of the earth itself but unless it possesses a soul it is simply a corpse.

The soul is, therefore, the purely non-material part of us. It provides our powers of growth, of movement, of reasoning and of will.

As the very life of us it must be responsible for all our physiological processes, including touch, taste, smell, sight and hearing. These perceptions first require stimulus from matter in order to activate them. That stimulus informs the brain which then makes practical sense of them to us.

Intellectual and spiritual aspects of life are also bound up with our senses because they require images from the material world in order to provide relativity, and to convey an understandable and communicable expression of them.

Nevertheless, the mind and spirit are also able to reach out beyond the purely material to conceive abstractions and ideas which are on another and higher plane — a completely non-sensual one.

We conclude, therefore, that the human soul works on two levels:

1. The physiological, whereby our bodies are kept alive and able to function in the material world of the senses.

2. The spiritual, whereby our thoughts, our emotions and the creative power of the imagination carry us into a realm which is not wholly materialistic but abstract. It is this level of the

soul which produces art, philosophy, all kinds of learning, and the religious impulse. Through it also comes the inspiration for man's noblest deeds and qualities and, unfortunately, for his worst characteristics as well.

But though our souls have this dual operation it is an error to assume we have two souls. There is but one soul, possessing two separate spheres of activity and faculties, which is united with the body to make of us a living reality in this world of matter, space and time.

Because of that unity the body and soul influence each other and know each other. In consequence any damage to the body will impair its ability to truly know, and be fully involved in, the physical world. In turn that can affect the mind simply because the body is the vehicle — the very temple — of the soul. Hence physical care and attention are vital to the full life.

When death occurs this unity of body and soul ceases. The body decays and will be no more, losing that form and activity which the soul gave it.

Because the soul is non-material, and accordingly not subject to the order of decay and extinction which is the property of matter alone, it continues its existence. But it is really incomplete, ever desiring re-union with the body.

Hence the triumphant emphasis which Christianity places on the 'new' creation wherein God clothes the soul after death with a new kind of body — a spiritual one, like into Christ's resurrection body — for its fulfilment.

There is what could be called a tug-of-war constantly going on within us between those two aspects of the soul, in which the body-soul seeks to dominate or mis-direct the higher aspirations of the spirit-soul.

This downward pull is the universal fault in mankind which religion defines as 'sin'. Sin literally means 'missing the mark' — a failure to reach the target of perfection which the spirit-soul conceives but, because of the contrary desires and weaknesses of the body-soul, can never fully realise.

So we speak of man as a 'fallen' creature — his potential perfection being ever marred by this universal grip of sin.

This truth about us is what the Bible reiterates and in the book of Genesis states its origin.

Of course the creation story in Genesis is a spiritual parable and not intended to be a scientific manual (even if such had been possible for its writers). Its aim is simple but profound — to express the great truth that God not only made us and all else but that He saw His creation was totally good, that He would sustain it, and continue to be lovingly concerned with it.

However, so that man might serve Him freely and not as a mere puppet, He gave him freedom of will. Inevitably with that free-will came the possibility of man choosing to pursue his own way contrary to God's design for him.

To that temptation earliest man (Adam) eventually fell. Thereby the good estate was tainted and evil entered in.

The original condition, then, of the first precursors of the human race was one of Paradise, a completely harmonious communion between God and themselves. At some stage in their development our primal ancestors lost their innocence, i.e. failed to accord absolute recognition of their Creator's sovereignty in all things. Using their free-will they chose to be masters of their physical environment. This constituted a rebellion against God — a usurpation of His supreme authority by challenging it in their material domain.*

In consequence of this disobedience to the Divine Will there were two results:-

1. Because they desired to rule matter they fell under its thrall and became heirs to its properties. Thus came fatigue, disease, suffering, decay and death, and all the limitations which the material world imposes.

2. Because they had misused free-will their will was weakened. As the will is the governing attribute of the soul the powers of the spirit-soul (which is pure spirit, even as are the angels) were greatly curtailed. The spirit-soul had capitulated to the body-soul.

Hence the full glory of man's nature was diminished so that now only vestiges of those originally perfect powers of his spirit-soul

---

* It is noteworthy that apparently unlinked cultures throughout the world contain the idea that at one time man enjoyed Paradise. It would seem, therefore, that embedded deep in our consciousness (or folk memory) is the fact that in earliest prehistory mankind knew God i.e. had a perfect and obedient rapport with the unseen world of the spirit. This would mean that at that stage man's spiritual powers were not subjugated to his physical ones.)

remain. These may be exhibited when the soul is freed (or partially so) from the body-soul's domination.

Such a condition only occurs during various states of trance (including morbid illness, e.g. somnambulism, hysteria, and depression). Then occur such phenomena as telepathy, clairvoyance, precognition, prophecy, divination, visions, healings, etc as well as certain physical feats which could not be performed in the normal state of consciousness.

The reason for all these lies in the properties of pure spirit for, as Abbot Weisinger reminds us, "a pure spirit is immortal, is not subject to suffering, can influence matter, has an understanding that knows all things to which it directs its attention with absolute clarity and possesses a will which holds fast to all that is presented to it by its understanding."

From that definition we can understand that all kinds of occult knowledge and behaviour may arise if the physical senses are suspended, i.e. when the spirit-soul is disencumbered of the body-soul by means of trance.

There is a constant stream of fascinating literature recounting the alleged results of trance. Some appear highly intriguing but they need no more involved an explanation than that the spirit-soul is simply exercising its peculiar extra-sensory powers during that abnormal condition.

What we observe is that the faculties of the spirit-soul are rudimentary because sin has diminished them. This accounts for the vagueness and imperfection of most records of the occult.

Until sin is overcome there cannot be pure spirit with all the fullness of its powers. The Christian faith assures its adherents that both sin and death have been dealt with by God acting in Jesus Christ.

After death, therefore, the Christian soul will be accorded a spiritual body and the completeness of the spiritual faculties, unadulterated now by sin.

The term 'trance' is not exactly a happy one for many religious people to entertain, but there is no other way to describe that condition wherein the sense perceptions and awareness of the body cease to operate.

There are, however, levels of trance from the crudest to the most mystical providing triviality or sublimity as the case may be. They arise from a variety of causes.

To begin with there are those trances which come about involuntarily due to the prolonged pressure of great anxiety or tragedy, or from a deep absorption in some mental or physical exercise (some folk, for instance, slip into a half-conscious state when playing a musical instrument, cogitating over some problem in their work, or carrying out some repetitive task which has become almost automatic). At such times the trance is usually very brief, providing flashes of extra-sensory perceptions, such as clairvoyance, telepathy, pre-cognition, or the sudden awareness of some mysterious spiritual presence.

Elementary trance can be induced by purely mechanical means, e.g. staring concentratedly at some material object such as a candle-flame, a pendulum, a pencil and paper (as in automatic writing), a crystal ball, a ouija or planchette board, etc. The result of such may often appear surprising by producing information otherwise not forthcoming in the normal state. It can prove of limited practical value, but it can also disturb the personality of the subject who is often dredging up knowledge from the subconscious which he has forgotten. It can also lay him open to possession by mischievous and deceiving entities. Such trances are not to be recommended for another reason, namely, that in time they debilitate the nervous system with the ensuing possibility of mental breakdown, and hence of harm being done to the body.

Trance can also be achieved through special breathing exercises and postures, by fasting, by listening to monotonous drum beats or other sounds, or by prolonged chanting. Of course the use of narcotics of all kinds can also cause a suspension of the senses but besides being dangerous is mostly hallucinatory (even as are most of the other practices for they limit the supply of oxygen to the brain).

All these forms of trance are of a self-hypnotic kind and any ecstasy or relief they provide is circumscribed and potentially self-destructive because they are largely uncontrolled.

Then there is the hypnotic trance instilled by another human being. Here we have the surrender of the subject's will to the hypnotist who can then direct it and even manipulate the sense perceptions. While this can have certain beneficial results (as in medical practice) it is questionable whether it is morally justified since God Himself does not impose His will upon us. There is also the danger that the patient's will may become weakened by repeated sessions of hypnosis (even as it can by excessive self-hypnosis)

A condition of trance also arises in certain morbid illnesses (e.g. somnambulism and depression) with deleterious effect upon the unhappy person.

All these forms of trance perform the same purpose — to suspend the normal sense faculties and so release the spirit-soul which will then be able to exercise certain of its own powers of pure spirit.

The purest form of trance is that of prayer. The most sublime and exalted of which is inspired by faith in Jesus Christ i.e. by devout meditation upon His life and teaching and what He has effected for man's salvation from sin and death.

Such prayer confers the highest bliss to the human soul and, in its most profound and disciplined form, the very vision of God.

The results of some of these various types of trance are recorded in the cases I have given in these pages.

PART ONE

Case Histories

PERILS OF THE OUIJA

Happily the ouija board craze is less prevalent than it was some years ago. Even so I am still counselling many who have been unwise enough to use it. Some persist with it because they have found it an effective means of producing extra-sensory perception, usually in the form of precognition: others because they believe it affords them contact with the spirit-world.

Of course for many folk the ouija has no effect whatever and is soon relegated, after a few abortive party games with it, to a junk corner in the attic. I have even found one innocently handed in for a church jumble sale! Needless to say I promptly confiscated it before it could fall into the hands of some over-sensitive person.

The group around the board place their index fingers upon an upturned glass or pointer and begin to ask their questions, or inquire if there is a spirit present who wishes to communicate. The glass or pointer then moves (sometimes!) towards letters in the alphabet inscribed upon the board to spell out answers to questions put by the group or messages to one or other of the members. As the indicator apparently moves under the control of an invisible force the group usually tend to assume that this must belong to some spiritual being for they are fully convinced that they themselves are not in any way manipulating that movement, whereas in fact the subconscious mind of one or more is usually responsible.

I would quote a typical example of the trouble this practice can cause.

A young woman came to see me with the plea that I should exorcise her. The belief that they have become demon-possessed seems to be the climax often reached by those who have 'success-fully' experimented in solitude with this iniquitous toy over a long period.

The reason for this is, I think, clear. There are those who, because they desire the experience so unreservedly and eagerly, can with ease hypnotise themselves by its use. Some indeed may enter upon the matter with the opinion that it is all nonsense but, because they are particularly sensitive, are prone to succumb to that peculiar atmosphere which serious attention given to it by others in the circle certainly arouses.

What occurs is that the individual's gaze being concentrated upon the glass and alphabet and his mind influenced by the general suggestion that a breakthrough to the spirit-world will occur or certain occult knowledge be vouchsafed, induces in himself a degree of trance. (Constant practice can actually produce this result quite rapidly). In consequence the spirit-soul is partially disengaged from the body-soul and so, with the dimming of the senses, extra-sensory perceptions may function. In some instances — and I have met all too many (in young people especially) — the 'success' achieved which is usually in the nature of rather trivial messages (although some can be sufficiently intriguing and arresting) causes the users of the ouija board to become obsessed with the practice. When that situation is reached (and ultimately it almost always does) great mental stress often occurs. Because he believes he has been regularly contacting the spirit-world the common reaction of the sufferer is that, by some mischance, an alien entity must have entered him during the course of that communication and is causing his tortured condition.

There is then a very real danger of mental collapse because the natural will-power, which generally safeguards human beings when they undergo the strains and demands of life, has been progressively weakened by the sessions of this type of self-hypnosis. Necessarily the latter is of a primitive order because it has been attained by a crude and soul-less means. Every difficulty or tragedy which dogs the ouija board addict from now on is considered by him as the vindictiveness of a demon which he imagines possesses him. He virtually abdicates all personal responsibility for his condition and begins to live a haunted and melancholy existence.

The dejection and fears, and often unpleasant images which are conjured in his mind can, in extreme cases, promote a suicidal state or even a homicidal tendency. But usually there befalls just a listless acceptance which makes its victims most painful and worrying persons to live with. I have known marriages which have eventually come apart because one partner (usually the wife) has habitually consulted the ouija board, initially in company with others but later doing so alone.

While it is generally true that the ouija board can develop an elementary extra-sensory perception that may furnish information which might not otherwise be acquired it is most likely that the messages received are actually the memories or urges which in the normal state lie hidden or subdued in the subconscious. A trance condition opens up that area of the mind and brings it into the conscious mind where it presents such mystification that the person considers it must be the spirit-world which is responsible.

Nevertheless there is the very real possibility that trance can open up the soul to the influence of spiritual entities which will be of a low and mischievous order just because hypnosis has been induced by a primitive means.

To return to my visitor, whom I will call Sarah. She explained that she had been encouraged to try out the ouija board after reading a magazine article about it which included the suggestion that it could prove useful for the successful placing of bets.

At first her boy-friend, Jim, had completely ridiculed the whole thing making the sarcastic comment that it was a wonder that punters had not long ago put the bookmakers out of business by consulting the ouija. But later he was to change his mind because Sarah began to make a number of accurate predictions of the winners of horse races.

Clearly the extra-sensory perception which had been caused to function in her was that of precognition. When I questioned her she said she had little knowledge of racing, had never studied form nor bothered hitherto to read the racing pages of daily newspapers. She simply went through the list of the names of horses, presenting each one in turn to the ouija board for winning or losing. Obviously her success rate was striking enough to convince not only herself but her boy-friend of the efficacy of using the board to make easy money.

Then came the anti-climax to the increasing tension and excitement of the whole affair. Suddenly there was nervous collapse and from being a bright and friendly girl, as Jim described her, she became morose and vindictive.

5

So altered in fact was she that whilst on holiday in the Hebrides with Jim and another young couple she would, for no accountable reason, suddenly assume a most antagonistic manner and on several occasions physically attacked the other three so viciously that they had great difficulty in restraining her from doing them very real hurt. In Jim's words "even her countenance changed to something savage."

When this last part of the story was disclosed I began to take a new view of the matter. The girl could well be right. She *might* be possessed since one of the signs of possession is just such a personality change. Although at first her dabbling with the board had simply heightened her faculty of precognition she had unwisely continued the practice to excess. Perhaps then, in an uncontrolled state of trance on some occasion, she had become wide open, not just to the irrational upsurge of her subconscious mind but to the malevolent entry of an evil spirit which could split the mind. I believe this to be one of the greatest dangers of the type of self-hypnosis which is attained by inferior methods such as the ouija board, crystal ball, etc.

I realised, therefore, that I might be facing a situation where exorcism would be needed.

The girl concluded her account, with the most intense anguish in her voice, pleading for exorcism.

I re-assured her that I would deal with her trouble forthwith. That statement appeared to calm her somewhat.

"What do you do?" she asked.

"First, Sarah, we must remember together that Jesus Christ is present with us now — in this room. He promised He would be if we truly desire it. Then we will place our complete trust in His power to overcome all evil."

I stood behind her chair, asked her to close her eyes and, placing my hands on her head, I prayed:

"Lord Jesus present in all Thy power and in Whom we have all our trust we come to Thee for the cleansing of the spirit of Sarah."

I could not feel her aura, not even a faint indication, and I realised that I must build up in the girl's mind a strong picture of Christ. I suspected she had made little or no attempt to reflect seriously upon Him.

I said: "Do you remember, Sarah, how He walked along the seashore and met His first disciples while they were busy mending their fishing tackle? Think, then, of being beside the sea, Sarah — anywhere you can remember well, say on holiday. Maybe, when you walked the coast of Iona with Jim recently. Think of such a scene.''

I noted that she was responding to my suggestion giving a slight affirmative nod of her head and that her tenseness and trembling had passed.

"Now think of Jesus, coming towards you, Sarah. Just like a figure from a bible picture, if you will. Now He is here with you, really with you. With us both.''

Her aura was now faintly coming through to my hands but there was a chill about it. The coldness increased and I was seized with a repulsive sense of a disagreeable presence which actually seemed to be coming up and out of her.

I began to feel the hair on my scalp rising and for a few moments I remained tongue-tied, completely bound to this strange and evil presence. It appeared to wrap itself around me. Suddenly my spine became ice-cold, and my flesh seemed as if it had dissolved. I no longer felt as if I were standing there in my cassock but that the garment was like some lifeless tube, stiffly erect but empty.

Of course such experiences beggar description. One can scarcely define them to oneself at the time because one is so lost within their awfulness. But fairly constant dealing with the spiritually distressed does provide a kind of armour which allows some degree of reflection even when one is wholly absorbed in such encounters. That fact, too, has its advantage as I have come to realise over the years of this particular aspect of my ministry. It allows some sense of final detachment, a last ditch stand as it were, wherein to resist the force of evil and commend oneself wholly to the almighty power and protection of God.

I called inwardly upon the Lord again:

"Be present, Lord Jesus, to strengthen me. May Thy holy angels guard me.''

Then I became aware of a transcendent power — beyond and above myself, assuring me of victorious control over the evil spirit which I knew was clinging on to the girl. A glorious, uplifting, wonderful presence was with me, in me and around me, and flowing joyfully through me.

"Out, out!" I demanded of that evil entity. "In the Name of Jesus, who has all power over thee and is now present among us, be gone!''

I could sense the ensuing struggle within the girl.

"Let it go, Sarah. Let it go. Let it go. Be delivered!"

The exultant power flowing through me had now taken complete possession of me and I sensed the transcendent beauty and exhilaration of it. I knew in that moment the battle was over and a victory of good over evil gained.

Suddenly Sarah gave a cry and her body momentarily convulsed. Then she began to weep. I sensed they were tears of joy and relief. The spiritual anguish had ceased.

Sarah's aura seemed to leap to my finger tips, vibrant, warm, pulsing with lively energy.

"Go spirit of darkness to that place which is prepared for thee. There is none for thee here — and never can be from henceforth and forever. In the Name of the Father and of the Son and of the Holy Spirit, Sarah thou art blessed and purified".

Under my hands, I could feel the strong surge of Sarah's aura. Now it reached beyond even the arc of my outstretched arms.

Then that unearthly, lovely peace which ever succeeds the laying-on of hands fell upon the three of us. I could sense it in the face of Sarah and in Jim's bowed head and still figure. O lovely, lovely peace!

A full two minutes of tranquil silence must have ensued. Only then did the ticking of my study clock begin to intrude and I knew that this spiritual experience was ended. Back now from the mount of transfiguration to the world of 'practical affairs' for all of us.

Then Sarah spoke: "Vicar, I saw something — a black shape — crossing the room and moving away so fast. Did you see it too? That was the evil spirit leaving me wasn't it?"

"There was something, Sarah." I replied. "You were right. But it has truly gone. For you that disappearing shape must have been the assurance of its departure. For my part my eyes were closed. But *feeling* the evil? Yes, I did."

The couple were filled with thanksgiving toward me.

"The best thanks of all" I said, "will be for you to promise me that you will leave ouija boards and all the paraphernalia of the occult strictly alone from now on. These things can be terribly upsetting. Dangerous to some — driving them out of their minds.

Remember the only healthy state of trance is that which comes through prayer inspired by our Lord Jesus Christ. Then we are kept safe from evil and we discover a truly beautiful spiritual experience."

From that evening Jim and Sarah were able to renew their former affectionate and untroubled companionship. Letters from them which followed were most touching, and I was glad to think that when a year later one of their many friends had become spiritually distressed over some matter they immediately asked if he too could seek my counsel.

2

A CASE OF BLACK MAGIC

The reader will have gathered how cautious I am in the use of exorcism because I have discovered that so often those who attribute their personal troubles to demon-possession are mistaken in their self-diagnosis.

Nevertheless there are cases where at first I have been very sceptical and then realised, during the laying-on of hands upon such persons, that there was indeed an alien entity indwelling them.

I would instance the following:-

Jane, a middle-aged woman, came to see me concerning, as she put it, 'a spiritual problem'.

"I read," she began, " *'A Priest's Psychic Diary'*[1] and afterwards I attended one of your healing services. I have been to healing services before but I have never experienced at them the kind of effect which accompanied that one."

(Though I did not enquire too closely I gathered that the services she had been associated with were those of Spiritualist Churches abroad).

"After you gave me the laying-on of hands" she declared, "I felt a flow of some peculiar power which seemed to envelop my whole system — literally flooding through me so that I came from the altar rail in a condition of felicity and exaltation such as I had never known before. I left your church as if walking on air."

At the time of that service she was on compassionate leave to visit her mother who was extremely ill in hospital in England. She and her husband were working in the Middle East at that time.

---

1   Published by S.P.C.K. 1977.

Actually she had come to my church to pray for her mother's healing and to receive, by proxy, the laying-on hands for her.

Now she had come to me with her own very unhappy personal problem.

It was a strange story she had to tell. Practically the whole of their married lives she and her husband had spent in foreign lands. They were devoted to each other. During one assignment, however, their relationship began to founder, not because of infidelity or any emotional difficulties but due, as she expressed it, to the attacks made upon their marriage by black magic.

This assertion, though made very calmly and unemotionally as if it were the most normal comment, caused me to wonder whether she might be a little unbalanced. She must have sensed my misgiving for she rapidly qualified her statement by saying:

"Oh, I know what you must be thinking. But, let me say this, I guess you only know the ways of the West. Believe me, there are parts of the world where the unpleasant side of the occult is practised and it can bring real harm. In England there is a very different attitude to life. There is a prevailing Christian influence and tradition — even if the people are not particularly religious.

But in the regions where my husband and I have spent so many years, often miles away from any other Europeans, evil can be an almost *tangible* force. Practitioners of magic can manipulate it in order to damage the minds — and thus the lives — of those they wish to harm."

She paused a moment as if to let what she had said sink in and then quietly added: "Even to the point of destruction."

I gazed at her. She was evidently an educated woman, and her sober, earnest manner made it impossible to dismiss the strange content of her conversation out of hand. I felt I must listen carefully and judge as best I could the real truth in what she was saying. Could she be the victim of some peculiar mania? It was certainly not the first time I had met those who were convinced of being under the spell or curse of some person who had exerted so-called magical powers over them. Such folk have sometimes become unstable by accepting as factual the more lurid fiction which abounds in occult literature. Probably some psychical or emotional upset combined with vivid imagination or naive suggestibility has set them off on what is really a path of escape from uncongenial personal responsibility or from the harsh truth of reality.

11

But the whole demeanour of this woman ran counter to that kind of diagnosis. One can usually gather after listening to a person for a while if one is dealing with a case of mental instability, and this woman impressed me as being a balanced and sincere character.

Nevertheless I remained convinced that there must be another, more rational, explanation than that of magic for whatever story she was about to tell me.

"Our last contract overseas" she said "brought us into a society which practised black magic. Its members tried hard to make us join them and were greatly annoyed when we refused to do so. Since our return to England we have been dogged with a series of misfortunes. All of them are fulfillments of the curses laid upon us by that evil group."

"What were those misfortunes? I inquired.

"To begin with" she replied "my husband, whose health has always been good, contracted a skin disease which persisted for months and seemed to resist treatment. Later I developed severe blood pressure and had to go very carefully and medication proved a long affair.

Then we had difficulty with a neighbour — a spinster — who gave great annoyance with her habits and behaviour regarding, among other things, the manner in which she kept the entrance to our apartment block. Persuading my husband to remonstrate with her ultimately brought a discordant note into our lives because of the many arguments we had in this matter. At one stage I feared the break-up of our marriage because my husband, who had originally been as upset as myself, began to take the woman's part, probably because he had got thoroughly tired of the whole business and decided to ignore it.

All these afflictions were, I could see, the fulfillment of the curses laid upon us by that weird 'society', which included those of an unpleasant illness for my husband and then the serious breakdown of my own health. It was also prophesied that my happy marriage would be in jeopardy..."

"But," I protested, "surely all these things could have happened to anyone as the pains and troubles which are possible afflictions in all our lives. I do not see that you should attach them so positively to so-called black magic."

"There you are" she countered "you naturally take that view. But when one has been at close quarters with such evil powers then, and only then, one realises their potency and their danger."

"What I think could happen" I argued "is that the power of suggestion can be formidable. There could be a predilection to tragedy through the mind ever trying to be on the look out for such dangers. Then anything remotely resembling the curses would be considered due to them — and to no other reason."

"Years ago" she answered "I know I would have agreed with you, but again I have to say, in a society where belief in evil powers is common and the practice of witchcraft not unusual one comes to a very different attitude...."

Perhaps I ought to be able to deal with it all through my own prayers but I find I cannot pray nowadays. Even the Lord's Prayer no longer seems to come from me naturally as once it did. Padre", she pleaded "I know you will discover that I *am* possessed by evil spirits if you pray with me..."

"Then we shall pray that prayer which Jesus taught" I said, "but first let us become mindful again of its significance. We remember that it is, of course, a guide for all our praying which is the desire that God's will may be done in us. It is indeed a pattern prayer and never a mere prayer patter! Recall also that Jesus did not teach it to the world at large. It is too wonderful and too intimate for that. It is a prayer for the truly *faithful* follower of Christ — a prayer, if you like, for the inner circle of His disciples. It is only for those who wish to be close to Him and to know Him, and therefore lovingly and faithfully to serve Him."

"Yes, padre. This I know and believe. Deep in my heart I do," she declared, "but I seem to have forgotten how to pray. Perhaps I have never prayed in that profound way save long ago when there came a deep personal problem in my life. I know I did pray then — and I found an answer."

"That is good. Remember that time" I urged "and let it serve to bring back your faith, and to recollect the help and guidance God gives to us in our hour of need when we call upon Him.

So let us reflect together upon our Lord Jesus Christ. He promised that if only two or three meet in their desire to experience Him then He will be truly present to them. We know, therefore, (not just believe, but *know*) that He is with us now in all His love and power simply because we long for Him to enhance and strengthen our lives in His service.

That prayer of His speaks of our daily need not only for material but spiritual bread. We cannot depend upon a stored-up larder, as it were, of spiritual resource from our past because that, just like ordinary bread, must soon become stale. Day by day and *every* day, we need to seek our Lord's Presence so that He may constantly refresh us with His spirit for each returning day.

We wish to be relieved of the burden we carry through our wrong deeds, wrong attitudes, wrong words. Our heavenly Father forgives us for them and offers us His newness of life on one condition. We cannot *earn* that forgiveness by fresh good deeds we do or by any new effort of faith but *only* as we are ready to forgive all those who, in any way, have hurt or wronged us."

"I know what you are getting at" she quickly interjected. "You mean I must clear from my heart any sense of grievance or grudge, or of revenge, concerning those who have harmed me in the past while we were abroad — and also this neighbour who is such a trial and causes so much contention. I feel I can truly say that I *do forgive* — that I empty myself of the resentment but I am still certain that there is fighting against me a demon which I cannot dispel — I believe I *am* possessed and need you to exorcise me..." Now her voice trembled and she repeated tearfully: "I *need* exorcism — I *know* I do, please, oh *please*..."

"Let me say this" I replied "I shall lay my hands on you and pray for the healing of your spirit. When I do so I shall know if I must exorcise. Although, let me say, it is not I but God in Jesus Christ whose power alone casts out evil spirits. Now, please, relax. Be calm and allow all your inner tensions to be surrendered...."

As I directed she leant back more comfortably in the armchair and folded her hands on her lap and closed her eyes.

Standing behind her chair I laid my hands on her head and prayed:

"Lord Jesus, we remember Thy healing Presence with us now. Thou hast said: "I am the Vine, you are the branches." So, then, we know we take our true life through Thee.....

Thy servant, Jane, comes with a loving heart to Thee truly forgiving all who have brought her harm and unhappiness. She comes with the sad and painful memories of experiences which have deeply troubled her. In Thy Name, Lord, cleanse and relieve her soul...."

At that point I found myself suddenly engulfed with a sense of horror. The shock of some evil presence which seemed to flow our of the woman was so overwhelming that I rocked on my feet and for a long moment felt I would have been thrown to the floor from the impact. A terrible cloak of icy coldness wrapped me from head to foot. I realised that the woman had been right. She certainly required exorcism.

"In Thy Name, Lord Jesus, Who art present with us now in all Thy power drive out this evil —."

Several times I repeated this invocation. Each time the horrifying atmosphere diminished slightly and the shuddering of my body would ease. Under my hands I felt the issue of something which appeared almost solid — and very, very cold.

Having had similar experiences in the past I knew I must keep my mind riveted upon the thought of Christ's presence and the sure victory of His power over all evil things. I forced myself to disregard, as much as I could, all these unpleasant physical sensations and to hold a living picture of Christ in my brain. I was greatly helped in the latter by the Flemish painting of The Risen Jesus which hangs on the wall of my study.

So, for what seemed far longer than the half-minute which it probably was, I maintained what could only be described as a battle between my concentration on faith in Christ and this evil force which appeared to be fiercely clinging to my own person even as it vacated that of Jane.

At length Jane gave a long gasping sigh accompanied by a slight shudder. Then the chill feeling under my hands was replaced by a warm prickling which betokened the release of her natural aura.

There ensued a long quietness during which I continued to sense the increasing strength of it and we both realised, simultaneously, that she was healed, exorcised of some evil entity.

Finally I offered thanks to God through Jesus Christ for this healing and for the support of His angels.

Jane was overcome with gratitude and departed with a most happy countenance and a confident stride so contrary to the tense and bowed figure who had first entered my study.

Later she was to write happily to me during the next sojourn she and her husband had abroad.

However, having said goodbye to her I found that on returning to the room it seemed odd and oppressive. It was as if the atmosphere had absorbed Jane's distress and whatever malevolent spirit had possessed her. I found it necessary, therefore, to complete the exorcism of my own person. Standing in the room and, describing a circle about myself with outstretched arms, I prayed — "Lord

Jesus, in Whom I have all my trust, surround me with the circle of Thy divine protection and may Thy Holy angels dwell here.''

This prayer gave immediate relief and a glow of sweet reassurance. A peculiar warming strength enveloped my whole person. I felt lifted up both in body and in spirit.

Afterwards I reflected that in all that recent conversation with Jane so preoccupied with evil spirits, one should ever remind oneself of the presence of angels whose light and goodness are equally as real and effective as the darkness and evil of demonic powers.

Note

The so-called art of magic is a very ancient one. Its alleged purpose is to perform miracles with the assistance of the Devil which is 'black' magic. If without that assistance it is 'white' magic.

It is very unlikely, however, that practitioners of the art are in actual league with Satan. Instead they are adepts at self-hypnosis by means of which, because their sense perceptions are dulled thereby, the faculties of their spirit-souls can be utilised. Some, of course, also fake things by conjuring and illusion.

The results may appear very puzzling, mysterious and unnerving to those sensitive and impressionable folk who assume they are being acted upon by the magician's occult powers. For example, they really do come to believe in the destructive force of curses. But the whole matter is really one which illustrates the power of suggestion over them, whilst the clairvoyance, apparent materialisations, healings, etc which so mystify them are the general manifestations of the liberated faculties of the spirit-soul of the magician.

It is clear, therefore, that the unscrupulous can pray upon the minds of others by using a ragbag of hypnotic tricks. Indeed, it is possible that some victims may actually become possessed by the evil force invoked in them by magicians and so require what is almost a form of exorcism to expel it. They certainly require spiritual healing.

3

A CASE OF POSSESSION

"I started using a ouija board a long time ago." So Mary, a handsome young woman, began her account to me of what, as she expressed it, was her psychic problem. "A risky thing to do" I interjected. "You really think so?" she asked. "Yes" I answered "and as you say you have come to see me about psychic trouble, I would guess it all began then".

"That's right, it did" she agreed. "You see I sat alone in my room practising with it for several evenings without results. Then, about a week later, at one o'clock in the morning the board began to move on its own. It gave messages to me of a friendly nature and I noticed a very sweet smell filled the room. During the following week I continued to receive messages and then I found I started to write notes of them. Gradually the pen started to write automatically.

Another week passed like that. Each evening the messages kept coming and the pen writing.

After that I started hearing voices in my head. They were very gentle at first but began to get louder and were of a violent nature.

Three weeks later I became very ill, always hearing voices and feeling freezing cold all the time. I was constantly shaking and often vomited.

One Sunday evening my head felt it would burst and it seemed both head and spine were being dragged from my body and my vision was blurred. Now the voices were more threatening and I ran from home in terror.

I found my way into a church and tried to join in a service which was going on, but discovered to my horror that I heard everything distorted. It seemed as if what I heard was relayed backwards to me. Likewise whatever I saw were distorted images — as if in reverse.

I ran from the church and back home. All the way I smelt heavy sulphur and charcoal fumes. I found I could not smoke cigarettes because they were also 'in reverse' and I just choked on them.

That night the voices were even louder and more threatening. My vision became so blurred I could see nothing at all. All was darkness. And again my head and spine felt as if they were being torn from me. The next morning, while dressing, I heard voices telling me to say prayers to God to save my soul. I prayed for over an hour and then ran again from the house in terror. The first person I met was a young man who kindly took me to the police station. There I gave the officer a false story — not telling him of the events which had led up to my awful state. The police, seeing my condition, took me straight to hospital.

There they examined me and found I had some cuts and bruises caused by my first frenzy and that I was suffering from shock. As there was nothing more I was sent home.

During the following fortnight though I continued to hear the voices. In the end I collapsed and was again sent to hospital. I was very ill there at first still hearing voices. But gradually these became quieter and now were of a more friendly nature. They kept saying they would take good care of me."

At this point in her story I mentally reflected that these kinder voices were probably the natural ones of nurses and doctors reassuring her.

"I stayed in hospital" she continued "for eight weeks and then returned to my family. The voices gradually stopped in my head but I found that they were contacting me in another way. About fourteen months ago they started talking in my tongue — as you would if your mouth were closed. I discovered I could talk out loud to them in my face and mouth which picked up the facial characteristics of the spirit talking to me at the time. These voices were not of an aggressive nature.

Five months later my head began to feel it was being pulled again and dragged about and once more I became very ill hearing the voices very loudly. Again I had to return to hospital for a further fortnight.

For the past ten months I have talked to the spirits. I am still doing so although not in my head but out loud. They always come when I am on my own for any length of time.

Although the voices are now mainly of a gentle kind I am still afraid of them and have had two nervous breakdowns because of them and I am in very poor health. I have bouts of feeling terribly scared and then I shake and vomit.

I am afraid these voices will never leave me alone. I need some help in this matter which has gone on for so long — nearly two years."

At last she paused and stared rather blankly at me and then pleaded:

"I've been so ill and afraid and yet I have told no one everything. Not even my parents know the whole story. I am looking to you, please, for help and guidance."

The pallor of her face which I had immediately noticed when I first saw her, seemed to have become even more extreme during the recital of her troubles.

"These voices, Mary," I asked "do you really want them to cease?"

"Yes — oh yes, I do. Would you like to hear them? They are talking to me now....." "I will hear them later if you wish" I interrupted, "but first, how many are there? Do they all speak at the same time? Can you distinguish them?"

"There are six" she replied "and they are all to do with 'rock' musicians."

"Ah", I said, "do you go to discos?"

"My boy-friend used to take me. But he has given me up since I started hearing the voices."

"I guess there was a lot of 'beat' music — very loud — and flashing lights at those discos?" I asked.

"Yes", she said "but I don't know why I hear the voices of 'rock' musicians because I don't like rock nowadays. And I don't go to discos anymore."

"Can you tell me the names, Mary, of those voices you hear?" I queried.

"There are six." she said "There's David, Stephen, Joe and Jesus. Do you think it is Jesus? He would speak to me, wouldn't He?"

"Of course in our prayers, Mary, Jesus is with us in a very deep and wonderful way. Maybe He does speak to you in your heart. But I am sure His voice would never make you afraid or feel sick"

"Then you think it may not be the voice of Jesus?" she asked.

"Not if the voice causes you pain and fear. No, Mary, I would say it was not Him who spoke. But you said there were six voices. You have given me only four. Who are the others?"

She did not reply to this but insisted that she must let me hear the voices. Her eyes narrowed to slits and she began to grimace and chew upon her tongue for some time. She was evidently passing into a state of trance.

A voice came from her at last, rather high-pitched, and said it was David.

"Who are you, David?" I asked.

With slow deliberation Mary mouthed the answer that David was a boy of twelve.

"But you said all your voices were of 'rock' musicians" I reminded her. "Would David be one at twelve yours old?"

She gave no answer to this but repeated:"David is twelve" and she began to smile as if to herself, presumably for pleasure at David's presence.

"Then, maybe, David died at twelve. Was he in an accident, or did he have a bad illness?" I asked.

"David is twelve" she simply said again, and vouchsafed no more.

"Perhaps David is trying to live through you, Mary? I ventured. "If so that is mischievous of him. He is a boy, but you are a grown-up woman. He can *never* be happy in you, can he? Therefore it is wrong of you to encourage him, Mary. Let us start by letting him go from you and giving him over instead to God's love and care. Shall we do that?"

After a long pause, during which I repeated my question firmly, Mary replied:

"Yes — but can we do that?"

"Of course, Mary, — if you really *want* him to go. Shall we say this together: "David, we want you to leave Mary *now* completely and go into God's gentle keeping."

She repeated this injunction after me and I bid her say it several times that it would enter deeply into her mind.

I explained that through our prayers we would help David to depart happily and find his proper place in God's heaven. I could see that she was now in a trance caused by telling her story, coupled with the effort to produce the person of David. On several occasions as I spoke to her she would munch her lips, drawing them inward, and then let her head roll from side to side or fall back upon the cushion which I had placed behind her to encourage relaxation.

At one point, after I had been gently questioning her as to who were the possessors of her voices, I teased her about them so that she laughed. For that moment she appeared to become perfectly natural and her amusement to be spontaneous. One might have thought then that the whole matter was really a joke — simply a game to attract attention to herself. But her peculiar pallor and strange faraway gaze unhappily belied such a possibility.

I could see I was dealing with a very ill person indeed whose mind was being split into several parts, unable to establish her real identity and to come to terms with the world and her part in it.

Standing behind her chair I bade her to relax. suggesting that she might like to gaze at the cross on the wall of my study, above which is a painting of the resurrection of Christ.

"The Lord Jesus is with us, Mary" I said. "He has power over all the spiritual world. No evil spirit can withstand Him and no restless departed spirit can remain outside the comfort of His healing and restoring love. In Him we can have our complete trust.

I want you to say, Mary: 'Lord Jesus, I know you are with me now — at this very moment'.

She repeated the words after me and then twice more we said them together.

"Now, Mary," I continued, speaking in a low, even and deliberate voice, as I noted the cessation of her grimacing and head-rolling, "let us consider what may be the reason for your voices. Those long sessions late at night with the ouija board in which you persevered until you got results opened up the deepest part of your mind — your very soul — to forces which were harmful to you, mischievous and perhaps lying forces which enjoyed possessing you for their own satisfaction. You might have remained unhurt by them had you given up practising the ouija but, while you were still under its fascination, your boy-friend began taking you to discos. There the flashing light and continuous beat music kept that deep level of your being wide open to those powers. Possibly also you were opened up to the muddled emotions and desires of all who were attending those discos. These peculiar disruptive powers have tried to take you over and use you. But they never will unless you yourself *want* them to stay.

Do you want them inside you, Mary?"

"No, no — I want them to stop. I want them to go away" she exclaimed. "Oh please, *please* take them away, I want to be myself."

"Then, Mary" I said "I shall lay my hands on your head and, in the authority which Jesus has given me, I will bid them to leave you. But first we will join in our Lord's own prayer."

With my hands a few inches above her head I noted, as we recited the prayer together, that Mary's aura was completely withdrawn. I guessed that she had probably taken some tranquillising tablets earlier (a surmise which proved correct when I questioned her later). This would have inhibited the natural release of her aura. But by deep concentration, in which I mentally willed her spirit-soul to respond, I began to feel it issue from her and start throbbing under my hands which remained a few inches above the crown of her head.

"...... and deliver us from evil". At that petition my spine chilled. I felt as if I had been clothed suddenly in ice. I fought to control convulsing tremors which shook me from the base of my neck to the soles of my feet. My very flesh seemed to be shredded away to leave me like a hollow frame. I feared I might lose control and realised the urgency of abandoning myself wholly to the protective supremacy of Christ if I were to be a channel of help to this unfortunate young woman. While my body was swept with this strange clamminess I had the sensation that some being was standing behind or beside me and was causing this unpleasantness. For several moments I felt compelled to repeat to myself that phrase 'deliver us from evil' before I could complete the Lord's Prayer. At length the sensation passed and I continued:

"Lord Jesus, Thou hast promised that when two or three meet together in Thy Name Thou art with them in all Thy power. Therefore we know that Thou art with us now. May Thy light dispel Mary's darkness. Lift from her, Lord, all confusion and perplexity and give her Thy wonderful peace ..... Lay Thy loving hands, Lord Jesus, upon her and heal her in body, mind and spirit."

Mary's head was now lying completely at rest upon the cushion. Her hands which has been so gesticulatory hitherto were now still and relaxed upon the arms of the chair. But her lips were still moving:

"David is in my tongue" she muttered several times.

"But he is going now, Mary" I said firmly. "Let him go. Don't hold him back. God has a place for him. You *must* let him go."

"I must let you go, David" she murmured, so quietly I could hardly hear her.

"Say that again, Mary" I urged.

"I must let David go" she repeated.

"Good" I replied. Though I tried to maintain a calm voice I felt grievously wracked within. I had to keep my gaze on the picture of the Risen Christ on my study wall in order to aid my concentration. I prayed over and over within myself "Christ be within me. O Lord, hear me. May Thy angels support us."

Then my voice appeared to gain strength and I felt a sense of complete authority. Half consciously (although I realised that it was I speaking) I knew that the power prompting my words was coming from a source beyond myself. All was changed. It was now a glorious experience which transported me from the previous sense of desolation and despair into a region of extra-ordinary light and serenity. The very atmosphere took on an illumination and gentleness which defies description. I think I can understand from it the meaning of St. Paul's phrase about being caught up into seventh heaven.

Now I could pronounce with total conviction and command:

"In the Name of Jesus in Whom we trust and Who has power over all the spiritual world, I exorcise you, Mary.

Go now, David, to God's appointed place for you and leave Mary in peace. Leave her, leave her, leave her....."

Mary's countenance became even paler, yet no longer sickly, but radiant. In the now gathering dusk I could see the shimmering haze of her aura, completely encircling her face and rising from the crown of her head.

"David has left me" she said almost in a matter of fact voice, but with conviction.

"Yes, Mary. David has departed. It was never right for him to stay. It is better for him know the spacious fields of eternity. Now he can find fulfilment....."

The vacant gaze Mary had when she first entered my study and which had persisted whilst she recited her troubles with mumblings and grimaces had now given place to a quieter, intelligent and lively expression.

"There is still Stephen" she said.

"I think we must let him be for to-night" I replied.

Then, with a side long glance at her to see how she would react, I added:

"We will forget the others, too. If you wish you can see me again about them."

She appeared to be unconcerned about those 'others' and said: I would like to come here again about Stephen, please."

Obviously deeply affected and relieved by our meeting and the 'exorcism' of David she stood up and, saying good-bye, lightly kissed me on the cheek.

"God be with you, Mary — and His angels protect you" I said.

A week later she called to see me about the continued presence of Stephen.

This time it was a fairly simple and speedy matter to guide her into a state of relaxation during which Stephen 'came through'.

Immediately she began to assume his voice and her face wrinkled into his expression as I questioned him.

Once more I established his name, that he loved Mary and did not wish to be parted from her. I ascertained from her that he had actually passed through death though he was very reluctant to accept this.

After further questions Mary stated that he had died at the age of twenty-three and had been a pop-singer, but not one of any fame.

I knew that one of my first tasks, therefore, was to reason with Stephen to ensure that he had fully accepted the fact of his death. Then I must persuade him to go on his way rejoicing and not to return to this earthly place, and certainly not to occupy the person of Mary.

For several minutes, therefore, I sought to impress upon Stephen that he had died.

"You have shed your physical body, Stephen", I reiterated "and are now clothed in a spiritual body. Because you have died you should not remain in the scenes of your former life. Thereby you cause disturbance and distress to those here."

I found the repeated efforts to make Stephen accept his true situation a great tussle of will which was most exhausting. Again and again I sought to project from my spirit-soul into his the thought of death and of accepting it. At last he agreed that there had been an experience which separated him from his body and from the life pattern he had known. I did not inquire how it had come to him, whether through some illness or accident or (as I intuitively felt) from drugs, since I did not wish to occasion any unnecessary pain or remorse.

I went on to explain to him the unwisdom and certain frustration of his 'possessing' Mary. But despite my remonstrances and reasonings Stephen stubbornly maintained that he would never leave her.

During this lengthy exchange I found that the duologue of Stephen and myself had become, in a sense, so natural that I felt I was dealing only with him and that Mary was indeed purely a vehicle for his expression. So intense was our exchange that I thought I could actually 'see' him in her face.

Several minutes of further conversation got nowhere, being merely a repetition of Stephen's insistence on attaching himself to Mary. Then suddenly I saw, by rapid questioning, an opening which would enable me to guide Stephen away from his thoughts of Mary. I had finally established from him that he was in his early twenties when he had died and I asked him whether any member of his family, or maybe a close friend, had passed through death.

No, his father and mother still lived, he said, but an aunt whom he admired had died a short while before his own experience of death.

Here was the breakthrough I needed.

"You realise, Stephen, your aunt is very likely wanting to greet you. She will be expecting you to go to her. She will wish to help lead you on in the world of spirit to your fulfilment. You will not be alone and that world is so superior to this one. It is far more beautiful, more rewarding, exciting and adventurous. There is much for you there but absolutely nothing for you here. You cannot live *fully* through Mary. You realise that?"

Gratefully I heard Stephen's reply:

"No, I cannot live completely in Mary but I do not wish to leave her".

"You say that now, Stephen. But if angels and your aunt are just waiting to welcome you and to accompany you is it not foolish to remain here with Mary?"

"It is foolish" replied the voice of Stephen. But then, in a whisper which trailed off to a low breathing, it added: "But Stephen loves Mary."

I should emphasise that in all his replies Stephen would partly repeat my questions after me and constantly add that he loved Mary too much to depart from her. I felt it necessary to make my statements several times over in order to drive home their meaning. Stephen never seemed to resent this repetition and after a while from his changing tone, I realised that gradually but surely I was getting through to him, helping him to reason out for himself the futility of lingering in his present state.

The same peculiar inner prompting which seemed to guide my intercourse with Stephen now led me to the appropriate moment for the laying-on of hands.

Rising from my chair I stood beside Mary and placed my hands about twelve inches above her head. Again an inner voice gave me the words of prayer which followed easily and naturally without my conscious deliberation.

"I am speaking to you, Stephen" I began. "You have just agreed with me that it is not sensible to cling to Mary."

"Yes" came Stephen's low voiced answer, "yes, it is not sensible but I love Mary."

"Because you love her you will wish to do the best thing for her. Isn't that so?"

"Yes, Stephen wants to do the best for Mary because he loves her." His reply, as so often, was almost a repetition of my own words.

"So," I said "I am asking you to leave her now so that she may become a happy person again, able to live her own life completely. There is for you the riches and wonder of a new world to know and to enjoy. A world for you to expand in and where you shall be fulfilled. Don't be tied here, Stephen. Don't spoil and interrupt Mary's life. Go forward in your own life. Receive even now the ready welcome of angels. Can you tell if your aunt is waiting for you?"

To the last question I received no reply and I did not repeat it.

Then, suddenly, Mary's lolling and swivelling head became steady. Her narrowed eyes began to open and the glaze go from them. The voice of Stephen still low, but no longer halting and monotonous, replied:

"I will go now. I love Mary but I shall leave her because that is what she wants, and she will be happy."

I summoned all my concentration and held on to a mental picture I had conjured of a real Stephen holding a normal conversation with me. I bade my spirit-soul to reach out in comfort, resolution and compassion to encourage Mary's release from her preoccupation with this other personality.

For a while I could feel within the depth of myself the intensity of her own struggle and I willed for her, with all the concentration I could muster, the peace and consolation of the loving presence of Jesus.

"Two of us — and maybe three of us — are gathered in Thy Name" I reminded myself inwardly. "Therefore Thou art here with us in all Thy power."

The strain began to ease and I became aware for the first time since my conversation with Stephen had begun of the natural world around us — of the walls of my study, of the ticking of the clock, of Mary herself as a single complete soul, a real person again. And I realised that she had found release. Out of trance she came and her demeanour was no longer bowed and distraught. She showed clearness of eye and her former screwed-up countenance was relaxed to give a natural, rather handsome and entirely lively expression.

"I feel good" she declared.

"Stephen has gone" I said. "He was happy to go in the end."

"I know" she answered simply "and I am glad, so very glad."

In reflection later upon this case I could see two possibilities to explain it. One, that here was a genuine case of possession caused by Mary's constant and prolonged use of the ouija which produces a vacuum in the mind, an empty trance which leaves the person open to whatever alien spiritual force is ready to gain access.

Alternatively, that Mary, an only child, might have fantasised for years with the thought of invisible playmates. A condition not uncommon in children, but in her case persisting into adulthood because of shyness and, possibly, of loneliness.

In that peculiar mental condition which arises when the trance state is achieved through inanimate, impersonal apparatus (e.g. the ouija) she might have drawn out of her subconscious the buried memories, reflections and consolations of her childhood and re-presented them to herself in, among other guises, the idols of pop music or similar.

From my own reaction, however, I am persuaded that it was a rare but genuine case of possession. I was glad to note that the other four voices of which she had first complained had ceased to trouble her.

In any event, whatever the true diagnosis, it was the work of prayer as well as professional psychiatry that mattered and which brought relief to Mary's tortured condition.

4

FOUR YOUNG PEOPLE
AND A DOG

Two girls, waiting outside my church one Sunday evening, asked me if I would lay a ghost which they said was haunting their lodgings.

Both were quaintly dressed but even more bizarre was their multi-coloured hair and the snow-white make-up on their faces. Like little circus clowns, I reflected, but so frail and undernourished. The one who spoke was in her late teens, the other obviously still of school age.

"Of course," I replied, "if that is what is really needed."

"We sure think so" the girl affirmed in a strong Scottish accent. Then she added "I'm Marie and", nudging her friend, "she's Jill."

Giving me their address, Marie added: Haven't been there long — just a month."

"Have you been haunted there all the time?" I asked.

"From the first night," she answered "but it's in the day, too, sometimes."

"Exactly what happens, Marie?"

"There's queer noises," she said "and it gets very cold and creepy like."

I promised to call on them as soon as I could manage. On the following Tuesday I arrived at their house and was astonished to find that it was a large, handsome residence with a recently painted exterior. Hardly the home I had imagined of these two young people. Then I noticed that there were no curtains at the windows but still did not guess the truth of the matter. At that moment a window at the very top of the house opened and little Jill's head craned out to see me.

"I'm coming" she yelled. There followed the quick patter of feet down what were obviously uncarpeted stairs. She opened the door accompanied by a large and ferocious looking Doberman. The dog menacingly bared its teeth and, eyes glinting fiercely, growled throatily at me.

"Shut up, Mimbo" said Jill.

"I hope he's safe" I said nervously. "he looks pretty wild to me!"

"He can be." she remarked laconically "He'll go for some types. Come on in. We are upstairs — at the very top."

As Jill and Mimbo preceded me I saw that the newly decorated hallway of the house was daubed with graffiti. Everywhere on the fresh white paint were thick black letters more than a foot high and various crude drawings. I could hardly believe that such an evidently well-cared for property could have been so abused.

The house was probably up for sale and had been left empty by its trusting owners. These girls, I guessed, had entered it in some way and were now squatting there.

I discovered a little later that they had 'inherited' the place from previous squatters. The latter had actually been responsible for the vandalised walls.

Jill and the still-growling Doberman led me into a small bedroom, devoid of all furniture, where Marie was lying on some sacks and old newspapers. She was smoking. Reclining on one elbow she greeted me. Her welcoming tone obviously mollified Mimbo who now coiled up quietly at her feet, although he still gave me a baleful glare.

This room, which the two girls had obviously made their living quarters, was also streaked with painted slogans on every wall and even on the ceiling. I could not help wondering how it could ever by cleaned for there was rubbish everywhere. The remains of the dog's meal, laid out on newspaper, stood alongside that of the girls' own supper plates.

Almost overwhelmed by the scene I could not concentrate (as I usually endeavour to do on first entering when dealing with a suspected haunting) upon gaining that early impression of 'atmosphere' which is often a helpful test as to whether the alleged phenomenon is of ghostly origin or not. Of course my apprehension of Mimbo had not helped in that!

"These noises you spoke of, Marie", I asked "where do you think they come from?"

"Not just here" she said. "They are mostly in the room opposite, across the stairs. But we hear them here, too, scraping and shuffling sounds."

"Not the dog?" I asked, with some humour.

"No, Mimbo gets upset when we hear them. Sometimes he seems afraid, doesn't he, Jill?"

Jill agreed. "yes, he shrinks back on the floor and begins to whine."

"Before I start" I said "can I ask you a question? I don't want you to think I am interfering with your way of life, but, Marie, whilst *you* are old enough to do as you please, surely Jill is still at school, even if on summer holiday at the moment?"

"We met in Glasgow" Marie replied, "She joined me in coming to London. She wanted to. I didn't try to persuade her."

"Unhappy at home, I suppose?" I said to Jill.

"That's right" she answered.

"Would your parents like you to return?"

"Yes, they would — I think" she nodded, "But I like it here with Marie."

"But what do you both live on?" I inquired.

"On my social security money" said Marie, "and we also go 'up West' every night."

"Do you mean you beg in places like Soho?" I inquired.

"There's always a pound or two to be got 'up West'" Marie replied.

I felt it best not to inquire more for fear of losing the confidence of the two girls, but mentally noted I must let the welfare authorities know the situation as soon as possible for the sake of the younger girl.

It was difficult to gain an unprejudiced impression of the psychic atmosphere of the place but I sensed very strongly that the previous squatters must have been drug-takers.

However, while engaging in small talk, mainly about the dog and how they could afford to feed him, I was able to switch off part of my attention upon the girls and Mimbo and to concentrate on what might be the underlying problem. I realised that the noises complained of could be those which can naturally occur in empty houses especially if they are old and of fair size. Natural noises which these two, in their youthful imagination, would blame upon evil spirits.

The dog might then react to their own nervousness.

Nevertheless I had what I can only call an overwhelming intuition that the trouble was really being caused by the use of drugs. I took note of the cigarettes the older girl was smoking. The half-empty pack lay on the floor beside her and was quite ordinary. However, I felt I must make sure.

"Do you take drugs — smoke cannabis or such like?" I asked.

Marie was quick to answer. "No fear", she exclaimed. "We are not daft. Actually, though, a couple of boys who stay in the room opposite sniff glue for an hour or two most evenings. They said they wanted to meet you. I'll ask them to join us."

She thumped loudly on the wall with her shoe and a few moments later two lads entered. It transpired they were still at school and, although living at home, a couple of miles away, made this house a hideaway where they could indulge in glue sniffing.

They were a dishevelled couple with drawn faces, long lank hair, and red-rimmed eyes. The odour as they came in was unpleasant.

I shook each by the hand and noted how cold and lifeless was their handclasp.

Their deadness of manner indicated to me that they were very open to self-destructive spiritual forces.

It was getting rather dark and the girls explained that there were no facilities of gas, electricity or water. Jill lit a candle and in the flickering shadows I explained to the four that I would say some prayers and give each of them the laying-on of hands. Thus, I said, good spiritual power would be released to overcome anything untoward. Earlier in conversation I realised that there was a large measure of superstition in these young people and that they completely trusted in the efficacy, not only of prayers, but in the fact that a priest was present.

We began with the Lord's Prayer which I was pleased to discover they knew by heart and readily joined in saying. Indeed I have rarely found a more moving response of greater intensity or attention. Even the restless Mimbo had curled up and appeared to be content.

"We have used the prayer Jesus Himself taught", I said, "So now we are in His unseen presence and therefore drawing upon His healing power.

As I lay my hands upon each of you any evil spirit which may be working in you to disturb this place will be driven away by the loving Spirit of Jesus."

All four were sitting cross-legged around me as I laid my hands on their bowed heads.

In the case of the two girls I felt almost immediately the warm tingling in my hands of normal auras. This increased in strength and compass as I prayed aloud for their deliverance from all harmful influences. It became particularly noticeable in the case of the younger girl and I gained the strong impression that she would soon be saved from her present moral and spiritual danger *by her own wish*. I sensed that her spirit-soul was now receiving encouragement to break from the situation she had allowed herself to be drawn into.

During the ministration I said to her: "Jill, you are being helped by the Spirit of Jesus to return to your family, where you will be welcomed and made happy again. We thank our heavenly Father for that."

The girl lifted her face and looked up at me with tear-brimming eyes: "Oh, vicar," she cried "do you think so? I thought I would *never* want to go back — never, never. Now, suddenly, I do. It's a strange feeling — so sudden."

"We shall see that you do return, never fear" I answered quietly but emphatically. "You will not mind, Marie, will you?"

Marie, without hesitation, replied that she would never prevent her friend doing what she wished and would certainly not attempt to persuade her to continue in her own nomadic way of life.

Then I turned to the two lads. It was with them, as I had expected, the most illuminating reaction occurred.

As I laid my hands on their heads they began to tremble quite violently. Their auras were very cold. One of them, whom I will call Jim, swayed so much that he toppled forward and would have collapsed to the floor had I not supported him by the shoulders.

He began to talk confusedly at first and then ¿

"I see things" he said. "What you do see?" I asked him gently, "good things or bad?"

"Most times they are bad. They frighten me. I see faces and crawling things which are going to hurt me. I can't get away from them — only when I sniff the glue. Then it is all quiet and there is nothing."

"And when my hands were on your head?" I inquired.

"That was good. It made me feel fine and there was something inside me that was happy."

"We call that the peace of God or the loving Spirit of Jesus, Jim." I said. "You are being healed — relieved of those awful sensations. But you must not go back to sniffing glue. It will all become unpleasant again if you do. Do you understand?"

Jim nodded in affirmation. His friend Peter broke in: "I felt something, too" he declared. "I felt it going all through me — like electricity. Even now I can feel it. It is good. Is it Jesus?"

"It is His power of healing, Peter" I said. "It takes away our sadness and give us hope for the future. But you, too, must give up the glue habit — from this very moment.

"Had either of you been sniffing it before I came in this evening?" I asked. They assured me that they had not but had previously intended to do so after I left.

"You will destroy yourselves if you do", I warned them. "Your minds will go and your bodies become weaker and weaker. I must tell you I have often had to take the burial services of young people, scarcely twenty years old, who have taken drugs. Sniffing glue can be just as bad. But others have told you that already?"

They answered that hitherto such warnings had meant nothing to them but now this one of mine did.

"Then we will ask God's blessing upon each of you — to help you keep your promise." I said. "Also you will find, all of you, that there will be no more haunting in this place from this night on."

"Does Jesus always come like this?" one of the lads inquired.

"Well" I replied, "each one of you say you have *felt* something — something happy. Now Jesus is not only in this special kind of experience. He is always present whenever we let our minds think gladly and trustfully about Him.

It won't always be like to-night — sudden and wonderful. And, remember, you won't need me to be with you. It is something each of us can know on his or her own. Sometimes you may think things remain just the same but deep, deep down in you the Spirit of Jesus will go on working to bring you new happiness, perhaps in some quite ordinary thing or event — and maybe to change your circumstances.

He continues to be on our side. Our part in it all is to remain true to Him — and *always* to trust Him. *That* is the love of Jesus."

Jill spoke up: "What sort of prayers must we say?"

33

"There is, of course, Jesus's own prayer which we began with to-night. That is a *very* powerful prayer if we say it thoughtfully. But it is not just *saying* prayers. It is having an attitude towards Jesus. Loving Him, desiring to live our lives well and with real purpose — as if He is beside us and we want to please Him by the way we are. Then His Spirit will stay with us and affect what we think and say and do."

"But I always thought Jesus could only help those who went to Church and all that sort of thing" said one of the boys very earnestly.

"By that, I suppose you mean you don't go to Church" I said "though I imagine you did at one time?"

"Yeah — I went to Sunday School" Jim replied, and the others agreed. One admitted membership of a Church choir for a year or two.

"It's a pity you don't go now", I continued, "because going to church is meant for life and not just while we were small. It is of the greatest help to us. But God is not just loving and caring only to those who go to church. He loves the *whole* world. Not just a bit of it or just some folk in it. Everyone — every Tom, Dick and Harry, every Jim and Peter, every Marie and Jill, the good and the bad, God loves. He will *never* stop loving everyone of us, even if we cease ever to think of Him. That would hurt Him like we are hurt whenever people stop loving or noticing us. But that will not stop Him loving us — and loving us forever, in this world and the next."

I felt, somewhat self-consciously, that I had given something of a sermon but the words flowed from me as if another being than mine was relaying them. While saying them I realised how great was their truth — a truth which I had preached often enough in a thousand different ways but not sensed with such underlying passion, happiness and conviction, as now.

Evidently the young folk caught the atmosphere of my own elation for there followed such a gentle silence, so richly charged with psychic power, that I knew deep within myself that comfort and healing had come not only to them but also to me.

With me they had reached out and, as it were, touched the very person of Jesus and received His healing love.

It was then that I perceived upon the heads of the four a shimmering glow which began to emanate also from their kneeling bodies like a golden sheath. No doubt the meagre light of the one candle had helped me to discern their auras. I ought to say that this candle was placed to my left, and slightly behind me, on the floor. It was not in a position, therefore, where its flame could have induced in me a trance. My own shadow actually fell across the group which was thus in added darkness.

But more lovely than this perception was when I looked upwards, in recognition of God's blessing upon us, because I saw a peculiar radiance in the corner of the room behind the young people. As I continued to look spell-bound upon it the light took on the shape of a glowing figure. There was no delineament of face or form that I could properly apprehend, but instinctively I realised it was an angelic presence. It remained for a few moments only but my sense of transport evoked by it was so sublime that I felt I must be out of my body. Though desiring that angelic apparition to remain it faded suddenly, but I continued to sense its joyful support and concern as I commended each of the young folk to the guidance and comfort of our heavenly Father. The ecstasy of the experience was such that I cannot recall precisely my words of benediction to them. They welled up as if from some other source than my own spirit and contained a strange force which left me feeling I had been raised several inches from the floor.

The stillness afterwards was charged with pulsating power which appeared to pour for several seconds from my right hand while it was raised in the blessing. Always in this particular function of pronouncing a benediction I try to hold a mental picture of Jesus with his own Hand similarly lifted in blessing. On this occasion that image was most vivid and powerful.

Now, in cool assessment of the phenomena, I realise that I had entered a deep mystical state produced by intense concentration upon spiritual things and by my earnest desire to bring new life to these stranded young souls. Doubtless those who seek so-called rational explanations would dismiss the experience as hallucination due to the emotional condition of my mind at that time. My answer must be that the visionary experience and the hallucinatory one are very different in quality and kind and certainly in aftermath.

As I prepared to leave one of the boys went into the next room and quickly returned with a tin of glue. It had never been opened and I understood it was their supply for that evening.

"We'll chuck this away, sir," he said "or *you* can if you like."

"It would be best if you do that yourselves" I urged, "it is good to make the positive effort."

It was several days later before I encountered Marie again. She was leaving a fried-fish shop with some other young people who, like herself, were clad completely in leather. They moved off to their motor-cycles parked at the kerbside, but she crossed the road to speak to me, clutching a bag of chips. Her hair was dyed in even more brilliant hues than before, but instead of the white make-up she had adopted large red patches on her cheeks and bright blue about her eyes. At least it looked healthier, I thought!

"How does it go, Marie?" I asked.

"O.K." she said. "I'm not in that house now. I left this morning and got somewhere further north. Jill went back the day after you came to see us — guess I'll see her again one day if I return to Glasgow. But she was looking forward to seeing her Mum and Dad." "What about the boys?" I inquired.

"They only came back once to the house after that night — just to say good-bye. They didn't use that glue and said they had thrown it away. They reckoned they weren't going to waste any more money on it. So I guess they've kicked it. Your prayers sure helped. Are you glad, vicar?"

"More than I can say" I replied "but what about you, Marie?"

"Don't worry" she grinned, "I'll be OK. Maybe I'll go home, too. Perhaps I'll live different one day. Thanks vicar — for everything."

The motor-cycles were revving up and their drivers called to her.

"So long" she said and, with another "Thank you for everything", she skipped lightly away to mount the pillion of one of the machines. She adjusted the black helmet which had been dangling from her wrist, upon her rainbow head and, cheerfully waving to me, she was driven away in a din of engine and a cloud of blue smoke — leaving me to muse upon the happy possibility that Jill and the two schoolboys were going to make a better life. Sad, though, that this might not prove so for Marie.

I could only continue to think prayerfully of her from time to time and hope and trust in Him who made it clear that He would never give up reclaiming even one lost sheep. Perhaps, above all, to thank Him for vouchsafing to me because of those four youngsters — and indeed *through* them — an experience of the loveliest exaltation.

5

THREE ADDICTS RECEIVE A BLESSING

Drug addicts sometimes complain of their homes being haunted or of themselves being possessed by demons. Generally their convictions are the result of hallucination. The drugs dull the sensory system and then the thoughts and desires of the subconscious mind come to the surface. However, the rational mind cannot relate these to the material world. In the constant, exhausting struggle to do so the unfortunate victim becomes caught in a web of fantasy and, ultimately, of mania. Hence the tendency after a while to believe that external forces, over which he has no control, are responsible for tantalising and tormenting him.

On the other hand the very fact of the sense perceptions of the body-soul being enfeebled by the effect of a drug may cause the extra-sensory perceptions of the spirit-soul to function. It is therefore possible that direct communication of the drug addict's spirit-soul with the spirit-soul of another person (or persons) may occur, or even with the spirit of someone who, though dead, is still earth-bound. Likewise there may take place communication with lower entities which are ever bent upon taking mischievous advantage of the situation.

Hence it would be wrong to dismiss every spiritual distress which is manifested under the influence of drugs as being pure hallucination. Let me quote a case where I believe it was possible that a genuine case of haunting had occurred in the lives of those who had embarked upon 'the drug scene'.

One day while making some pastoral visits a young man hailed me from a doorway.

"You are the local vicar?" he asked.

"That's right," I replied. "Can I be of help to you?"

"I think you can" he said "I believe you are one of those who do things about haunted houses?"

I nodded: "You mean exorcise them? Yes, I have done so on a good number of occasions. Do you think your place has a ghost?"

"We are sure of it" he answered: "Can you spare the time to come in?"

I followed him into the house — a small very decayed terrace dwelling with the main door opening directly on the street.

I took stock of my questioner. He was extremely thin, his inadequate clothing for such a wintry day hung loosely upon him, more than a size too big. The complexion of his peaky face was unhealthily pale and his manner decidedly nervous.

I was immediately impressed by the entrance passage of the house. It was painted entirely in the darkest blue, relieved only with a profusion of stars of various sizes fashioned in silver paper and glued everywhere on the ceiling and upper half of the walls.

I reflected to myself that the occupants obviously felt they were being very 'arty', but this bizarre decoration made the narrow passage seem more cramped than ever. Indeed I felt the walls might tumble in at any moment, so claustrophobic was the effect.

The young man led me into what was evidently the main living room. This, too, was strangely decorated to give a weird atmosphere — black painted walls and ceiling with rather tawdry paper cut-outs of gross beasts and demons in bright red and green applied to them.

Here another young man, more robust and a little older than the first, greeted me. A large fair beard which covered most of his face did not, however, hide the fact that he, too, had an extreme pallor.

"Do you" I asked, "have the same experience as your friend?" He nodded affirmatively.

"Can you describe it to me?" I asked.

The eyes above the beard looked rather vacantly at me.

"Its the same," he said, "just the same", and he lapsed again into a trance like silence.

"But what is it?" I repeated. "There are usually tell-tale signs, you know. It could be cold feelings or odd smells. Maybe unaccountable noises, of course. What is it you both *feel — and when*?"

The thin young man, after glancing expectantly at his friend, as if hoping he would make the explanation instead, spoke up at last.

"Like Mike says", he began, "it's the same for both of us. Just suddenly we feel there is someone here and then it's real scary. It just sends us!"

I took a long look at both of them trying to make up my mind about the situation. At that moment I heard a lavatory flushing and soon after another young man entered the room. Like the others he was dressed in faded blue jeans and a sloppy sweater. He was smoking and the peculiar smell of the cigarette made me suspect cannabis, though at that time I had only a little knowledge of the drug scene.

Inwardly, I thought: "Ah, just as I guessed — these chaps are having drug hallucinations."

The third man was monosyllabically apprised by Mike and the thin young man of why I had come. He welcomed me much more forthcomingly than his two friends and appeared most ready to supply not only details of 'the experience' but to make his own diagnosis of it as well.

"I'm Lance", he said, speaking with an American accent, "I am damn pleased to meet you, father. I guess this pad is haunted sure enough," he continued, as we shook hands. "You see, we get together and smoke a joint or two and have one or two beers. Then John-o... That's John-o (here he pointed to the thin young man). Then John-o begins to feel scared. He was the one to feel it first, soon after we got this place fixed up..."

He broke off to wave his arm around the room in evident pride of what had been achieved in its decor. "By the way, how do you like it? Don't you think it's great?"

"Certainly unusual" I murmured and then, as I noticed the rickety table by the window strewn with a jumble of paints and brushes, I enquired: "But why these dancing devils and queer animals all over the place? That would create a queer atmosphere surely? — especially if one were tired."

Lance replied: "it was John-o's idea — he's good at them isn't he? We are all artists, father, and we've all shared in this but it's John-o's devils. Aren't they just great?"

He looked somewhat reproachful at what I had said and I sensed that my criticism may have hurt the feelings of the three. I must rectify that quickly I thought, or I will lose their confidence. After all they obviously liked their effort at unusual decor. Certainly not to my taste but then heaven knows how shabby and dilapidated a scene the house may have presented before.

"It's jolly striking I must admit" I conceded. "I've never seen anything like it before." Then, jokingly, I added: "except perhaps in a horror film."

This sally obviously pleased them and they smiled as if my comment was the best flattery they could have received. Ease between us was restored.

"Well, anyway," I said, "what about this haunting?"
The American continued:

"Yeah — John-o gets this feeling that someone has joined us. He gets stiff with fright and then usually we both feel the same thing. There just has to be a ghost here. Once or twice we have seen a shape move across — by that window."

This looked out upon a tiny patch of garden raggedly covered with scrawny grass and piled with an assortment of litter.

Mentally, I reflected, this all sounded like a case of suggestion. The thin young man's preoccupation with devils, as portrayed by his mural efforts plus the fact that he was taking drugs had, I conjectured, dragged out of his subconscious a disordered fantasy. When at the same time his companions were likewise in a semi-trance induced by drugs this spiritual impression was communicated to them.

A case of hallucination, and nothing more, I felt certain.

Not wishing to say as much bluntly to the three, because I thought they might take offence, I extricated myself saying:

"I'll look in again to see how things go. But let me know immediately if you sense anything at any other time than when you have been smoking 'pot' together."

This appeared to satisfy them and, explaining that I must now continue on my way to visit a sick parishioner, the three accompanied me in single file down the narrow passage to the front door.

"Thanks, father," said the American, "you really will come again? I'm sure we'll need you."

"I will," I reassured him, and after handshakes all round I emerged into the street.

At that very moment an elderly man passed and spoke to me:

"Queer lot in there, vicar, aren't they?"
I smiled: "You could say that. Actually though they are a bit bothered about the house. They feel it is haunted."

"That's more than likely" replied the man. His answer surprised me. Often enough people's reaction to talk of ghosts is immediately one of scepticism or outright amusement.

"What do you mean?" I asked.

"Well," said the man, "I don't know what the place is like now but it always was a bit of a hovel. To my knowledge there have been a couple of suicides there in the last few years."

"Do you know the details?" I enquired.

"No — I'm sorry I can't help you there but I think in both cases they were youngish fellows, probably on drugs."

Suddenly I felt a sharp twinge of conscience. Maybe I had made too hasty a judgement about those three young men in their assertion of a haunting. It could be, I reflected, that an uneasy departed soul (or souls?) was earth-bound to the place after all. In that case the drug-induced trance condition of the thin young man, John-o, might render his spirit-soul receptive of the distress of such a soul. Most likely the other two young men would not receive this impression directly themselves but, in their own drugged state, they might pick up telepathically the effect which had been made upon their friend. I felt I must go back to the three as quickly as possible. This I did immediately after I had made the sick visit.

The trio were greatly pleased to see me again so soon and even more so when I said that I would say some prayers in their living room. Instantly they became most earnest and attentive when I asked for a small bowl of water. Requesting them to stand around me I blessed the water by making the sign of the cross on its surface and prayed:

"O Heavenly Father, our Creator, may this water be to us a sign of Thy cleansing, of Thy protection, and of Thy love for us. So we bless it in the Name of Thy dear Son, Jesus Christ, in Whom every soul, living and departed, can find peace and fulfilment. Amen."

Then I bade them remain silent and to take several deep breaths together with me. This they did with great concentration when I explained it would help us to be in spiritual union with each other. Then I reminded them of the promise of our Lord Jesus that when two or three meet together, truly desiring Him, then He would be present among them in all His power. The Lord's own prayer, I said, would help us to come spiritually close to each other and to the unseen world.

They joined me in that lovely and most potent of prayers and how I thanked God that at sometime in their youth they must have been taught it, however immature in other respects their religious understanding appeared to be.

Their sincerity was obvious by their relaxed features and in the confident gaze of their upturned faces. I was most impressed by this latter fact because most folk in prayer usually look downwards and close their eyes. here it was as if the three realised the majesty and ascendancy of the Lord Jesus — looking up, as the disciples of old may have done, in expectancy of Christ coming down from heaven. Certainly it occurred to me then that it was as if they were truly seeing Him Who is invisible.

In the happy knowledge of their spiritual earnestness and simplicity of faith I continued in prayer:

"If there be among us any who have passed through the veil of death in distress and perplexity, thinking by taking their own life all would be solved, but who now remain in unease and anguish of spirit let us tell you that your sadness has been felt and recognised. But take courage that there are those around you in spirit who are ready to help you and who can take you to where you will find a peace and understanding you can never find here. The Lord Jesus waits to reveal Himself to you in a new way. His angels work for you. Go, then, happily and with complete assurance, knowing the love and compassion of our Heavenly Father."

The three companions were marvellously quiet and there was a transcendent feeling of gentle peace being powerfully generated in the room.

With the bowl of water I moved towards the window and made the sign of the cross upon the frame in the lower left and right hand corners. I did the same on the upper lintel of the door.

"May all who look through this window and who come through this door enter this home in joy and peace and leave it in true friendship. In the Name of the Father and of the Son and of the Holy Spirit. Amen."

After a few moments, throughout which the presence of spiritual power and peace continued, I moved amid that little group of three and, laying my hands on each of their heads in turn, I said:

"Receive the blessing of our Heavenly Father, the assurance of the unseen companionship of Jesus, and the continuing life and help within you of the Holy spirit. Amen."

Their countenances were so alight with happiness that I found it difficult not to weep for the extraordinarily beautiful effect our meeting together had produced. It was a most moving and profound spiritual experience. Some days later I called upon them again. The American was in the process of making coffee for his two companions, one of whom was reading, while the thin young man was busy with his brushes. "Painting more devils, I expect," I said to myself, but I saw I was wrong judging from the half finished sketch.

"It's all OK now" John-o said and then, seeing my gaze upon his work, he added shyly: "I do paint angels as well, father ... do you see?"

"That's good, I'm glad of that" I replied, "because I believe I met one just a day or two ago..."

They looked at me. "No kidding" said one of them.

"It's like this." I answered. "When I first left you I met a man immediately after you had said 'good-bye'. He was passing your very door and told me something which made me decide to see you again promptly. As you know, I did so — within the hour. That is sometimes how angels greet us — through another human being who happens to be at a certain place at a certain time and who says something to us which triggers our action which otherwise we might never have performed. That's what *I* believe anyway..."

They did not press me to reveal what my 'angel' had said that day. It was as if some intuition on their part happily and naturally accepted my explanation. When I left them all three were smiling and their faces showed great content. It even seemed to me that their peculiar pallor had disappeared. They never complained again about their 'haunting'. I am left to reflect that, whether there had been a genuine ghost or not (and I do suspect there was) our prayers together had certainly exorcised their minds of their fear or their hallucination. And that, too, is spiritual healing.

6

A HAUNTING EXORCISED

A woman who felt sure her new flat was haunted asked me to exorcise it. She explained that earlier she had lived in an apartment above. When the opportunity to move below was presented she was glad to accept because it was more spacious accommodation. However, very soon after settling in she had been disturbed by a peculiar atmosphere and certain strange happenings. These were the unexplained movement of small objects in the flat, an occasional ill-odour, and a generally oppressive feeling which was particularly strong in one bedroom. Here her young daughter complained of being unable to sleep, often experiencing cold and eerie sensations which frightened her at night. Her bed which in the former flat was always favoured by the dog to sleep upon during the day was now completely spurned by the animal. Moreover, the dog absolutely refused even to enter this bedroom, crouching down whenever it was led towards the door and exhibiting signs of great unease.

The woman said that, till then, she had not really considered psychic matters, had never thought seriously about ghosts, nor known anything like her present experiences before.

I pointed out to her that the moved objects and bad odour could have perfectly normal explanations. Temporary forgetfulness, the mischief of the dog, a blocked drain could be the causes! To this she was prepared to agree although very reluctantly because she was positive each time that no one could have been responsible for the movement of household objects, items of food, etc. other than herself.

On the ground floor in those days were the premises of an undertaker which included a small chapel of rest. She wondered if there were any connection between her experiences and maybe the restless spirits of deceased persons still attached to their bodies.

I agreed that there was some possibility of this but thought it could be discounted by the fact that her account indicated a continual haunting of the flat while the corpses would only be kept for a few days at most in the chapel awaiting the funerals. Moreover, this chapel was not always in use and one could not believe that the soul of *every* deceased person whose body was brought in would be a disturbing influence.

There was, however, something I learned which at the time of the woman's early days in the flat she was not aware of, namely, that a murder had been committed in the house which adjoined her flat. It was a notorious and, for a long time, very baffling case.

The body, before being dramatically disposed of, had first been temporarily hidden in a cupboard. This was in a room on the other side of the dividing wall separating it from this woman's 'haunted' bedroom.

A corresponding cupboard, backing on this one, was constructed in that bedroom also. The bed was placed lengthwise across it. When this was pulled aside and the cupboard door opened there was a peculiar coldness. Not, perhaps, to be unexpected as there was a chute below. But the kind of chill I experienced when I stood before it was not a natural one and emphasised what I had been conscious of at the very moment of entering the bedroom. This I remember thinking was in itself most unusual because in most cases I find I must concentrate a while in prayer before I gather any special impression or atmosphere.

While I stood before that open cupboard the hair on the nape of my neck bristled and I felt swathed in a peculiar aura which made me aware of a prickling all over my body. Energy seemed to be leaving me from every pore. As from some guiding inner light I knew that I must be resolute and above all *definite* in my approach to the situation. I must go straight forward, as it were, and deal with it in *absolute* assurance of the power of God, without the slightest trace of hesitation. There is only one way to be able to direct such a confident attitude: to *know* (not just believe) that God cares for the release of every human soul from whatever binds it and destroys its peace.

I knew I must not care about any personal psychic unease but trust only in the power and love of God. Such knowledge perhaps only comes with oft repeated experience of exorcism. Would that I could have come to it more certainly in earlier days! But I sm sure that it is wholly important if one is not to become unhappily affected afterwards or debilitated by the repeated practice of dealing with disturbed souls or the discord caused by difficult entities. In actual fact a true exorcism should be followed by a lovely kind of peace, an elation, a glorious inflow of spiritual power, which raises the soul to what can only be called ecstasy. The reason for this should be obvious.

The exorcist has offered himself wholly to his loving Creator and is an instrument through whom His peculiar grace is being effected. What a blessed fellowship!

So, in such resolution, I stretched out my hands, thereby endeavouring to encourage in myself a spirit of welcome, a kind of greeting, which would give assurance to the unseen presence.

Then I said:

"Friend, I know you have been through a terrible experience. As others do I understand your fearful anguish and frustration. Believe me, there awaits you a great comfort and consolation, if only you will now accept it. Your ordeal *is* known to this world. But now it is all over and the fuller life of the Spirit with all its glory and wonder, is calling for you to enter it fully. Be sure there are no bounds to that life."

I sensed that I *must* give emphasis to underlining the genuine compassion of those who were shocked and grieved by the murder. So, after a short pause, (during which I continued to feel the oppressive gloom of an unhappy presence), I repeated my assurance:

"..... we *know* your pain; we realise the horror of your death and the anxiety of the long, long days before it was revealed. We share your agony over the mystery which still lingers about it. But the loving God Who made each one of us for a blessed fulfilment bids you into the greater light and peace that He wills for you. There is joy sublime for you and perfect understanding of your spirit. Enter that beauty and rejoice in it even now....

Friend, let me call you friend, for I bring only good tidings — I shall now say the Prayer of Jesus who is ready to accompany you on your happy journey to release ...."

I then repeated, gently and very deliberately, the Lord's Prayer. Great comfort came to me as I did so and the chillness began to disperse. Then I added: "The holy angels wait upon you and those who knew and loved you. Your friends and family, who have passed through death, are wanting to renew your fellowship. Do not let them go on waiting. Be ready to join them .... as they bid you welcome."

During these last words, which came most naturally from the very heart of me, I enjoyed a sweet easing of my concern and an ineffable feeling of tranquillity. It was like the breaking of sun through black clouds. The strange coldness gave place to reassuring, caressing warmth and pure elation.

I am sure in that last statement I was but echoing a jubilant fact. Angels and departed loved ones were indeed present — and were welcoming, at that very moment, that forlorn spirit.

I closed my ministration with a prayer of gratitude to God: "All glory be to Thee, Father, and thanksgiving. May Thy blessing rest now upon this home and may Thy holy angels ever protect those who dwell here. This we pray through Thy dear Son, Jesus Christ, who is our Lord and our Saviour. Amen."

The woman, who had been standing by me with eyes closed and clearly intent upon all that I was saying, added her own obviously heartfelt 'Amen'.

Later she explained that she had only learned of the murder a day or two after asking me to visit her. This was because she was a comparative newcomer to the district.

"I was rather surprised" she continued "that you conducted the exorcism so *informally*. I had some idea that there would be a special ritual. What I felt sure of, though, as you were speaking and praying, was that it was being truly effective — and that it all seemed so real and natural. I cannot put it more clearly than that ..."

"Yes" I replied, "I know many do think that an exorcism must follow some set pattern of prayers and so forth. Indeed that could have been true years ago in an age when folk were more in accord with religious faith and practice.

But that kind of situation has not generally pertained for several generations as we well know. Of course if I had reason to believe that a haunting was due to an event in the distant past I might well approach the matter in a more stylised and ritual way."

"I remember", I continued "after giving a lecture on psychic matters to a church group, a deaconess in the audience approached me, very seriously, saying that she and her vicar had met a situation which they came to believe was a genuine case of haunting. They had conducted, therefore, a service of Holy Communion, but were dismayed to find that this did not produce a satisfactory exorcism. The haunting had continued just as before.

I put it to her that if she were in some deep spiritual trouble and I had simply said that I would celebrate Holy Communion especially for her, would she think that to be an entirely satisfactory answer? Would she not expect that first I talked over her problem sympathetically and, if possible, provided advice and counsel? Surely only after that had been done would the special spiritual support of Holy Communion be realised. Furthermore, I went on, supposing a person in spiritual anxiety was not, like herself, a regular churchgoer or communicant, would not the most important thing to him or her be one's personal compassion and undivided attention? Then the person would more likely be in receptive mood for the follow-up of prayer and its blessing..."

The deaconess immediately saw the commonsense of this. "Likewise, then," I said, "one must approach exorcism in the same natural way as we would give to any disconsolate human being."

The aim of exorcism is always to reassure an unhappy departed spirit of God's eternal love and of the welcoming support and guidance given by the members of the spiritual world. If quite definitely evil spirits are at work the exorcist must recognise the authority in which Jesus himself cast out devils, namely, through the power of God and *only* through that power. However, it is to be remembered that the power of God works in and through us whenever we seek His will which is eternally compassionate, comforting, merciful, understanding and infinitely good.

So it follows that in dealing with a departed soul which is earth-bound because of intense frustration, anguish, remorse or whatever strong emotion, we *must* reflect that same love, care and understanding, and that intimacy of knowing, which God has towards us all. Clearly that must mean treating that departed soul exactly as what he or she indeed is — an unhappy being who rightly deserves sympathetic attention and the reassurance of not being alone or disregarded. Most of all to underline the radiance of life in the nearer presence of God for which death is meant to be the exodus, that is, the 'way through'.

The more natural, therefore, we can be in exorcism the more efficacious it is likely to be. Histrionics and dramatic gestures or ritual patterns simply will not do. While it is true that there may be hauntings of such grossly evil kind that what can only be described as a great tussle must ensue, even to the point of the spiritual, mental and physical exhaustion of the exorcist, they are extremely rare. It may even betoken (though, in charity, we must say not always) that the exorcist is falling back upon his own strength and personality rather than offering himself wholly to God and acknowledging only the Divine Authority for his task.

Much more often the exorcism required is of a gentle, tranquillising nature; the simple use of the God-given power of sympathy and a desire to impart the comfort which arises from the exorcist's own faith in the all-loving Father.

It so happened that the day after this particular exorcism my wife and I left for a holiday in France. When we returned home the woman delightedly informed us that her flat had been completely dispelled of the strange, brooding atmosphere immediately after my visit, and that her dog had, for the first time, gone into that bedroom without hesitation or any untoward behaviour, exactly in that homely manner to sleep on the bed as had been its custom in the former apartment.

This latter fact was highly significant for when animals as well as humans react to a haunting it is a positive indication that the haunting is genuine.

7

DISQUIET FROM A DEMON?

The psychic experience of many folk who have confided them to me over the years, as well as my own, have convinced me that help, guidance and inspiration are received from those whom we 'have loved and lost awhile.' Such assurances may come to us through some rare moment of psychic awareness (usually when our attention is directed away from ourselves). I believe that they also arise in other ways, through occurrences which appear natural and even ordinary. Consequently in such cases we are not conscious of the fact that aid, consolation, encouragement or sudden upliftment is really due to the angelic ministration of our departed loved ones acting indefinably, but nonetheless truly, for our blessing.

So I do not question the fact of communication from the unseen world but I do hesitate to believe that the trance of a medium necessarily provides genuine contact with a particular departed soul. That is certainly not to impute fraudulence on the part of the medium but to suggest that the latter may unwittingly draw out, clairvoyantly or telepathically, some deeply buried memory from the subconscious mind of the sitter (who may have long forgotten it) or even from the medium's own. Moreover, we cannot assume that the realm of the spirits is an arena of total purity and light. There could be spiritual darkness, mischief and deception practised there even as in our present world.

Our difficulty on this side of death is that our extrasensory or spirit-soul faculties are imperfect. Hence, in our attempts to communicate with the unseen we may unknowingly make contact with entities who could be masquerading as our departed loved ones.

A measure of wishful thinking during a seance might seduce us into believing we have truly contacted deceased members among our families or friends. Very little positive proof of identity may be demanded or desired by us for fear that we would be thought insulting them, to the detriment of receiving their message.

No doubt lying spirits dwell in the immediate reaches of the unseen world. They include malevolent departed human souls who have remained earth-bound and seek opportunities to continue to trouble this world. Maybe they are just unhappy and undeveloped souls who are ever intent on drawing our attention to themselves for their relief. Or they could be spirits which are demons who take pleasure in creating disorder, disquiet and mischief whenever they can contrive to do so.

I will quote just one example of what I mean. A middle-aged woman sought my advice on what she described as a very worrying spiritual problem.

"My husband died eighteen months ago" she said. "We were very close and I know I have never really become used to the loneliness. But I have not allowed myself to mope. I took up a little job which gives me much happiness and a degree of satisfaction, as well as keeping me in daily contact with other people.

Nevertheless when I return home I still feel the ache of no one there to share my life. Well, just lately, I have been enduring a most strange and disturbing sensation when the day is done. Often I think I hear footsteps behind me or peculiar noises in the house as if someone else is there. I feel there is a presence in my home which seems not just to be accompanying me but actually trying to get inside me. I could say it has *possessed* me. In consequence I am constantly troubled and have begun to have the most morbid thoughts"

"What do *you* think of all this" I asked.

"I wonder" she answered, "if it is my husband — though I cannot believe he would do anything to upset me."

"You have told me how greatly you loved each other and the happiness you shared," I replied. "I am quite sure, therefore, that this haunting is *not* your husband's doing for he would not wish to frighten you or cause you distress of any kind.
It is just possible, of course, that he might be endeavouring to complete some unresolved business which was important to you both. In other words to direct your attention to it."

"There can be nothing like that," she affirmed. "His illness was prolonged and he became aware of its seriousness some weeks before the end and put all his affairs in order. We talked quite freely about dying — there was nothing held back."

"Then it is clear" I said "that this peculiar presence within you could be a disturbance of your own subconscious mind brought on by the pain of bereavement. On the other hand it might be caused by some mischievous entity gaining a foothold in you through the long ache of emptiness which your soul has experienced.. When you are alone, do you think much upon the past — through concentrated reverie almost enter, shall we say, a trance?"

She looked at me and after a long moment nodded.

"I think you are right about that," she said, "I do conjure many pictures of the past, sometimes they are quite vivid and I feel I am living in them again."

During our conversation I had noted that she was a very intelligent person of open countenance and frank disposition, but that she was trying to assume a composure and detachment which her words and their content belied. As our conversation proceeded she indicated that she had begun to wonder if she were possessed. In some diffidence she asked if she might require exorcism.

"If that proves so" I said, "I shall know it during the laying-on of hands which I am now going to do."

Having first requested her to relax in an armchair we maintained a minute or two of complete silence. At length I felt moved to place my hands above her head and prayed for her protection by Jesus Christ and His angels.

She remained calm, and obviously entirely relaxed, during this ministration but soon after its commencement I felt an unpleasantness which made my flesh suddenly seem very cold. By maintaining the thought of the spiritual help of Christ this very disconcerting sensation gave place at length to a consciousness of tingling warmth from my hands (positioned several inches above her head) and finally there broke through the reciprocal flow of energy between her aura and my palms and fingertips. This throb of energy continued for probably half a minute and then began to subside. Throughout I maintained the thought of Jesus being present with us, using a mental picture of Him as suggested by a general one which I have always conjured of Him from the healing narratives in the New Testament.

At the end of the session we thanked God for His healing through Jesus Christ and then spoke encouragingly to her of the marked improvement in the strength of her aura. It had, I said, appeared at first so withdrawn as to be almost non-existent. This was obviously due to her inward unease over the past months which had culminated in such fearful apprehension.

She looked most relieved and even happy as I told her this and it was delightful to observe that the intense, somewhat faraway look she had first displayed to me had given place to a relaxed countenance and a healthy brightness of eye.

"You will find great relief now" I said "when you get home. If, however, you do feel at any time any sign of your recent distress I suggest you say a prayer for Christ's protection and, of course, before you go to sleep commend your soul into God's loving care. Always remember that God made our souls to be in His sublime keeping. Put all your trust completely in that marvellous truth."

It transpired that after one further similar session of prayer and laying-on of hands she came back to report her complete cure.

"The night after I left you" she said, "I dined with my married son who, incidentally, knew nothing of my trouble. Some hours after he had left to return to his own home I suddenly felt strangely exalted. At that moment it seemed something fell from my shoulders. Turning about I saw a black shape, like some giant beetle lying on the floor with its legs waving in the air. Almost immediately it disappeared and there came over me the most sweet reassurance. I knew, then, that whatever it was causing me so much distress had left me — so that I could be normal and happy again. I want to thank you."

Then she added: "Do you think I was possessed? One thing I am sure of now is that it was nothing to do with my husband. But *could* it have been an evil spirit?"

"You are right to say that it was certainly not a haunting by your husband" I replied. "The love we have known and shown continues in us beyond the grave. Though glorified it is not altered by our death. Hence, in that greater light, we shall not do anything which would diminish that love — rather to transcend it with a knowledge and beauty which can only be hinted at here on earth.

After the trauma of your husband's passing and your deep sense of loss, maybe your subconscious mind became disturbed and the black shape became an effective symbol to you of the end of your anguish.

But it could have been possession by an entity where again the strange shape was a spiritual token to you of final exorcism.

Because of the peculiar intimation I usually receive during the laying-on of hands, my belief in your case is that you were laid open at some time during your repeated periods of great loneliness and sorrowing to possession by a base entity. This was ready for its own satisfaction to deceive you into thinking that it was your husband's spirit, knowing that you might reach that conclusion despite your belief that he would not cause you such distress.

I do not think you should agitate yourself over finding *precise* answers as to why you were haunted or by what. The simple joy, given you by God, is that you have not only been delivered from your anxiety but that you know, deep within yourself, that this is so.

Let me offer you one more thought. I believe that our departed loved ones seek to support us unobstrusively, in our times of perplexity, sorrow or depression. I think they share our joys, too, in a transcendent way. May it not be, then, that your husband, realising your distress, was also spiritually able to help lift it from you?"

Looking intently at me, her eyes shining with relief and new-found contentment she said, quite simply, "That, I feel sure, is true."

8

FUNERALS AND PSYCHIC EXPERIENCE

Officiating at funeral services has brought me its own range of psychical experience. Particularly during the words of committal I have known a truly lovely serenity. At such times I am no longer aware of my body but transported to some gentle and happy spiritual company. My spirit soars and I sense another dimension, another realm. This elation has generally communicated itself to the mourners who, on numerous occasions afterwards, have vouchsafed their own intense feeling of great comfort and a peculiar uplifting of their spirits during that especially sacred and poignant part of the funeral service.

Such experiences are joyful and memorable, serving to stimulate and confirm my belief in the fusion of our physical world with that of pure spirit. So I have been assured, again and again, of our alliance with 'angels and arch-angels and all the company of Heaven' as the Book of Common Prayer so beautifully expresses it.

Nevertheless it is not always so. There are times when a funeral service has, despite all my desire to give comfort and hope to those who mourn, maintained an air which has been distressingly chill, almost empty of any feeling.

I have found this is so when there is great friction within families, dividing them into groups who are usually seated apart, rigidly refusing to come together even for such an occasion.

The funeral service should sound triumphantly the twin notes of God's infinite love and perfect understanding. It is certainly not a time for painful questioning or uncharitable attitudes. All our human affection, however imperfect it may be, is a reflection of the Divine Love and Mercy. If our love has changed to hatred or resentment or indifference there is bound to be created a spiritual vacuum or, at best, discordant vibrations which must wreck the harmonious interchange of the emotions of those assembled.

Because the auras of those present are being held back within themselves instead of being released in warm, outgoing sympathy and love, previous good memories and supporting affections cannot be telepathically shared during the service as they ought to be if its purpose is to be fulfilled, namely, of providing a union of our souls with that of the departed and with the spiritual host of the unseen world.

How grievous and wicked, therefore, that human contention should ever be retained in the presence of the death of one who may indeed be equally loved by the warring sides of a family. Such will most surely inhibit that joyful, hope-filled atmosphere which should permeate the funeral and shine through all the natural sorrow of much felt loss.

Then, of course, there is the suicide. This often causes such profound anguish and perplexity, or such a desperate sense of shame, that the mourners cannot raise their spirits above the shock which they have sustained nor come to terms with the fact that such a thing has really happened, let alone discern the reason for it.

In such cases at the commencement of the service God's mercy and understanding must be most clearly and firmly emphasised. That comforting note should be sustained in the commendation of the departed soul to our Heavenly Father's care. I have found that a quiet sense of peace usually descends. However, I have sometimes noted on very distressing occasions that there is a peculiar haunting presence which makes me feel I must console it with my own faith, and personally endeavour to assure it of the welcome and support of the angels. This I do during the moments of quiet time I allow in every service. I have no doubt that this presence is that of the departed soul seeking reassurance. I believe that the soul of the suicide may often remain earth-bound, for a while at least, after the trauma of what it has done. It needs to accept that its connection with this world has irreversibly ended, and that the understanding which it may continue to seek from those it has left on earth is now freely accorded by them in their love. Moreover, that the help and guidance of the spiritual world is wonderfully ready to heal the anguish and darkness which caused it to seek its own death, and to usher it now into a haven of light and peace.

Naturally, the funeral of one who has been murdered can be a most crushing experience. The more violent and premeditated the act has been the more intense, frightening and repellent can be the atmosphere created. At times (and I have had the painful duty to officiate at a number of funerals of murdered men, women and children) the aura of fear and the feeling of great chill in the congregation and about the coffin have been almost overpowering. It is so important to use every ounce of one's spiritual strength (given through faith in God's mercy, coupled with the certainty of future life and fulfilment for the victim), in order to raise the service to that level wherein consolation and support may be bestowed on those who mourn and also (as I believe) on the victim.

During many funeral services I have become acutely aware of what I deem to be the presence of the deceased's soul and of other spiritual beings. I believe these latter may include the departed's own welcoming dear ones who have already entered the unseen world and also, most assuredly, ministering angels whose service it is to accompany the soul in its first encounter with the spiritual world and thus bring to it ease, enlightenment and reassuring love for its ongoing journey.

Such intimations have sometimes been so strong that I have had, most reluctantly, to force myself to relinquish the beauty and transport of them in order not to prolong the service unduly in consideration for the mourners. During such experiences I have sometimes received knowledge hitherto unknown to me about the departed.This, I believe, is because the special atmosphere generated by a funeral can afford a measure of extra-sensory perception. The following is a case in point. During the service I found my attention irresistibly drawn to a small posy of garden roses. They were lying on the coffin amid a welter of large and very expensive wreaths. At the same instant I had a sudden mental picture of a small man in a brown overall coat standing in a garden. He was attending to some rose trees with secateurs. The image was very fleeting but I noted that he was aged in the middle-forties and had very dark wavy hair.

In the midst of the prayers I was saying a little later in the service I felt compelled to mention the deceased's particular love of roses. I had no reason for this save that I had received a strange intuition in that moment to do so. I have never known the dead man or anything about him. Moreover, there was nothing in the position of the roses to give them prominence and thereby suggest any special significance being attached to them, indeed they were almost hidden by the profusion of other flowers.

The mourners appeared very grateful for the service and afterwards thanked me most warmly for it. One of them drew me aside and said:

"I want to thank you very much for the service. You must have know Bill very well."

"I am sorry to say that I did not." I answered. "In fact I never met him. I only know what the funeral director told me just before this service — simply that he was married with two sons and two daughters, all of whom were in the front pew."

The man looked at me almost unbelieving.

"Yet you know how much he thought about roses." he countered "and the time and care he gave to cultivating them?"

"About that" I said "I have to tell you that I had an intuition of it during the service. That is all."

"How very strange" he replied, "but absolutely accurate. As a matter of fact I have a photograph which shows him and myself at a local Flower Show where he is receiving the first award for his roses."

Then he opened his wallet and produced the picture. It showed a man, middle-aged, with black wavy hair and rather short in stature. He was taking a prize which had just been awarded to him by an official beside whom was standing the man who was now talking to me.

It is likely that in the profound concentration which I always give to funerals I had picked up telepathically the thought of this man for his friend, or a special memory of one of the other mourners as they remembered the departed during the service. Later I checked on the age of the man. He was forty-three.

The clairvoyant insight of my spirit-soul, acting under what amounted to trance, had been accurate about the deceased regarding his age, stature, dark wavy hair and his exceptional passion for growing roses.

I must also acknowledge that not all my experiences in this regard have been a delight. I recall one such during the committal of the body at a cremation service while my back was temporarily turned towards the congregation and my right hand uplifted for the Commendation. I suddenly felt so violent a blow between my shoulder blades that it was with great difficulty I did not lose my balance and stumble headlong. For the moment I felt sure someone from the congregation must have stepped forward and struck me. I thought there must be an unstable and violent person present and fully expected others to come forward to restrain him. The whole matter was over in a second or so and when I turned back again, after the coffin had moved away behind the curtain, I could see that the congregation was wholly respectful, still and silent, and obviously unaware of any unpleasantness.

I knew then what I had in my deepest being suspected (for it was only the intensity of the blow that made me assume it was a physical one delivered by a living person) that there must be some extreme annoyance on the part of the deceased. During the concluding prayers I had the strong feeling that perhaps the dead man disapproved of the service.

This indeed proved to be so for although the widow and her family expressed their deep appreciation of the service, another relative on the way out of the chapel paused to say to me:

"Thanks, padre, for such a sympathetic and most helpful service. For my part I am really glad and grateful that he had this Christian farewell — and I know his wife dearly wished it for him. But, you know, the fact is that *he* certainly never wanted it. He was always very positive about that and would get very argumentative whenever the subject arose and if anyone was opposing him on it. At one time he belonged to the Communist Party and although he gave up membership years ago the anti-religious bit of it remained very strong. He would have disapproved greatly about today, preferring no service at all. He could become quite violent in his objections over anything like this." Then, shrugging his shoulders, he added, "Well, as *you* might say, everything is in God's hands now."

Little wonder, after this unsolicited conversation, I was certain that my intuition concerning my uncomfortable experience was correct. The departed had certainly registered his disapproval!

Phenomena like these provide further endorsement of the theory that great concentration upon prayer is likely to diminish the sense of the body so that extra-sensory perception may be aroused and thus give knowledge and communication of a kind which otherwise would not be apprehended.

9

A CASE OF OBSESSION

The attribution in some religious quarters of every mental and
psychological affliction to the malice of devils can be very obstructive to the advance of spiritual healing. The fact is that although
demon-possession may superficially appear to be a satisfactory and
reasonable diagnosis it is usually a completely mistaken one. Certainly
in my own experience I have found that actual cases of possession
are extremely rare.

Most disturbances of a psychic kind have nothing whatever to do
with alien spirits gaining hold upon the personality. Some are caused
by a fragmentary knowledge of the supernatural percolating from the
subconscious to the conscious mind which produces bewilderment
and chaos for the unhappy victim.

On many occasions people have come to me with the plea to
exorcise them but few actually require this kind of cure. Usually
it has been a case of an imagined condition of demon-possession.
I quote an instance of this kind.

It concerned George, a young man, Czech by birth and most stu-
dious of appearance, who came to live in my parish for a while.

In the beginning he gave me much cause to admire his brilliance concerning philosophical issues. Whenever we embarked on
a theological discussion he insisted on reading from the Greek New
Testament to make his points. His translations were always fluent
and precise. After a time I prepared him for Confirmation and
found him a most zealous pupil. During the period he resided in
the parish he proved a regular and devout communicant.

All seemed well with him for some months until the time came
when he was closeted with me for a couple of hours during which

he expatiated on the origin of life and the nature of the universe. At first I found his theme coherent enough although over-complicated. However, as he pursued his subject I became completely out of my depth. Trying to follow his train of thought and the seemingly unceasing flow of words left me feeling numbed and my head swimming.

The same situation was repeated on several occasions when he came to see me. At the last of these I managed to get him to cease talking by promising to read a thesis which he said was almost completed and on which he had been employed long before I met him.

Sure enough a few days later he brought me a voluminous script, carefully typewritten and appearing (as far as I could observe from the first cursory glance at it) to have not a single alteration made to it.

By reading the written word I felt I might extricate the theme he had poured out so volubly over recent weeks.

The thesis started in a promising way — logically moving along if rather long-winded. But by about the seventh page the thread was completely lost to me. Ideas were going off in unconnected tangents, each one expanded into lengthy passages suggesting, in a vague way, some sort of sense but getting nowhere. Then the script swerved into an entirely unintelligible dissertation upon the importance of — a dewdrop! This continued page after page rambling on until I found myself unable to pay any attention whatsoever. Presumably it could have continued thus ad infinitum for George intimated that: "Of course, there was more to do before it were finished."

He had allowed me to read without interruption. I noted, whenever I looked up from the page, that he would be staring abstractly ahead, his eyes dull like black coals.

When I placed his opus aside he roused himself from his apparent trance to say:
"Will you do something for me?"
"Of course — if I can" I answered, intuitively sensing that whatever his request it was sure to be a strange one.
"I want you to exorcise me." he said simply.
"Why do you ask that?" I asked, studying his face carefully,
"Are you sure you are haunted — or possessed? Could you describe the symptoms?"

He gazed back at me earnestly, very tense now and sitting forward in the chair to emphasise the depth of his concern.

"I just *know*, that's all." He spoke in clipped sentences so unlike his former profuseness. "It's in me — making my head ache. It follows me around. It's always with me — and it's evil. It's a demon, you see. *You* can make it go away."

It was then I became sure that the opinion which I had been forming during our recent meetings was correct. He was the unhappy victim of mania.

There are persons, often of above average intelligence, who at some moment in their lives gather a piece of information from their subconscious minds. The reason for this is obscure. A debilitating illness could trigger this peculiar illumination or a grievous shock arising from some disturbed human relationship. Sometimes it occurs during excessive study, as in young persons who become over-anxious in preparing for their examinations thereby causing what is generally termed a nervous breakdown. Whatever the psychological cause, the subconscious mind (which is pure spirit) by exercising its extra-sensory perceptions acquires a degree of occult knowledge, some aspect of spiritual reality, which could not be gained by the normal working of the mind. This intuitive 'flash' rises into the conscious mind where the person then endeavours to translate it into the world of sense perceptions.

The victim of such an intuition agonises over it, trying to rationalise it. He returns to it over and over again, worrying it like a dog with a bone, in an unceasing attempt to formulate it clearly and exactly so that others may know his experience and share in what he conceives is its tremendous importance.

By its very nature this is an impossible task. The frustration thus incurred can build up to a dangerous degree as the percipient becomes absorbed by his strange glimpse of a purely spiritual reality to the extent that, in his fevered imagination, life itself must depend upon it. Only the sufferer himself can know the depth of anguish involved in his unending desire to express the special insight he has obtained.

The likely next stage is for the sufferer to assume that because he cannot deal with the problem it must be the activity of something outside himself, alien to him — even antagonistic.

Unable to accept that it actually originates from his own soul he objectifies it as being pursuit by a demon which, having fastened itself upon him, must needs be driven out. Exorcism then appears to him to be the only solution of the mental torture he endures.

As time passes and this tension continues the matter fills the whole picture of life. It can lead to the unhappy victim slipping into a dream world where preoccupation with tracking down that elusive spark of spiritual truth or contesting the demon is all in all. This chasing of a shadow can eventually cause the mind to break altogether.

We have to remember in all this that the soul of the unfortunate person is not ailing because as pure spirit it cannot be afflicted by sickness.

This fact can give comfort to those relatives and friends who have the heartache of loved ones who are mentally ill and may imagine their dear ones are destined to experience continued restlessness after their death. Indeed, what happens after death is that the spirit-soul then understands perfectly what caused the confusion and frustration on earth and can fully relate it to the spiritual realm.

Having realised what was the trouble with my Czech friend I sought to deal with it accordingly. If I explicitly expressed doubt as to his case being one of demon-possession and therefore requiring exorcism I felt I would risk losing his confidence. In any event it would be unwise to try to change his view at that juncture because it was not only very strongly held but was actually providing him with some sort of life-line to reality, however inadequate and misconceived.

Consequently I implied my rejection of demon-possession in a delicately oblique way bearing in mind his exceptional intellect.

Placing my hands on his head I prayed:

"Lord Jesus, present in all Your power, we know You make all things new. We have all our trust in You. Our lives are open to You. Deliver your servant, George, from the burden which now weighs so heavily upon him — and make him new. Cleanse and restore him utterly. By Your own light shining within him grant him all those things which belong to Your perfect peace. So bring to him Your joy, hope and spiritual renewal. Drive out all his fears and enlighten him in his perplexity. Make him assured of Your infinite love for him."

The initial coldness of his aura (a fact I have often noticed in those who are anxious or mentally strained) gradually gave place to a marked warmth and vitality. I sensed we were being united in a mystical experience of profound ecstasy.

I continued in prayer:

"In most joyful thanksgiving we praise and glorify Your Holy Name rejoicing in the victory which You have won, O Lord, over all that is evil, all that harms us. By our faith in You we take to ourselves Your pardon and the blessing of Your perfect life wherein there is no disharmony but only clear purpose and sure guidance. Into your dear hands, Lord, we now commend ourselves wholly — body, mind and spirit."

My hands felt the vibration of psychic power while my words came effortlessly, as though responding to the unhesitating prompt of an inner voice.

Spiritual healing rarely has an instantly obvious effect. Rather it achieves, at first, the restoration of tranquillity and confidence to the core of the personality. From thence it works, as it were outwards, to influence the body and so promote physical well-being. In those cases where the body is unimpaired (as yet) and the illness is purely within the mind there can sometimes be an immediacy of healing. Not always, simply because of that imperfection of faith which is due to human frailty (or sin), in both healer and patient.

Further counselling of the patient may therefore be necessary, more opportunities be made to let him unwind, more time for prayer and the laying-on of hands must be given.

This was to be so for George, but gradually the cloud was lifted from him and normal behaviour regained. That first session with him was, however, outstandingly beautiful, altering the intensity of his countenance and general demeanour quite markedly and encouraging him to continue to seek my spiritual help in further sessions. Often, as in George's case, there is the conviction that the person has obtained some profound illumination upon the source of life, a unique unveiling of spiritual reality. Such, of course, is the experience of the mystic who attains (through *purposeful* prayer and meditation upon a spiritual truth) what he describes as a vision of God. But, unlike the mystic, there is an inability to relate that experience to the world and so gather spiritual exaltation from it. On the contrary the result may be one of depression, melancholia, and even mania. Such had been George's own plight until this spiritual healing finally released him.

10

A CASE OF TRANSCENDENTAL MEDITATION

Richard, a correspondent from the United States of America, introduced himself by stating that he had read *A Priest's Psychic Diary* and was therefore asking me for advice concerning what he defined as 'a haunting'.

He had, he wrote, become plagued by voices which were destroying his ability to concentrate on his work as a journalist. Hitherto he had written articles which had always been readily accepted for publication. Indeed he had become a leading authority in his particular field. But latterly his publisher had been disappointed in his work and had refused it. Richard had found it more and more difficult to pen his material at all but had been urged by his 'voices' to engage himself in writing articles upon occult subjects which had not proved marketable.

His letter showed obvious distress and it concluded by asking me to pray for him and to suggest ways in which he might exorcise himself.

Several times I wrote back to his further anguished letters, suggesting prayers he might use and giving him what spiritual counsel I could.

Repeatedly I urged him to talk over the matter with his doctor and with his priest (he had informed me he was a devout Roman Catholic and regularly attended Mass).

Eventually a letter came in which he said he would be coming to England and could he make an appointment to see me in London? So, at last, we met. A man with a pale, sensitive face, gentle and withdrawn, greeted me very hesitantly.

His initial shyness was laid aside at last as I sought to arouse his confidence by rather general conversation while at the same time exercising the habit, which I have always adopted where there is obvious reticence, of inwardly willing him, through my spirit-soul, to open up the barrier with his own.

Now he spoke quite freely. With little prompting on my part I was able to gather details which he had not disclosed in his letters. These made clearer to me the reason for his predicament.

He explained that he had gone to stay for some months in Italy, partly for a holiday but also to gather material for a series of articles he had been commissioned to write. While there he had fallen in with a group of American and English expatriates who were devotees of transcendental meditation (TM).

They had spoken enthusiastically of this practice and one of them had encouraged him to take an interest in the occult, with the special purpose of contacting the spirit-world. This fellow began by flattering Richard (as I saw it) by saying that he would make a particularly sensitive medium and that TM would help in this.

It was not long before Richard became completely addicted to spiritism and regularly attended seances with his mentor.

Then one day while sitting at his desk in a trance state induced by TM, he heard voices directing him to write at their dictation.

Daily the same phenomenon would occur following his regular session of TM until he had accumulated a monumental pile of notes purporting to be from the world beyond.

Sometimes, he explained, they were the revelations of persons who had died either recently or in the distant past, and at other times the messages were from pure spirits of superior knowledge. The friend told him that he obviously possessed a great and special psychic gift and that he must foster it. He urged him to submit his 'spirit' writings for publication. However, they never proved acceptable to any publishers. After reading some of those which he asked me to peruse I could well understand why. They struck me as neither informative nor well written — in fact rather repetitive and boring and in great contrast to the articles he had written in former days which I had found excellent and absorbing.

After a while he began to complain of headaches and discordant noises in the head and became disinclined to write at all. His friend maintained that he must now persevere with his 'automatic' writing and that these symptoms would pass. He insisted that he must prolong his sessions of TM and join the group in theirs. Richard maintained that this was very helpful to him. "Why, then", I asked, "did not your concentration return and your previous successful writing be re-assumed?"

This he could not answer but admitted that his work suffered so badly that he was scarcely ever doing more than sit with a blank sheet of paper before him until, in trance, he found his hand begin to scribble without effort his occult information from 'beyond'.

His normal talent had deserted him and the very act of concentration upon it seemed to induce the condition which brought on the 'spirit voices'.

As he was a highly intelligent and serious-minded person I knew he could take what I had to say and so I spoke freely and openly:

"The first thing I have to say, Richard, is to warn you of the perils of transcendental meditation. Now I know that may sound like heresy to you because you clearly believe you have been helped by it. Nevertheless, for someone as sensitive and artistic as you, it *is* dangerous.

What happens during TM is this: the repetition of the mantra relaxes the senses so that the body-soul becomes subdued and the faculties of the spirit-soul begin to operate. A condition of ecstasy can then occur. You may say "surely that is a good thing" and, indeed, have probably found it so ...."

He was nodding in agreement.

"I can only answer" I continued "that for some folk — and I do repeat *some* — TM can have a beneficial effect physically. It can serve to calm a person, relax the body, reduce blood-pressure, etc. But it can also do something else for some people — and clearly you are one of them. It throws up from the subconscious mind that which can confuse and distress the conscious mind so much that there ensues the loss of ability to concentrate. Haunting nightmares, irrational thoughts and fantasies may follow. Indeed a whole world of unreality can begin to take over until you begin to think that the world of spirits is really controlling you and that your own will counts for nothing — and can effect nothing.

You are one of those sensitive souls who should never experiment with the occult. It was a dangerous — I would even say a wicked — thing on the part of your friends to encourage you to do so.

You are a religious person. Your Christian faith, the teaching and sacraments of your Church, are not only the best for your spiritual

elevation but they are the safest. Wholesome and complete, tried
and tested through the centuries. Adhere only to them and be
content with them. The genuine mystical experience for you lies in
the Mass. Let that be enough — for it *is* enough; and be guided
by the advice and warnings of your priest. Does *he* agree with your
TM sessions?''

"He doesn't actually speak against it" Richard answered, his countenance now more solemn than ever.

"Nevertheless, I am quite certain he would not agree with your seeking contact with spirits by means of it." I countered. "Anyway, leave
it alone. Don't be persuaded by anyone to practise it again."
Rising from my seat I said:

"I am going to pray with you and give you the laying-on of hands."
However, as I placed my hands above his head I received a sudden
intuition. Looking hard at him I said:

"You are receiving psychological help — are you not? It is fairly
recent isn't it?"

"Yes" he replied, somewhat startled. "Yes, only a couple of
weeks before I came to London. But how did you know?"

"These things come sometimes," I said, "often I can sense it
from a person's aura. I can tell, for example, during the laying-on
of hands if tranquillising medicine has been taken. I do make it
a general rule not to intrude into a situation where medical help
is being given unless in accord with the doctor. However, I can
certainly adminster the laying-on of hands with prayer."

"Lord Jesus" I prayed "present now in all Thy power Who
hast bidden us to come to Thee with our burdens, let Thy Holy
Spirit bring peace to Thy servant, Richard, whose trust in Thee is
complete..."

The word 'peace' began to assume great importance. It seemed
to stand out in my mind's eye in letters of brilliant whiteness. I
could virtually *feel* the word working through my hands, through
my entire body.

"Peace," I said again "deep, deep peace. O let Thy peace descend
upon us and fill us. May we see Thee Lord — Thee only — and
know Thy peace now..."

Then that peace came, a tranquil loveliness which seemed to clothe
us and to shut out entirely the physical world. How impossible it is
to define in words the beauty of such an experience. How ineffably
precious every recollection of it. And Richard was knowing it,

too. The stiff attitude had gone. his steady, gentle breathing and complete relaxation was now allowing his aura to come through and to be firm and lively beneath my hands. Gradually widening the distance of my hands to arm's length from his head I could still feel the throbbing power of it. Surely this was the peace which passes understanding.

"Lord," I prayed, after a long pause, "we thank Thee for Thy peace which is now filling our souls. Always we shall think of this hour and, recalling it, will remember the light Thou givest to dispel our darkness. This day shall be as a rock of faith to us — to remind us of how our trust in Thee brings the blessing of new strength into our lives. These moments, Lord, speak to our hearts of Thy loving and eternal presence with us. Amen."

Several times thereafter Richard visited me. On each occasion he would report that after the laying-on of hands with which I always concluded our meetings, days would pass without 'the voices' and that he was now working more happily and successfully than ever. Things were easier all round. Faithfully he attended Mass.

Then he went back to Italy. At first he wrote gratefully of the times he had visited me and how well matters were. Then, at last, a letter came in which he said the old trouble had recurred.

In vain, he wrote, he had tried to cling on to and uphold in his imagination the uplifing experience of those consultations in my study. His letters began to show increasing panic. Clearly great mental pressure was building up. I did what I could in my own correspondence, endeavouring to hearten him, assuring him of my continued prayers for him, and always asking how his medical treatment was progressing.

Some months later he wrote to say he would be back in England and could he, therefore, please see me again?

So we talked once more, face to face. As I suspected he had fallen in with the old crowd and had been persuaded to take up TM again. There had followed in due course the same disorder of automatic writing, the hearing of 'voices', the inability to concentrate. Even the normal everyday matters of life were in jeopardy.

It was a repeat performance which underlined for me the correctness of my opinion that TM can prove harmful. In the final analysis it is a means of self-hypnosis and a rather mindless one in many cases. Though its advocates may declare a mystical experience arises from it, their claim is generally spurious.

In any case it is not an experience which has either the depth or wholesomeness attained through substained Christian prayer.

There was only one course to follow with Richard. After the laying-on of hands he regained his composure and then I bade him promise me to sever completely his association with his friends in TM because they would only succeed in enticing him again into their peculiar spiritual activities.

This time it was advice he followed and he returned not to Italy but to his own country. From the USA I received letters assuring me that the episode in his life of experimentation with TM and spiritism was a thing of the past and would ever remain so. Photostat copies of some of his recent magazine articles clearly indicated that he had recovered his great talent once more.

11

A HAUNTED SELF

My introduction to Jane came through someone who, having attended one of my lectures on psychical subjects, believed that I could help her.

Jane was an Asian girl whose childhood and early youth were spent in Goa. It was there she was betrothed and later married. Typically it was a marriage arranged by the parents of the two families. During the engagement period the couple were, as is the native custom, constantly and carefully chaperoned. Until the very day of the wedding — a Roman Catholic ceremony — they had never been alone together.

Things went very badly in their relationship within weeks after the marriage. Even whilst Jane was carrying his child the husband was acting cruelly and unfaithfully towards her. He completely deserted her after the birth of their son. Jane then sought the help and advice of her priest.

As there was a good case to show that the marriage had been made without fair consent of the bride — in fact that she had been under some duress to marry at a youthful age — the priest felt that there was sufficient cause for her to obtain not a divorce but an annulment. He explained that he would forward all information to the Vatican and she must await its decision.

She waited many months without hearing anything. She spoke to the priest about the long delay and he agreed that the requisite papers might have been lost or mislaid. He would, therefore, prepare them afresh and post them again to Rome.

The months became two or three years and no reply to her petition was received. It then happened that her family left Goa and came to settle in this country bringing her with them.

Here in England she finally procured a civil divorce on the grounds of her husband's desertion. After that she ceased to pursue her appeal to the Church authorities for her marriage to be recognised by them as annulled.

She settled quite quickly, and more or less happily, to life in this country and soon secured good clerical employment in which she showed great aptitude and industry.

After a time she became independent of her family and moved with her son, now fourteen years old, into her own accommodation. Life was now fully occupied with her job, the chores of home, and the care of her son who showed excellent ability at school.

However, all was not entirely well for her because her health began to suffer from what she described to me as 'ghostly knocks' and 'strange footfalls' in her flat after she had gone to bed. They occurred with almost unfailing regularity every night.

The constant sleeplessness caused by these phenomena had so upset and nervously exhausted her that when her friend mentioned my lecture to her she was so eager to consult me that she immediately telephoned for an appointment.

Here I ought to say that I knew no details about her until she revealed them to me during our first meeting. All that her friend had told me was that Jane was suffering, as she put it, from a 'haunting' and therefore could I find time to see her.

Jane visited me after her work one evening and when I opened the door I saw what I first took to be a young girl scarcely twenty years of age. To my surprise I was to learn later that she was thirty-one.

This point has some relevance because poltergeist phenomena are usually associated with young persons or with those who are somewhat immature. In talking to her I discovered she had a gentle, rather winsome, naivety — no doubt due to the sheltered and restricted life-style of her upbringing. Despite the tragedy in her life this very unsophistication had probably preserved her youthful appearance.

I questioned her in detail about the phenomena of her alleged haunting. It appeared that she would be aroused from sleep by a knocking sound on a bureau near her bed, as it someone were striking it with their knuckles. Later, when she was fully awakened, she would hear a noise as of footsteps — quite heavy and deliberate ones — which seemed to pace back and forth across the room.

The footsteps particularly alarmed her and she expressed the conviction that her husband was harassing her through the spiritual projection of himself. Evidently she fully believed him capable of this by his exercise of occult powers which many times he had told her he possessed.

Because she felt that people would not believe her experience she had attempted to take tape recordings of the sounds. She had, however, been unsuccessful in obtaining any clear results on the tapes. I took careful and significant note of this.

After months of these experiences taking place nightly she had become extremely exhausted and her nerves frayed. For a long time she had been receiving tranquillising pills from her doctor but still the phenomena were being repeated and she failed to get proper sleep or any sign of returning vitality.

She was in almost hopeless desperation when she had learned from her friend of my deep involvement in spiritual healing.

I inquired if she had talked the matter over with her priest. (She was, and is, a most regular practising Roman Catholic) She nodded and said that he had come to her flat and blessed it with special prayers, but the trouble still persisted. Again I noted the extreme significance of this.

She was seated in an easy chair and I had taken a seat beside her. I began to ask a few more questions, requesting her first to hold my hand while we conversed. I find this physical link with a distressed person is very helpful in securing their confidence and in setting them at ease.

"Does your son live with you?" I asked.

"Oh yes" she answered, "and he is a great help to me. He is quite clever at school for which I am so thankful."

"Do these phenomena only occur when he is at home?"

"No" she replied "because quite often he is away staying at my mother's place. She makes much fuss of him, you know."

"Well, then," I said "I do not think your flat is haunted. A blessing carried out in it would not therefore settle this matter. I suspect this is poltergeist activity. Mostly such phenomena are caused by young persons — often when they are passing through a particularly distressing puberty. But as your son is sometimes absent when the phenomena occur we can, I think, rule out the possibility that any psychological disturbance on his part can be the cause. In any event, from what you say about him, he seems too well balanced and happy to be drawing attention to interior stresses in himself by these means."

"At present" I continued "I discount the 'psychic' projection of your ex-husband because I feel he is fully occupied and now settled, from what you have told me, in his life with his second wife. It is very unlikely, therefore, that he would be concerned with giving you further hurt, even though you have heard his present marriage is also foundering. Again I cannot agree with you that this is a genuine case of haunting by a departed spirit which is earth-bound and requires exorcism. I say this because you tell me that these experiences have gone on at other addresses which you have occupied as well as your present one. That indicates the haunting — if haunting it is — is not of a place but of your own self.*

She gazed at me wide-eyed but it was clear that she followed my reasoning.

"So you think *I* am haunted?" she queried.

"Not really," I replied, "you see, Jane, it is like this. It is evident that during the years you have spent in this country you have had opportunity to see the customs and outlook of people here. You will have noticed above all that our young girls have almost unlimited freedom to form relationships with the opposite sex — to be able to *choose* their boy-friends, to get to know them. Thereby they are better able to assess their own minds and feelings and so generally shape their own futures.

"You have seen that very closely in your own office. that is why I asked you about your work and how well you have come to know your colleagues. I think you have realised how different your own life has been from theirs. You feel now the loss in your own case of that freedom which you see all around you in others — and that an unhappy marriage could have been avoided."

"Yes, I do," she concurred immediately.

"Let me put it like this, Jane," I went on, "rather naturally you have a sense of resentment about this matter — indeed you would like to have had the chances for free choice which you observe the young people around you so clearly enjoy. Am I right?"

---

* We might note the distinction between hauntings which affect a particular individual wherever he lives and those which occur in a certain place and are experienced by any psychically sensitive person who enters it. The 'haunted' person is generally described as having a poltergeist.

"Well, yes," she conceded, "I do feel like that. At times very much indeed. Though I want to say that I have always tried to make the best of things as they are."

"I'm sure you have" I replied, "and I admire you for the way in which, against so many difficulties, you have achieved independence and met your responsibilities so well.

"All I wish to point out is that the years of unhappiness and frustration may have upset you so much deep deep down that, despite all the busy preoccupation on the surface of your life, there is an area within you which is crying out to be noticed — and to be healed. It is that tension going on inside your soul — turning it into a mental boxing-ring — which is producing the phenomena which have for so long caused spiritual unhappiness and brought on insomnia. This in turn has induced the activity of certain powers of your spirit-soul which are the reason for the odd noises you hear.

Sometimes, you see, inner unhappiness and insecurity will activate peculiar powers within us whereby we are actually able to create the signs of what we then come to think are those of haunting."

"What, then, do you think can be done?" she asked, and her manner showed scarcely controlled agitation. "Can you help me? I just can't go on like this much longer."

"Yes, certainly I can help you" I replied," — or rather our Lord Jesus Christ will. Through faith in Him our healing comes. You will remember His promise that if we meet together to think of Him He will be truly with us.

"We will pray together, therefore, to acknowledge His Presence. I know you are deeply religious. Your faith and mine will bring God's peace to us which will refresh our souls.

"Relax now. Let your whole body go limp. Think of yourself on the sand of a beach. The quiet water is just passing over your feet and legs. It is rising to cover you, softly, gently — but at the same time restfully supporting you."

Even while speaking I noted that she closed her eyes and the previous tenseness of her countenance had cleared.

I noticed, too, that the constant nervous gripping of her hand in mine had ceased. her grasp was now quite still, very firm and assured. So I continued:

"Our trust in Thee, Lord Jesus, is complete. Thy beloved Jane brings her deep need to Thee in this hour — the resentment she feels about her unhappy marriage. Remove the anguish from her, Lord. In Thy loving mercy restore to her the beauty of that inward peace of mind which flows from Thee. Make her to know the brightness of her future from this day on.''

With my free hand I made the Sign of the Cross on her forehead ''In the Name of the Father and of the Son and of the Holy Spirit we have made our prayer.''

Her head relaxed even more as I said this and she appeared to fall asleep.

I left her thus for a few minutes although still holding her hand. At last when I freed it she opened her eyes and smiled happily. There was such a sweet calm about her — almost childlike.

She came once more to see me. Again she received the laying-on of hands. This time more for the opportunity of repeating the experience of complete relaxation and peace than because she was still bothered by her 'haunting'. Six months later she wrote to thank me again for the elimination of her 'poltergeist' and to say that since then she had been a totally new person. A further piece of good news she wanted to share with me — her engagement to a young man. They were both, she wrote ecstatically, so divinely happy and they hoped that I would be able to participate in their wedding ceremony.

Several years have passed since then during which she has sent regular letters, always repeating, amongst news of the family, how marvellously happy she is now with a truly loving, companionable husband who, like herself, is deeply religious.

In that confident and reassuring new relationship there is also, of course, a rich source of healing for her.

12

THE APPROACH OF DEATH

Of course a priest must often minister to the dying. In my own frequent association with death I have come to realise that it is then the spiritual world makes itself specially evident.

A ninety-four year old lady, hitherto remarkably active, had to take at last to her bed and it was clear that her earthly life would soon be over. During her last weeks, tended by her devoted unmarried daughter, she remained as bright and entertaining as ever for a good deal of the day but, by early evening, there was a tendency to fall into a half-sleep while visitors were conversing with her. At these times she would appear to become completely detached from those present and talk instead to invisible persons.

Her daughter, concerned about what she felt must be the off-putting behaviour of her mother before her friends, approached me about the matter.

I was able to put her mind at ease.

"You must not think your mother has, as you put it, become senile or 'peculiar'," I said. "Not a bit. Senility is obviously out of the question since her mind for most of the day is as lucid as ever. I believe at those times when she is apparently slipping away from us that she is actually in close touch with spiritual beings. You have said that often on these occasions she speaks as if to her mother and that sometimes she seems to be addressing your brother who was killed during the War.

"Don't be troubled about this nor be put off by those who say that her mind is simply wandering. I believe that she *is* in the company of her mother then and that she *does* converse with her son. Remember the strong belief she has always held about the

Communion of Saints — which, as you know, she interpreted so rightly as the eternal and unbroken fellowship of all believers in our Lord Jesus Christ. She is discovering the reality of that more clearly now ... That is all."

Her daughter nodded appreciatively her agreement to my last remarks.

"So you don't think she is just rambling?" she enquired. "But don't people sometimes go on like this under anaesthetics, for example?"

"I'll agree with you up to a point" I replied. "When the body-soul powers are suspended through unconsciousness or semi-unconsciousness it is true that there can rise up a jumble of forgotten memories which have been stored away. Usually it is all rather incoherent — though sometimes it can be quite surprising, even illuminating to those present. But this is not wholly the case with your mother. Of course her bodily strength is very frail now and when quite exhausted, as it is by early evening, her spirit-soul faculties then become active. Spiritually she sees and hears what you and I cannot see or hear. But it is not nonsense or hallucination — it is reality, the reality of the spiritual world which is always close to us, though we are rarely aware of it because in our present vitality we are dominated by our physical senses."

"I can't always catch what she says," her daughter added "and sometimes it seems incomplete so that I cannot make sense of it."

"That, too, is understandable," I said. "Her physical faculties, which are translating her spiritual intimations into words, are weak and so the matter appears fragmentary, maybe even incomprehensible so far as we are concerned. Nevertheless her spirit-soul is perfectly attuned, wholly susceptible, and fully communicating. She *is* receiving messages and her own correspondence with the realm of pure spirit is exact."

Later, while sitting by the bedside of the old lady, I had some confirmation of what I had explained to her daughter. After maintaining a fairly animated conversation with me the spare little figure suddenly relapsed and a look of quiet peace came upon her face, giving it a very sweet loveliness.

I had been holding one of her tiny hands while she had been talking and now, telling her I must leave, I said that first I would join her in a good-night prayer.

This mention of prayer accelerated, I believe, her slipping into unconsciousness at that moment, doubtless because she was composing her spirit for the act of prayer.

Her hand relaxed in mine and I began to recite the twenty-third psalm. During this she suddenly appeared to become fully awake and, opening her eyes, began to speak.

She was looking towards the window and suddenly the half-drawn curtains billowed unaccountably. There was no draught to cause this and the windows themselves were completely closed.

"Mother is here as I told you" said the old lady quietly. "There she is ...." Her eyes seems to point, even as did the delicate hand, towards the curtains.

"She is very beautiful, isn't she?" she added.

Almost immediately after this she sank back on the pillows and fell asleep again.

I reflected how happy and contented she looked and how the room seemed to be occupied now by another, and very lovely, presence. The old lady's lips continued to move for a little while as if she were still in gentle conversation but I could distinguish no words.

The following afternoon death came and so she entered fully the unseen world. There was a peacefulness which I can only describe as angelic in the room. It seemed to envelop her tiny corpse and lingered most sweetly about the bed.

Some have asked me the significance of the moving curtains. Could they betoken another presence and, if a purely spiritual one, why such physical manifestation?

I cannot answer but can certainly say that I had a marked intuition at the time that the strange movement of the curtains and the sense of another presence in the room did have a definite connection.

I hazard the guess that conversation between spiritual beings, one of whom is still holding, albeit lightly, to the physical world as in the case of the old lady, requires some material energy to effect it. Perhaps then, the exchange of energy in such communication could give rise to a physical distrubance which caused the curtains to billow.

It has often been my joy and inspiration to note how around the body of one who has recently died there lingers for some time a peculiar feeling of unearthly presence which has encouraged me to believe that not only the soul of the departed may still be in the room for a while but also the spirits of angels or of loved ones who have pre-deceased that person. No doubt the latter would be welcoming the newly departed.

I have no doubt also that the emanations of great love created by sorrowing relatives and friends may conjure their continued presence even after they have reverently and lovingly viewed the corpse and gone away, each holding so dearly and vividly his or her own thoughts of love and of precious memories.

Let me quote but one of many experiences of this nature.

A day or two after arriving in the South of France to begin a month's locum duty as a chaplain at Holy Trinity Church, Cannes, I was asked by his French wife to see George, an Englishman, who was seriously ill in hospital. He greeted my first visit with evident pleasure but was most forthcoming and honest about the neglect of his church-going. "I have been too lazy, padre, on the one hand" he said "and too concerned with business and golf on the other."

We talked much about many things and when I was about to leave he asked me with great enarnestness if I would please visit him again.

A few days later when I saw him his condition was very grave and he was now well aware of it. He wished to talk about spiritual matters, about prayer, the forgiveness of sins and life after death. He told me some of his experiences as a soldier in the Second World War and of how certain events concerning comrades during battle had convinced him of immortality. It was clear to me that, for all his lack of church-going, he had been most deeply moved spiritually on many occasions.

I told him that his years of concern for others and his present desire to be at peace with his Creator were most precious things and assurances of God's infinite love for him. He held my hand as we prayed together. His grip was surprisingly strong for a man so considerably weakened and only days away from death. While I kept our minds on the thought of Christ's Presence with us it was as if, in the strange pulsing power which vibrated between us, the very life-force which flows through creation was making itself signally felt.

I had spoken to him of death as the exodus, or way through, to the life of glory.

"And what do you mean by 'glory.' " he had asked with something of a teasing smile upon his gaunt countenance.

"Now you are disarming me," I had replied "and a good thing too! We parsons often use marvellous phrases without due thought. Well, by 'glory' I must first mean the character of God. But to be more specific I think of the life beyond as the realm in which, as pure spirits, we reach fulfilment in a new kind of body. It is, of course, a wholly transcendent condition beyond our present imagining. Space and time are not to be considered but personal relationships are of supreme importance. I am certain that the immediate experience after death for us is one in which we shall be greeted and guided by those of our dear ones who have preceded us — and certainly there will be the exhilarating help of angels.

"In short, George, death means the most exciting and adventurous transformation for us. So I feel there is no other way of putting it than to say we enter 'the life of glory'..."

I would have tried to say more but George gently halted me, saying:

"Of course I know what you mean, padre — and that it *is* all beyond our understanding until death comes — just because dying is an experience that is absolutely individual and for once only."

Then he added, with his eyes intently looking into mine:

"And I'll let you know of the 'glory' " There was a pause and then, slowly, the words *"if I can."*

Through the slight banter sounding in his reply I detected nevertheless a very serious note. I was to understand later what he meant.

In the mid-week which followed our conversation he died.

An hour before the funeral George's widow felt she could not endure the ordeal of viewing his body — something which the undertakers requested before closing the coffin — and so she asked me to perform this duty for her.

His body reposed in one of those elaborate rooms variously furnished in ornate styles which are to be found in some fashinable funeral parlours abroad. The idea, no doubt, is to convey a gentility and comfort about death for the sake of the bereaved. Maybe it succeeds for some although for my part rich brocades, elegant furniture, and the deepest pile carpeting induce a rather distracting atmosphere, when one is mentally comparing such either with the simplicity of the hospital bed or with the relatively prosaic but natural surroundings of the average home where one last saw the dying person.

Yet, despite the unnaturalness of the room, when I looked down upon George's face I found my thoughts completely emptied of any reflection other than of the living George whom I had known only for that brief period of his last days in hospital.

The wax-like features seemed so strangely unfamiliar and unlike his countenance that I had to gaze intently before I could make a true recognition. I must have looked for a full minute and then the face seemed to become shrouded in a mist which blotted it from my sight altogether.

I realised later that my prayerful concentration must have induced in me a measure of trance which would account for this.

But within that very mist I caught an impression of something utterly transcendent, a perception not of this world. Burning into the very depth of my being came the words, not spoken, but printed as it were in exhilarating radiance: 'The life of Glory'.

It was a revelation, enthralling and reassuring, beautiful and over-flowing with peace and sublime happiness — the complete attestation of the reality of the unseen world. It remains etched indelibly in my memory as a most precious and exalting experience to treasure always.

I have no doubt that in some unique way George had been able to carry out that hoped-for promise he had made to me — to inform me if it were possible for him to do so — of the truth which here on earth we only know by faith that beyond death is a form of life for us which is transcendent, beyond all human superlatives, the life indeed of 'glory'.

13

TWO CASES OF HARMFUL HYPNOSIS

Hypnosis by others can have a very dangerous consequence as the following cases indicate.

A youth and a girl, in their late teens, sought my advice on a matter which was increasingly troubling them. In the final year at school they had come under the influence of Henry, a young man in his late twenties, who had encouraged them in what he rather grandly termed 'the study of the spirit and the occult.'

That study was not very profound but certainly flamboyant. Early in my conversation with the couple I realised that their tutor had, in fact, scant knowledge of his subject but was largely influenced by a combination of highly colourful books about the occult and of science fiction. The consequence was to prove again the adage that a little knowledge is a dangerous thing. However, what he lacked in knowledge he made up for by his ability to bring impressionable youngsters under his spell. He was a person endowed with a crude hypnotic power which he was recklessly ready to use to enlarge his own ego and to gather around him obsequious disciples who hung upon his every word with blind devotion.

Fortunately one of the youngsters who came to see me had some years previously been a conscientious member of one of my Confirmation classes. Later she and her family had moved out of London. Something of those classes had obviously made its mark and had encouraged her to make the long journey with her boy-friend to seek my counsel.

At long last she had begun to feel uneasy about the domination of their 'guru' over the personal lives of herself and her friend and to wonder about the wisdom of remaining in his group.

First of all the youngsters produced a small piece of sheet lead which had been quaintly shaped. They told me it was regarded by them as a potent talisman given to them by their young master with his strict instruction that it must never leave their possession. They were told that it had been especially blessed with protective properties during one of the ceremonies which he made his disciples attend. In the event of their doubting his wisdom or disobeying his commands instead of protecting them the talisman would produce calamity. The most serious accidents, misfortunes and disappointments, would assuredly befall them.

They held the metal shape with evident respect and, handing it to me, asked my opinion. I could make nothing definite of its shape and suspected it had been roughly sheared from a piece of church roofing. My surmise was, they affirmed, correct. Evidently their 'master' was astute enough to see the added superstitious value to young minds of material which had come from a sacred building.

Next the girl drew from her bag a cassette tape and asked me if I would play it through. We sat listening to the recorded voice of their leader and I noted the serious and rapt attention which my young visitors paid to it.

As I listened to the voice I recognised that its owner clearly possessed a strong theatrical talent. Indeed, when I inquired if he had received stage training they nodded assent, stating that he had been to a drama school but, as far as they knew, had never acted professionally. Apparently he was of independent means which may have blunted his industry and necessary discipline in securing any acting work.

The message on the tape opened with a flowery and extravagant statement of how his disciples were blessed with acquiring special understanding of their souls and of their future path through life because of his expert knowledge and teaching. Attendance at his group lectures and observance of his individual counselling, which would be regularly accorded to them, was essential.

The voice ended with the command to intone for five minutes daily a chant — the words were at first gibberish to me but they were uttered with dramatic solemnity.

'IMARETSAM', the youngsters informed me, was the phrase which was somewhat difficult to transcribe from the tape. It was repeated a number of times in monotone at the beginning and close of the recording. Scribbling the letters in block capitals on a sheet of paper was an immediate help to me as it is fairly obvious that on simple inversion they become "I am master". Evidently the young folk had not realised this because it had never occurred to them to translate. They simply accepted it as some dread occult phrase which they had been commanded to repeat in the presence of their 'teacher', and also at various times on their own as a preliminary to meditating upon some theme he had prescribed to them during the week. If they had thought about it they might have realised much earlier that their 'guru' was on an ego trip which he shrouded in pseudo mysticism.

The tape recording thus confirmed my suspicion that the youngsters had become the mesmerised victims of an unscrupulous, egocentric person. Perhaps frustration over his lack of theatrical opportunity had made him resort to this means of commanding an audience. Most dangerous of all was the fact that Henry obviously had considerable, if untrained, skill as a hypnotist. There appeared to me to be a carefully rehearsed tone in the recording. I could well imagine that the owner of such a voice could dominate the wills of young people to a degree where, as in the case of these two in my study, they believed they could make no personal decisions without first consulting him. Fortunately it had not yet reached a situation where the most simple decisions in their lives — and loves — could not be undertaken unless under his direction and according to his opinion. They were on the verge, however, of becoming his completely hypnotised subjects.

The first thing, therefore, was to apprise the young couple of the unhealthiness of accepting the dictate of their 'guru' with such unquestioning obedience. They had met, I explained to them, with a person who revelled in gaining control over others. He had an ability, I said, to achieve this by the power of suggestion. He was an hypnotic, megalomaniac character such as makes a minor Hitler. The danger was not simply in accepting his bizarre esoteric beliefs and injunctions, but it was the making of him into a kind of god who demanded blind worship.

They must surely see, I continued, that he was not without human weakness and could not be infallible in his judgement and counsel.

What they had intimated about him had all the hallmarks of a tyrant — a fact wholly borne out by the tape recording. The purpose of the talisman he had given them was to ensure that if they were out of his presence his hypnotic influence would constantly be brought to mind when they handled it.

The little piece of shaped lead was, I explained, the necessary focus for their attention to become riveted upon their 'teacher'. It induced in them a level of hypnosis whereby his power over their wills could once more be re-asserted.

It took me sometime to argue them out of their long standing allegiance to him. But in this, of course, I was greatly helped by the fact that they had already begun to wonder if their discipleship was wholly wise and somewhat concerned as to how the matter squared with their earlier Christian teaching. Despite their gullibility they were very intelligent young people and my explanation of their predicament convinced them to the point where they themselves asked me if I would pray for them.

This was a welcome and promising opening for my ministration which I told them would consist of the laying-on of hands with special prayer for the freeing of their wills from the shackles imposed by Henry upon them.

They fully accepted that by their faith in Christ their souls were preserved from evil and they agreed that they now realised that Henry, by his desire to dominate them, was serving the cause of Satan. "Could we be exorcised?" they asked me.

"In a sense that *is* what is needed" I replied. "Although this is not a case of an evil entity possessing you there is a parallel in that, by a hypnotic practice on the part of Henry — you are, as it were, being possessed by his spirit. The power of Christ's own spirit will set you free."

Laying my hands on the head of each of them in turn I prayed: "Lord, Thou knowest how these souls, who would only love and serve Thee, have been diverted from Thee in paths which would lead away from Thy wisdom and goodness. Now, dear Lord, impart to them the unconquerable power of Thy Spirit which protects from every evil that can be wrought by man or the Devil. Invest them again with unshakeable and true faith in Thee, purify them from the spirit of Henry and relieve them of the power of his will over them"

Then I asked them to join with me in the Lord's Prayer, after which I pronounced a blessing.

"Go, each of you, upon your future way in God's protection, always in the safe keeping and companionship of Jesus Christ and His holy angels."

Deep silence followed for several minutes and I noted how intently concentrated the young pair were. There was a tranquil atmosphere about them now. Gone was the nervous and halting manner in which they had begun their visit.

Unhesitatingly, and with evident great relief, they left behind the talisman and I knew that now they were freed spirits. Henry's hold over them had been completely broken. They never returned to him.

Hypnosis likewise caused the distress of a young woman whose mother, having read in a woman's magazine of my spiritual healing ministry, brought her to see me.

The girl had recently returned home from a year's stay in South Africa. There she had come under the malign influence of a group who indulged in black magic. She had participated with its members on many occasions in occult ceremonies of a most reprehensible kind which included sexual activities of an unpleasant nature.

Heading the group was a man who said that he had received occult powers from personal contact with Satan. The extravagant and ludicrous claims he made apparently did not appear ridiculous to his young convert who had first been attracted to him but later ended up in terror of him. She was still living in that fear, and sensing his peculiar power over her, even these hundreds of miles away.

She must have been very frank about everything with her mother for the latter, who was present throughout the interview, supplied details whenever her daughter did not make herself fully clear to me.

During my questioning I thought the girl evinced signs that she was still deeply absorbed in what had transpired in South Africa. Clearly she was very strongly tied to her memories of it and particularly of the strange group she had joined there. Indeed I suspected that for her South Africa was that odd company and nothing else.

The breakthrough in our conversation came when she made the comment:

"I believe an evil spirit is in me. It was given me out there. I know because they told me so. Sometimes everything is so black. I feel I can't escape the darkness. If you would exorcise me, please. Please, please .... that is what I need."

As I have constantly said I do not immediately take the view that exorcism should be the first consideration Even less so when a person requests it for so often they are mistaken in their need, subconsciously seeking a scapegoat for their illness or behaviour. Consequently, while not actually dismissing her appeal outright, I told the girl that the laying-on of hands would help her.

I asked her to relax in the comfortable armchair in which I had seated her. As I stood behind it I realised that she must have been subject to hypnotic influence — perhaps on many occasions — because at my request to relax she responded promptly despite the fact that only a few moments before she had been so agitated. The suggestions which I usually need to give to people how to relax were quite unnecessary in her case. Almost immediately she adopted an easy posture (whereas before she had been sitting forward in a tensely rigid manner) and, closing her eyes, exhibited a trance-like demeanour. I spoke gently but with studied emphasis so that her mind might fully absorb my meaning. First, as always in my healing work, I mentally bade my spirit-soul to instruct her own and then, aloud, I said:

"You believe fully in the healing power of Jesus Christ and that He is present when two or three come together to seek Him?"
She nodded and added a quiet "Yes, I do."
"Have you a special picture of Jesus that makes Him real to you?" I asked, "perhaps a childhood one from a pictorial Bible, or ideas from the Gospels..."
Sometimes I think of a picture on a card at home" she replied, her eyes still closed "He is holding a lantern outside a door..."
"Ah, yes" I said "Hunt's Light of the World, I expect.
That is good. Concentrate on that."
A slight wrinkling of her forehead indicated her response.

Then, laying my hands a few inches above her head, I said:
"Lord Jesus, lay Thy hands on this, Thy child...."
· I could say no more because in that instant the tranquillity was completely shattered I felt a most violent convulsion throughout my body and became aware that the girl's aura, which had seemed rather weak and subdued under my hands, had now become ice-cold. I had the greatest difficulty to maintain my balance and, even more, my concentration as some blustering and antagonistic force seemed to have been suddenly released in the room. My hands shook uncontrollably and I felt completely drained and empty. The alien force seemed intent on engulfing me and rendering me powerless. It was then I realised that this was the activity of an evil entity —

the preliminary resistance to its exorcism — and I must call upon God's help lest the demon should seek to regain its hold over the girl — or to jeopardise the spirit of the mother or even my own in its desire to find a dwelling place.

Exerting every effort of will and concentrating wholly upon the thought of Christ's presence with us, I commanded:

"Out! Out! In the Holy Name of Jesus and under the authority of God, I exorcise thee. Leave now this world and us and depart to that region of the spirit-world where you will trouble human souls no more."

I looked down at the girl with my own composure returned. Her face was utterly drained of colour and she was breathing quickly.

"It is alright now" I said, "the evil thing has left you and you are clean."

The pallor began to leave her and after a few more moments she opened her eyes and gave a wry smile of obvious relief.

"Thank you", she said simply. "Thank you. I feel ..." she searched for a word "I feel fabulous — so full of light. And this room is so full of light — everything around me is ·...."

"Thank God, really" I answered. "But you must promise me something — that you will never open yourself to that nastiness again. In its place you must build up your trust in God's unbounded love for you and regularly recall the companionship of Jesus and His angels. Better if you do not return to South Africa — at least not on your own — and certainly do not meet up again with that evil group of people.

Now let us pray that henceforth your soul may be protected."

Taking her hand I prayed that Christ in Whom there is no darkness at all should fill her heart with felicity and grant her guidance and confidence for the future.

The girl responded by gripping my hand tightly as if clinging to a life-line. I felt power passing through me and into her — a pulsing, vibrant flow of energy which seemed to come from the very atmosphere around us. For a fleeting moment I thought how true is the phrase "in God we live and move and have our being."

Gradually the girl's breathing which had become rather quick during this, became normal and she said:

"I *was* right then, wasn't I? I *knew* that something had got into me. It left me — while you were praying..."

For answer I placed my hands once more on her head and pronounced the blessing of God in the Name of the Father and of the Son and of the Holy Ghost.

Now I felt her aura had become strong and warm. Making gentle stroking movements with my arms fully outstretched I could still feel under my hands its steady pulsing. I continued this action for more than a minute until I sensed that the healing flow through me had subsided.

When the mother and daughter rose to leave there was such a relief upon their faces that I knew the work had been truly done. Their grateful letters afterwards were welcome testimony to it.

14

A POLTERGEIST

Poltergeist phenomena may have increased in recent years. If so I suspect it is due to the peculiar stresses and materialistic disappointments of modern society which cause so much mental illness and family instability today.

'Poltergeist' means a noisy spirit whose racketing behaviour causes a variety of peculiar, and apparently unaccountable, annoyances. Mostly these are of a telekinetic nature. Small objects in a room are moved about, or even violently thrown, by an unseen force; switches and taps are mysteriously turned on and off, etc. I recall a missionary priest telling me of an experience he had in the home of a friend. He witnessed several pictures crashing to the floor after a certain member of his friend's family had declared to everyone assembled in the room that they were about to fall. Apparently this individual was a frail young woman who suffered from hysteria. She could 'will' this phenomena from time to time by directing her attention to each picture in turn causing great consternation on each occasion and thus, very effectively, drawing complete attention to herself. The popular idea that these phenomena are the antics of some discarnate spirit is not generally borne out in my own experience of dealing with the appeals of persons who have complained of such incidents occurring in their homes. In most cases I have been able to conclude that the cause is a disturbed mind in some member of the household. Usually this is a young person who is psychologically agitated ¿ perhaps enduring an unusually difficult puberty.

Emotional stress can make the subconscious mind cry out for attention from what is felt to be an unnoticing, uncaring world.

In the case of a child it is the longing to receive from adults (particularly the parents) special consideration and reassurance.

Those periods of day-dreaming which are normal to most children can become increasingly intense and prolonged in those who suffer the isolation of an unhappy or unstable home. A similar state can occur in very shy children of frail physique who are hypersensitive to their inadequacy amid the robust activities of their fellows.

The day-dreams of such disturbed young souls are a way of escape into a more congenial, albeit imaginary, situation. Day-dreaming of such intensity dims the sense perceptions and can stimulate the function of extra-sensory ones. The result may then be the exercise of elementary telekinetic power which is capable of moving small objects, interfering with simple mechanical devices, etc. Thereby the distressed personality illustrates its frustration in not gaining sufficient recognition and understanding.

So the strange and apparently mischievous '*apports*' of the so-called poltergeist are more than likely to be produced by a confused and disconsolate human being than by some unrelated entity or demon.

I would quote one such case in which a family requested me, as they put it, 'to exorcise' their apartment.

The idea that exorcism is necessary is one which is often evinced where psychic disturbances and phenomena are concerned. This may be due to that mass of literature, so popular nowadays, which relates rather exotic tales of demon-possession and hauntings, accompanied by all the bizarre trappings of the occult.

In actual fact cases requiring exorcism are rare but naturally folk may be loath to think that the poltergeist is within their own family. Parents certainly find it difficult to credit this if their children are asleep or in another room when the phenomena occur.

When I visited the apartment I did not know there were any children in it but I soon realised that the couple who had asked me to exorcise it had a peculiar life-style. Another couple who were introduced to me apparently shared completely in all the living arrangements giving the whole establishment a bohemian flavour.

The entrance passage of what was a fairly spacious flat had arrested my attention immediately. The walls were covered in a sombre hessian which completely subdued the already inadequate natural light. I found it rather depressing, if not forbidding. This feeling was not much relieved on entering the living-room which had the same heavy hue not only on the walls but on the ceiling as well. It did have the merit of large windows but even these were heavily draped in dark brown velvet and in a half-drawn manner so as to reduce considerably the daylight.

I began to wonder what possessed this strange foursome to desire such oppressive surroundings. They immediately withdrew after explaining to me the nature of the phenomena which consisted of small ornaments being transferred from one place to another and little piles of loose change being mysteriously hidden or scattered when the room was unoccupied. (Incidentally most of these articles were out of reach of a child). I found their prompt exit strange since most people who request an exorcism usually like to watch the procedure and, indeed, one usually encourages them to participate in the prayers if they will.

Evidently they assumed that the flat was haunted and that I must therefore get on with the business of 'laying the ghost', presumably judging that to be my province and not theirs. They left me alone in the hall to wander at will through the apartment.

There were three bedrooms which were evidently used also as sitting rooms although their occupants were absent at this time.

On entering the first of these rooms I stood quietly praying for guidance and the help of angels. I then became vaguely aware of a sense of ill-intent near the window. This overlooked a large communal garden. Intuitively I surmised that there had been a burglary recently in the flat and that entry had been gained through this window. In conversation later with one of the tenants this proved to be the case.

The next room, however, furnished me with my first clue to the possible origin of the poltergeist, for it was obviously a child's bedroom. Normally one of my first enquiries is whether there are any children in a 'haunted' household. But on this occasion I had omitted to ask that question of either of the two couples before they had left me alone. Their obvious desire to withdraw so rapidly had driven the query from my mind.

Turning a corner of the long passage I perceived the kitchen. The door was ajar and I could see a boy of small stature for the twelve years of age which I later discovered him to be, who was seated at a table eating a bowl of cornflakes. He was just pouring some more from the packet when he caught sight of me. He stared blankly and I smiled to put him as ease.

"Hello," I said "and what is your name?"

"Harold," he replied.

I thought there was something very frail and pathetic about the little chap. His face was extremely pale and his eyes, large but unlively, made him appear very withdrawn.

At first conversation with him was difficult. His replies to all I said, which was simply intended to encourage his responsiveness, were monosyllabic. Even these were mainly inaudible so that, apart from constantly repeating my questions, which I thought would be unwise, I could only guess the answers. But I did gather that he was the only child of the man and woman who had asked me to perform the exorcism.

Having asked him about his school and what subjects he preferred I expanded on his replies in a gentle and purposely uncontroversial way in order to win his further confidence. Inwardly I prayed that my spirit-soul might communicate with his. In a little while he began to show some real interest and suddenly broke in with:

"I know who you are — the man who runs the Church."

I smiled at the way he had put it and nodded agreement.

From then it was fairly easy.

"I've come to say some prayers here", I said, "because things are being moved about and we are not sure why. You can help me if you like." He gazed straight at me. His look was quiet and serious.

I left the kitchen and crossed the passage to his bedroom-cum-playroom which was almost opposite. Harold followed close on my heels. Standing together there I said the Lord's Prayer. He joined in this quite naturally. All the while I had one hand on his head. During the prayer I mentally carried on a separate prayer-thought for the stilling of what I felt sure was the restless distress of his soul. Could, I wondered, the strange relationship (as I had sensed it to be) of his parents and the other couple in the flat have caused the boy's psychological upset?

I believed now that this was so by a peculiar intuition. I felt, however, I could not discuss this matter effectively either with the lad or with any of the four adults. In the latter case I thought they would be so blasé that I would achieve no satisfactory response.

The only alternative was to command my spirit-soul to convey to the spirit-soul of the boy the reassurance and interest which I sensed he desperately needed from the adult world

94

I knew that I must largely depend on a telepathic communication of such sympathy and so I silently prayed that God would empower and control it. It was then that I gained a flash of insight.

"You like drawing, don't you Harold?" Although I put this as a question I knew that it was a fact which had been psychically revealed to me in that moment.

The lad nodded. "That's good" I said, "I like people who can draw."

He brightened visibly and said shyly: "Can I show you my painting book?"

My immediate reply that nothing would please me more brought an equally rapid response. For the first time he appeared to come fully alive as he dashed to a wardrobe drawer to take out from the jumble of playthings in it a large sketch book. He thrust it at me eagerly.

I turned the pages and became fascinated with their contents. Repeated many times were drawings of strange creatures which had rather grim suggestions about them. Mingled among these were human faces which likewise appeared unfriendly and decidedly ugly. Children are often fascinated by the bizarre — after all, much nursery folklore is rather terrifying — yet these drawings seemed to me to be no mere childish evocation of horror but rather to declare a sense of spiritual abandonment — a longing for consolation and concern.

I was now fully aware of what I can best describe as a current of psychic sensitivity through which I was being given the right things to say and increasing insight into the child's spiritual need.

Here, I felt assured, was a classic instance of a young soul desperately craving the attention of the adult world in order to be assured of personal identity in that world and anxiously desiring the demonstrative response of human love.

In his forlorn condition he had created a fantasy world to escape into but this was one where he manipulated, through his drawings, the discomforting and ugly world he knew. It was not a world of beauty or of love for these were qualities he had not been made truly aware of in his short life.

I could see that his drawing-book was a cri-de-coeur. The clear path for me, therefore, was to convey sympathy for him and an appreciation of him as a real and vulnerable person. When the soul of a young person is in torment it can retreat from unhappy reality by excessive day-dreaming (often carried over also into actual sleep). The soul may then draw attention to its plight by producing the so-called poltergeist phenomena. This is because the spirit-soul is largely disencumbered of the body-soul due to the prolonged state of trance incurring by such dreaming and can thus exhibit extra-sensory faculties such as telekinesis (i.e. the moving of small objects, raps and peculiar noises, etc).

After showing more interest in his artistic work and warmly applauding him for it I was pleased to note the evident pleasure on his face. At length there was a complete change in his demeanour which, previously so dull, was now quite bright. He was obviously keen to gain even more of my attention and admiration. I continued to listen therefore for some time to his chatter and evinced my delight in seeing several of his favourite toys which he showed me with much pride, indicating how some of them operated. My appreciation of all this gave him considerable happiness and ere long he was clutching at my arm in order to impress me still further with what he wished me to enjoy with him.

Finally I suggested to him that he should draw some happy figures in his book. Forthwith he began sketching a train and then a motorcar in which the drivers appeared as rotund and jolly, then came more figures of children dancing about a maypole. I reflected how very different were these from his other drawings.

All the while I continued my silent prayer for his comforting, and for his release from morbid brooding upon his disenchantment with the grown-ups in his world.

Eventually he accompanied me to where the adults were gathered. I assured them that prayers had been made and that the phenomena would probably cease, but they must all give a greater measure of time and attention to the child so as to relieve his present introspective solitude. In any event, I said, the phenomena would gradually decrease of their own accord. Indeed this is usually the way with the poltergeist. The young person will quite naturally cease to have a disordered subconscious after a time as he or she comes to terms with any sense of personal insecurity, or any difficulty in relating to the grown-up world. The phenomena will then cease as suddenly as they began.

In this case I was to hear no more from the parents about their poltergeist annoyances.

15

CONFIDENCE RESTORED AND A GUIDED JOURNEY

The removal of a state of anxiety and replacing it with one of composure and confidence is an important accompaniment of spiritual healing.

"I am afraid, very afraid. I have to admit, vicar." an elderly lady said to me towards the end of a visit I had made to her in hospital. She had been there for a week and told me that she was expecting to undergo an operation.

"They will perform it when I am a little stronger" she said. Then added, with a wry smile "They are fattening me up for it."

"It is the first time in my life I have ever been in hospital" she went on, "and the thought of an operation scares me. I really am afraid. I know I shouldn't be, but I am."

"It is natural enough to have such a feeling" I said, "particularly as you have never been operated on before. But you believe, as I do, in the help of Divine Healing through prayer and the laying-on of hands. Isn't that so?"

"I do indeed" she replied. "I have heard your talks about the subject especially during last Lent. One of the reasons why I started coming to your church is because you had something to say about it."

"Well" I said, "I would like you to think this way. You are the person who is going to have the operation and it is, therefore, up to my spirit to give confidence to yours. That's how God intended we should be to each other in this world — helping someone else who is temporarily afflicted, with the strength and health we are enjoying ourselves.

A Priest and the Paranormal

Will you take my hand in yours and imagine that you are drawing strength *through* me? Because your own mind is a little agitated and mine is not I can be in fuller communication with the Divine Healing Power.

First, I shall pray in order to help both of us concentrate and then, in the silence, your spirit-soul and mine will be in accord. You *may* feel something passing between us but whether you do or not is not really important. Feelings don't count all that much in this, but our faith *does* — absolutely. Our faith in the healing love of God."

Drawing a stool to the bedside I sat down and took her right hand in my own.

"Rest back on the pillows." I said. "Let yourself relax as completely as you can."

I could see that she complied remarkably quickly. Her body was soon in good repose and she had closed her eyes.

"Lord Jesus" I prayed aloud "present now in all Your power, we remember how You said that we should not be anxious or afraid and that all our needs are known to our Heavenly Father. May we become aware, deep within ourselves, of Your Healing Presence. Cast out from this, Your servant, who puts all her trust in You, every fear. Grant her the assurance of perfect peace and a good courage. We pray, too, for our Father's blessing upon the skill of the surgeons and nurses who attend her. We pray in Your Name."

Her hand was firmly grasping mine but there was no nervousness, no twitch of anxiety. Opening my eyes for a moment I saw that her face was composed, serene.

I concentrated again, willing that my spirit-soul should relay to hers the confidence I had in the Healing Presence of Christ with us in that hour.

Between our clasped hands there appeared to flow a pulsing energy. A veritable stream of life was rising from the deepest recesses of my being. It prompted me to think of the words of Jesus: "If any man thirst, let him come unto Me and drink. He that believeth on Me ... out of him shall flow rivers of living waters."

It was such a beautiful experience that I thought we were caught up into the loveliness of the eternal world.

After a while I placed my free left hand upon her brow, saying: "May God's peace remain with you."

98

I now moved this hand along her recumbent body at a distance of about twelve inches or so above it. Between my palm and her body I could feel a throb of mysterious energy — the life force. The space between appeared to become quite solid and I was constrained to exercise a gentle stroking motion as if I were massaging a turbulence into steadiness. All the while the coursing flow between our joined right hands was maintained.

I held the thought of peace in my mind, by quoting to myself the words of Jesus: "Come unto Me and I will give you peace ..", "Peace I leave with you ..." My peace I give to you ..." "Come unto Me all that are heavy laden and I will give you rest ..."

Thus I sought to communicate to her spirit-soul the idea of gentle harmony and courage.

I continued the stroking movement of my left hand and became suddenly aware of the fact that I was concentrating over the area of her stomach. it was now clear to me that in this part of the body her physical trouble must lie. Possibly a cancerous condition, I conjectured to myself.

When the sensation in my left hand abated I felt impelled to conclude by making a brisk emphatic sweeping action with it, as if to brush away any lingering malignance.

For a minute or two longer our right hands remained joined. When at last we disengaged them she opened her eyes. She flicked them several times as if coming from sleep. There was a happy light in them and the drawn look I had seen on her face at first had completely disappeared. In fact she now had the countenance of a person many years younger than I knew her to be.

"l am not afraid any more" she said simply, looking at me with a smile of real contentment. "I have felt closer to God than I have ever known — and it is so beautiful. I'm not the least afraid now, come what may. Thank you so much for this."

"We both thank God for it" I said. Then, with a sudden flash of intuition, I added: "I feel you will not have to have an operation after all."

Then I left her. My wife, who had been waiting outside the ward, now went in to see her for a few minutes as they were great friends.

Afterwards my wife said to me:

"Goodness, something pretty marvellous happened didn't it? She told me that she feels completely different since you prayed with her. She was terribly anxious about her coming operation but now she isn't in the least. Did you know it is something to do with her heart? So she tells me.''

I had not known that and indeed had thought it best not to inquire of her what her physical trouble might be. However, it was revealed later that my surmise was correct. It was cancer and not, primarily at any rate, a heart condition though the latter may have been the compassionate suggestion given to her by doctors or relatives.

Soon after this the old lady was transferred to a nursing home thirty miles outside London. She was destined after all not to have any operation and her last three weeks were ones of continued contentment and serenity from that day of our prayers together.

My wife and I continued in our prayers for her until one day we suddenly decided we must visit her again. We set aside the afternoon for the journey saying that we would leave home by a certain hour. The peculiar thing about this decision was that we felt a most compelling urge that we must go on this particular day and must not delay leaving, even by five minutes, from the time we had set ourselves.

My drive in the car to that nursing home was one of the strangest I have ever known. All the way I felt I was being guided by an unseen presence urging me on. Although I had never been to the place before and had no map of it I had to make no enquiry about my direction. This, despite the fact that when we reached the town where it was situated there was a maze of one-way roads and a veritable cobweb of streets to pass through to it.

When we finally parked the car in a side road by the nursing-home I noted that we had covered the miles in a surprisingly short time despite the heavy traffic en route.

We discovered that the old lady was in a coma when we enquired of a nurse as to which room she had been transferred. Members of her family had gathered to see her as they had been informed that she might not survive the night.

They left her bedside when they saw me and I was alone with her. She was a wisp of her former self. Her eyes were closed in her now tiny face and she was scarcely breathing.

I stood silently at her side holding one of her hands which were crossed on the coverlet.

I asked that God would use my spirit-soul to convey to her own spirit-soul the prayer that I was making for her commendation into His gracious keeping.

Then I began to quote aloud the words of Jesus from St John's Gospel:

"Peace I leave with you, My peace I give to you ... in My Father's Home there are many dwelling places ... I go to prepare one for you ..."

I bent forward to speak into her ear the Twenty-third Psalm: "The Lord is my shepherd. I shall not want. He maketh me to lie down in green pastures. he leadeth me ... He restoreth my soul ... Yea, though I walk through the valley of the shadow of death I will fear no evil for Thou art with me ..."

When I had concluded the Psalm I made the Sign of the Cross on her forehead and said:

"God is with you, my dear, forever and ever. Amen."

For the first time her eyelids flickered in recognition that I was with her. I sensed her utter tranquillity and I felt a sweet and gentle presence all around me. It was wholly beautiful.

When I returned to her waiting relatives they asked me what I thought about her condition.

"It will not be long now" I said. "She is ready and so happy to go. Perhaps a few hours."

But inwardly I thought it would be a matter of minutes.

A short while after returning home we received a telephone call from one of her children. His mother had died, he said, only ten minutes after we had left the nursing home to go back to London.

I believe that she had waited until I could see her that day and that her spirit-soul, so active in its faculties now that her body was fast declining, had guided me not only to visit her on that particular day before she died, but throughout that wholly unfamiliar journey so that I might arrive at her bedside in time to have our last prayer together.

16

WHEN WORDS FAIL

We often find that our inability to help or advise others as well as we could wish is due to the difficulty we have in expressing ourselves adequately to them in words. This frailty may be overcome if we remember that our spirit-soul can communicate our deepest feelings of love and compassion to the spirit-soul of another person without the medium of words. The prerequisite is that we first enter silently into a deep communion with Christ. This we do by realising His Presence through that great attribute of the soul called faith.

That exercise liberates the spirit-soul which can then act as pure spirit and so may illumine another spirit-soul with the consolation, wisdom, healing and joy which it has itself received from the Spirit of Christ.

Thus not only bodies and minds but also broken human relationships may be healed by the activity of one's spirit-soul when it is influenced by faith in the reconciling power of Jesus Christ.

One of the welfare problems with which I was concerned during my chaplaincy in the Royal Air Force concerned a young airman who wished to divorce his wife and marry a girl whom he had met while serving in his previous station. Talking the matter over with the Commanding Officer it was decided I should make a visit to the wife and try to sort the matter out since, apart from an unhappy and incoherent letter from her, we only had the airman's rather vague and unsatisfactory side of the story.

As he worked for motor transport he was requested to drive me by Staff car to his home. The journey took several hours and during the first half of it I found my companion rather sullen and very uncommunicative. He did make it clear, however, that in his opinion my visit was an infringement of his personal liberty and in any case a waste of time.

"Whose idea was it?" he asked. "Yours, padre, or the C.O's?"

"Actually neither, Richard. It was mutual. After all something had to be done when you started talking of getting a divorce and desiring to marry this girl. We *are* concerned about you, you know."

"All I want is a divorce" he said. "My wife has been unfaithful. That's a good reason isn't it?"

"Yes, certainly. But divorce is not quite so easy as that. You say she is unfaithful, but have you any proof?"

"A neighbour told me she's been seen with the fellow. Seen them going off in the van he drives."

"Hardly conclusive — that kind of hearsay." I said. "You would need better evidence than that. Surely you realise that?"

He did not answer and there was a long silence.

"Look" I said at last, "much as I may disagree with divorce I'm not saying you shouldn't seek it. It might even be the best thing. But, you see, we know very little about the whole affair — just that you want to marry this other girl. We are, despite what you may think, trying to be helpful. But you've got to face facts and as far as you have given them they are pretty one-sided. Your side and not your wife's. That's where I come in and why I am seeing her. Perhaps I can find out a bit more. Clear away the fog a bit, Richard, that's all. Of course it would help a lot if you told us more about your married life. How it went wrong. It wasn't always bad, was it?"

"I've told you she is unfaithful" he repeated gruffly. "She goes now with this other chap. I don't want to talk to her again. I hope you won't expect me to see her when we arrive. I draw the line at doing that. We've finished and I just want the divorce."

His face looked hard. He was obviously determined not to discuss the matter further.

"Speak to him, Lord", I prayed again and again. " Speak to him. I *know* there is something he wants to say to me. Give him the courage to say it before we reach his home. Please, Father, do this for Jesus' sake."

The car sped on and then, quite suddenly he spoke:

"As we shall be at my place in about half an hour I ought to warn you."

"Warn me?" I queried. "What on earth about?"

"You've seen slums, have you padre?"

"Why yes, Richard, I've seen some pretty poor places in my time — and some tragic circumstances. Of course."

"Nonetheless, padre, I guess my place will give you a shock. You see when I was called up for National Service the slums were all I knew. So the RAF was like a great adventure. For the first time in my life I knew what it was like to take pride in my appearance, to be able to wash properly, to have decent clothes, to eat well. I couldn't understand at first some of the chaps who were always grumbling about National Service and longing for it to be over. For me it was marvellous. It was as if I had never known a real family before — being cared for, that is. That's why I decided to sign on. The RAF is my life now and I love it."

After a long silence he continued:

"My wife doesn't understand how my life is now. I tried to tell her but she just can't see it. She's always lived the way I used to do and it's impossible to make her otherwise.You'll soon see what I mean when you meet her. Jean is quite different. We get along just right."

Jean was the girl he had come to know while serving his previous posting and whom he wished to marry.

I felt that I must make some answer even if I put at risk the new confidence which I hoped was growing between us.

"Are you saying, Richard, that while *you* were able to change when you experienced life in the RAF that you think your wife never could? Don't you think that if *she* had the chance like you have had to get into a new kind of world that she might find happiness too? It does sound, Richard, as if you are being, shall we say, spiritually snobbish. Are you afraid that she won't do you credit? If she had never had the opportunity to make something of herself don't you see that you owe it to her to get her out of the slums? I've no doubt that we could work something out as soon as possible — getting you married quarters on the station, that is, or a decent hiring in the town ..."

Then I realised I must be talking too much. The words were coming too fast and I checked myself from elaborating further. To my dismay he made no further conversation and the deep brooding look was hardening his face again.

I began to regret my answer even though I felt the truth was in it. I returned to my silent prayer and the remainder of the journey

passed without a word. At last we came to a stop in a gloomy road
with tall gaunt buildings on either side of it. Rain was now falling
to add to the general air of dejection of the district.

Then Richard spoke again.

"It's here — just two entrances ahead." he said, and then added
"Remember, padre, I won't see her. I don't want her to talk you
into it."

"Fair enough, Richard" I replied "you've made your point. I
will not force the issue. Just wait for me in the car."

The staircase of the tenement I entered was sombre and very grimy
with a dank unpleasant smell on each landing. I found Richard's
house on the third level, and when I knocked a fair young woman
appeared. She looked extremely frail and the severe pallor of her
face made me wonder if she were ill.

"Mrs D-?" I asked. She nodded but looked apprehensive. "I've
come from your husband's station" I said. "We have been very
concerned about you since you wrote to us. Can I come in and
talk?"

She beckoned and we walked straight into what I discovered
later was both living room and bedroom.

Though it was only mid-afternoon it was so dark inside that it
was some time before I could make out the surroundings. In fact
I talked with the young woman for nearly ten minutes thinking
we were alone before I discerned a huddled shape on a chair by
the empty fireplace. This, it transpired, was the girl's grandmother
who was fast asleep the whole time I was there. Bit by bit, as my
eyes grew accustomed to the gloom, I also became aware of the
presence of the baby half-hidden in one corner lying on the floor
upon what seemed to be a heap of old clothing.

It was not long before Elizabeth, Richard's wife, had poured out
her troubles. She maintained that she and her husband had been
happy together until he decided to sign on in the Royal Air Force
while still doing his National Service. Aparently he then became more
and more distant in his attitude towards his wife. After a while he
made only rare visits home and whenever he did there were fierce
rows which ended in some violence. I spoke to her of her husband's
conviction that she was associating with another man.

"I know that's what he says" she replied. "He tells everyone
that. The chap he means is someone who lives in this block. He's
married. He's felt sorry for me and baby Jimmy and has taken

me sometimes in his van to the shops, that's all. I've always had Jimmy with me. His wife is kind to me, too."

I did not interrupt her and she went on" "Dicky has been real cruel the last few times that he has come here. He makes me crawl naked across the floor and hits me with a belt ... I can't tell you how awful it is ..." She began to cry.

I looked at her pathetic figure and could find no words. I prayed that God would tell me what to say. The cramped room with its dark and cheerless atmosphere became oppressive. Elizabeth was sitting on the floor by my side for the only chairs in the place were those two which were occupied by her sleeping grandmother and myself. In the corner the baby began to whimper a little. I could see and understand for myself the pitiable plight of this fragile creature whose thin frame was now shaking with an uncontrollable sobbing.

I continued to pray inwardly that my spirit-soul might communicate with hers — and her husband's ¿ convey the healing guidance of God, to bring a happy issue out of this tragic situation.

When the flood of tears had subsided she began to appeal to me: "If only he'd come to see me again" she said. "Can you get him to do that? If he would just talk to me again I believe something could go right. But he's written to tell me that he'll never come home again or speak to me. Would you ask him to see me, just once more — *please*?"

I found the answer almost too hard to make in the face of her agonised pleading. "I'm afraid he seems to have made up his mind, my dear, not to see you again. I tried to get him to do so today."

"Before I go" I went on, "shall we ask God to help?". I stood and laid my hands on her tiny head. She felt like a wraith who would fade away at the least unkind breeze. "God who loves you and cares for you be with you now. May Jesus Christ guide you and protect you in your great trouble. May He heal your marriage and bless you and your husband."

There was quiet between us. Beautiful in its stillness and sense of peace. There were tears in my own eyes, too, when I removed my hands at last from her head. There was a strange light shimmering about her and the unhealthy pallor of her face had changed to a glow which seemed to come from within it, rising up to the surface, as it were, to make her countenance radiant. All around us was the depressing darkness of the room with all its unwholesomeness. Yet here, in the midst of it, was this wondrous beauty and tranquillity.

How long I stood before her kneeling figure I do not know. The atmosphere was like a spell which I felt I would break if I made any movement. I longed for it to remain forever to enhearten and solace this tragic soul. God grant, I said to myself, that I may remember this experience of transcendent loveliness forever, and may it heal all the wounds and sadness of this heartbroken girl.

She clung to my hands as I was about to leave. "Thank you, sir, so much." And then, quite simply and without her former tenseness and anxiety, she added "Try to get Dicky to speak to me again. Just once more."

I left the wretched dwelling still sad of heart but supremely fortified by that strange glory with which my visit had ended. When I returned to the car Richard was reading a paper-back. Without a word he started the engine.

"Won't you reconsider, Richard?" I asked. "Elizabeth dearly wants to see you ... to talk to you, even for a few moments."

He shook his head with definite determination and we moved off into the gathering dusk. As we went I saw the little figure of his wife standing in the shadow of the tenement entrance. This pathetic sight haunted me as we drove on. I realised that there was no more I could say but in the forefront of my mind I continued to find a powerful reassurance in the final good outcome of this day's journey, despite the obduracy and discouragement of my companion. I must simply resort to prayer. I must cast the whole depressing affair into the loving hands of God and trust completely in Him to deal with it in His way.

So I mused over and over again upon that interview with Richard's wife in that forsaken, cheerless room and the marvel of its concluding vision of hope and joy.

At the deep level of the spirit-soul I now sought to communicate the anguish I felt in that melancholy experience to Richard, but also the sense of reconciliation within it as well.

Time and again I willed my concentration on these things so that he should become sensitive to them and react with warmth and understanding. Yet we drove on out of the city until the light of the main road ceased and we were in the deep darkness of the countryside. There was no word between us for almost an hour during which I could not let up in my desire to have some response from Richard.

Then, quite suddenly, it happened. He pulled up sharply at the side of the road and made a complete turnabout so that the car was heading back.

"I think I must go and see her — like you say, padre. I hope you don't mind the delay" was all he said. His tone seemed to tell me that he had had a fight within himself to make this decision. Against pride perhaps — or his gentler self — or my battle to win him to Christ?

"Of course not, Richard" I replied. "There is all the time in the world for something worthwhile to be done." I was determined not to say more in case I jeopardised what I began to feel was the beginning of a change of heart in him. It was best to leave him entirely to his own thoughts and I began to pray silently that when he saw his wife there would be a reconciliation or, if parting there was to be, then one which held no rancour in it.

There was no further conversation between us until we reached his home once more. "I won't be overlong" he said quietly as he left the car.

"There's no hurry, Richard. God be with you." I replied.

When he had disappeared into the building I concentrated upon his meeting with his wife. I prayed that God would surround them with His love and understanding. Then I created in my mind a picture of them together in that room not, however, in its gloom and bareness but transfigured with light. I tried to see it bathed in beauty, enlivened by flowers and furniture and pictures. I built up this mental image with meticulous detail and became so involved in it that I felt I was there myself. Also, though an onlooker, I began to feel that I was nevertheless sharing in some strange way in the reunion of Richard and Elizabeth. I prayed for gaiety and joy to come to them. The scene of all this became so vivid and substantial that I lost sense of time.

At last, however, I became conscious of the ticking of the car clock and noted that nearly an hour had passed since Richard had gone. The rain was now quite heavy and the surroundings appeared even more depressing because of it. I would have wished to leave the car and stretch my legs but I thought that if Richard came out and saw me pacing up and down he might feel embarrassed at keeping me so long.

I had a wonderful feeling now that he and his wife were in a happier relationship. I must do nothing to disturb that. So I remained in the car and endeavoured to sustain that encouraging sense of optimism about the affair which I had received in my long reverie. I did so by continuing to dwell upon the mental picture I had created of their reconciliation.

About twenty minutes later Richard returned to the car. He apologised for the long wait he had given me and then said: "You know what you said about trying to get Elizabeth and me a married quarter on the station or a hiring? I would be grateful if you could do that, padre. I believe we shall make a go of it together."

What a joy it was to hear him speak like that! Yet because of the lovely vision I had had of them it came as no surprise to me, only a sense of inner affirmation of the certainty I had received from it.

Looking at me with frank eyes, in a manner he had not shown all day he continued:

"I've got to admit, padre, that I didn't think I'd ever feel this way. But something came over me, you see, that made me want to turn back. It was queer. I just didn't have any idea then why I should go back or what I would say or do when I returned. Then when I went into our house the strangest thing happened. It was as if the place was suddenly changed and I could see it all so differently — with curtains, flowers, decent furniture and that sort of thing. And Liz seemed different to me. I felt there was something good ahead of us and now, quite suddenly, I'm not thinking of Jean anymore. It's as if she had never come into my life. I know the three of us, Liz and me and baby Jimmy will be OK from now on. God knows what happened. I mean that, padre, though I hardly ever think about God. Now I realise I ought to, for I certainly never thought today would end like this..."

The long journey back to the RAF station was made in an entirely different atmosphere from that which had prevailed during our outward one. There was a lightness and warmth about Richard which made him now a most agreeable companion. And the outcome proved equally happy for he and his wife both came to live on the station shortly afterwards and their marriage proved stable and contented. Spiritual healing with a difference. Not physical illness overcome but a human relationship restored. Yet the principle is the same — re-creative prayer, using one's spirit-soul to convey the reconciling power of Christ.

17

ANGELS OF CHILDHOOD

The Church generally maintains a belief in angels but it is hardly a strong point among Protestants. As for guardian angels they are scarcely ever mentioned.

I believe that unseen beings do offer their help to us but it is certainly not of a nature which can be said to rob us of our identity, our will or our initiative.

Though not taught such a doctrine in my childhood, nevertheless I see now that an assurance of this kind was awakened in my early years. Maybe this awareness of angelic assistance lies there deep within us as an inheritance of the subconscious of the human race. Certainly its reality for simple and primitive people is very evident in their cultures. Perhaps as babes we inherit the sense of it but the ever growing sophistication of man causes it to fade until it is not only dim in us but is finally discarded as being impractical if not untrue.

When I was about ten years old my companions and I had a favoury walk along the perimeter outside a large recreation park. It was a dusty lane deeply rutted with wheel tracks — mostly of horse-drawn carts, but an occasional motor car did venture down it.

After heavy rain it became an intricate pattern of pools and gullies difficult to negotiate without arriving home ankle deep in mud.

On one side lay the recreation ground edged by iron railings. These were screened by odd patches of scraggy blackberry bushes which might surrender a tiny handful of minute fruit after extensive searching. On the other side of this lane were private allotments always smelling strongly of manure and decaying cabbage leaves, and tended by those who found their own gardens inadequate for their agricultural aspirations. A multitude of corrugated iron and wooden shacks cluttered this area, which added to this special interest for small boys.

It was altogether a most enticing place for youngsters who were brought up in a big city and for whom this was the nearest taste of country.

We would always stop at one place where stood the fascination of an old-fashioned pump. It rose up from a platform of rickety planks and, if one persisted long enough at the shaky handle, it was possible to draw up a dribble of dirty water through the rusty spout.

On this particular day there had been rain and my friend and I had gained this platform in a fairly unmuddied state. This was something of a miracle in view of the conditions!

No one seemed to be around — probably because of the recent downpour. My friend began to work the pump but without much success. When he tired I took over. With gusto I heaved at the handle and sure enough the spout gurgled at last a thin stream of dirty water. Then it happened. The rotten plank on which I was standing cracked with a stomach jerking suddenness and my legs disappeared through the fractured timber. Being still in the grey short trousers and grey woollen stockings worn by schoolboys of those days, the splintered wood badly scored my legs and knees. But the worst was the fact that I found I could not move.

Firmly wedged in this position I called on my chum to try to heave me up but his added weight and exertions only succeeded in cracking the rent still wider so that I now felt in imminent threat of disappearing altogether into the inky darkness below.

The pump handle of course was now beyond reach. No 'allotmenteers' either were in view and the situation began to make me feel frantic and frightened. My friend moved away from the danger zone and said he would try to find a stout piece of branch or a piece of discarded wooden paling to extend across the treacherous board so that I could pull upon it as he held the other end. I think his mind had been arrested by some thriller he had seen at a local cinema in which a dog had exercised the same brilliant solution for his devoted master who was disappearing into a particularly loathsome bog. He had been rescued in this way at the eleventh hour even as his head was about submerge. Such optimism, however, did not encourage me very much especially as meanwhile I was unable to get a handhold at all on to anything stable and the splintering planks were creaking ominously with every panting breath.

The fact that I had lost sight of my friend as he wandered off in his search for the necessary length of wood — for I dared not turn my head to see where he was — did not help to reduce my panic either.

Then it was that I began to experience real fear at my condition. Something however prompted me to try to keep perfectly still. The creaking and cracking of boards ceased. And I prayed. Oh, a simple enough prayer — *"Dear Jesus, please help me."* As I have said before Jesus was very real to me. There was never any doubt in my mind that He was the One Who, when human help was not forthcoming, came to us when there was danger. All my childhood training had clearly implanted this as a wonderful fact. At that stage of life, of course, moral struggles were not all that intense so that my belief was then along what might be called mainly practical and physical lines. Jesus Christ was a Saviour. Yes — and He would indeed save me in this, my hour of need!

And then something happened. I use the word 'something' carefully because to this day I cannot say how or what it was. I know that when my friend returned and found me standing several yards away from the gaping hole and ruefully contemplating the grazes and scratches on my shins and knees, I could not explain to him what had transpired to extricate me. All I can say is that I knew it was an answer to prayer. I had not the shadow of doubt about that. It was a complete mystery and has remained one. To my companion I said it was a kind of magic but I did say also that Jesus had saved me. In those days at any rate (whatever may be the case today) boys of nine or ten could accept without question the mysterious workings of faith in the unseen aid of Jesus without scoffing and, indeed, without undue surprise. Therein, I believe, lies a great power. Childhood is the age of trust, of belief — of magic if you like. But just because of that simple unquestioning acceptance of unseen powers those self same powers can be most potent.

It is the years that take the toll of our early vivid insight into the spiritual realm. Of course we must learn to rationalise, to break from childish concepts, to let loose the reins of superstition, to face the stark realities of our material environment. It is a pity though if our hold on the world of spirit, which childhood's creative imagination makes so real, is allowed to fade entirely away. Maybe we need the occasional agony of the apparently insoluble problem or the anguish of a great sorrow to galvanise us into recovering in our later years some fraction of that absolute faith known to the infancy of the human race — to revive the unquestioning trust in the unseen world which was so much a natural part of us when we were young.

Be this as it may, I know that this personal encounter as a boy of ten with a power which words cannot describe, or the mind fully comprehend, remains one of the signal experiences of my psychic journey.

Another — not quite so dramatic perhaps but obviously of sufficient intensity to linger on in the long corridor of memory — was an occasion when I had gone on an errand to the grocer's shop for my mother.

On the way back I had the sudden idea of buying her a little iced cake. This I did at her favourite shop. I was only a small boy and so excited at the thought of the surprise I would give her that I started to run in order to reach home sooner. This proved fatal for I took a short cut through a narrow alley of adjoining houses. A few yards down this path I was suddenly confronted by a very large black dog which barked furiously at first and then began to snap fiercely at me.

At that time I had a pronounced fear of dogs. I understand my mother had been severely frightened by one when she was carrying me in her womb. Whether or not this had implanted in me my deep apprehension of dogs I cannot say, but I do know that for many of my early years these animals, especially if boisterous, were a real bane to me. If alone I would always make a wide circuit whenever possible in order to avoid crossing their path.

Anyway, this particular creature was a real terror. I believe that some time afterwards complaints of its vicious behaviour were raised and it may subsequently have been destroyed. Certainly not so very long after this particular incident it ceased to be seen roaming at will in the neighbourhood.

Terrified, I tried to back away down the alley but the creature seemed to gather more ferocity as it sensed my timidity. Not only, I remember, was I concerned about my own safety but I feared also for the little iced cake in its fragile paper bag.

What mixed up feelings there were! Fear, distress, the misery of having my present spoiled or even destroyed, and the fact that both my hands were encumbered — one holding the bag of groceries and the other clutching the precious cake. And no grown-up in sight to scatter this growling beast for me!

Then, as the situation grew more unbearable, I stood at last stock still, and thought of Jesus and His invincible power. In those few seconds of stillness my terror left me completely. Like the raising of a heavy blanket which has become intolerably oppressive, I suddenly felt immeasurably strong, daringly bold. I had all power. The power and safety of the great Lord Jesus were with me!

Now, instead of backing away, I found that I could walk steadily *forward*. And the dog? strangely it began to move backwards for a few steps. Looking at me, it stopped its racket of barking and prancing and then turned tail and, completely disregarding me, sidled off ahead sniffing in odd places. Elated, I passed it at a steady confident pace and gained the open road once more.

One more experience of my early life may have served to strengthen the view which has grown in me down the years that angelic beings are not a pure figment of the imagination, or the left overs of a very ancient theology, but that they do indeed exist in their own realm, maintaining at the same time a loving concern with ours.

Two brothers were among my regular companions when I was about eleven years old. One day, when we were out together during the school holidays, they were eagerly talking about a film they were going to see in one of the local cinemas. As I recall it concerned the adventures of Robin Hood, or it may have been of William Tell. Whatever it was it contained a good deal of archery.

Shortly after they had seen the film they made some bows from bamboo canes. Quite powerful they were, too, firing arrows made from smaller canes with a fair degree of accuracy.

The next time I met them they had become enthusiastic archers and I was treated to an hour or so of their prowess. I handled the older brother's bow myself but failed to match anything like his marksmanship when I aimed at the various targets he selected.

Then, unaccountably, in the midst of this quite absorbing play in which I was thoroughly enjoying myself a most odd sensation came over me. I suddenly felt quite detached from all that we were doing. The best description I can give is that the feeling was akin to a cold numbness which totally robbed the afternoon of any further attraction. As I say, this feeling arose suddenly and without apparent reason. Nonetheless it was compelling enough for me to decide to leave my friends therewith even though I would not be expected to return home for another hour or more.

So I left the brothers still playing in the park despite their pleading with me to stay.

Many times I have asked myself the question as to what made me take a course which I had never taken before, viz, to leave my friends before it was necessary for me to do so. I had, as always, been told to be home by a certain time. That time was more than an hour ahead. What strange prompting had caused me to forsake that remaining playtime with my friends? Most certainly it was not boredom for I was thoroughly enjoying myself and quite absorbed in all we were doing.

I was to learn later how fortunate my departure was. For it transpired that some short while after I had said goodbye to them, the older boy had aimed at his brother who was then acting the part of any enemy of Robin Hood. The arrow struck the boy in the right eye. The immediate consequences must have been terrifying for by the time the two had reached home after the accident the sight of the eye was destroyed.

I can still remember the series of weekly visits we made to the outpatients' department of the hospital in order for the poor lad to have treatment. I must say he bore the whole sad affair with amazing fortitude. He never complained and even gave us some macabre amusement by removing now and again his new glass eye.

I have realised much more in after years how easily this accident could have befallen me instead of him. If I had lingered until the game had turned from inanimate targets to include ourselves I might well have been the one to be blinded.

Is it so fantastic to believe that some higher and protective power sometimes urges us to adopt a changed course?

In the main we do not heed our inner promptings and premonitions. But on the occasions when we do how often we can afterwards perceive how narrowly we have avoided some great harm or been prevented from making some dreadful mistake?

Let me conclude this chapter with another reminiscence of childhood because, as I believe, it testifies still further to the reality of angelic assistance.

A Priest and the Paranormal

During the First World War, in April 1917, HMS Swift, a vessel of the Dover Patrol, together with HMS Broke, engaged the enemy in the Channel. It was a successful encounter as the country came to know when Commander Evans of the Broke made his triumphal return to Dover.

Either during this battle or in one of the many patrols the hull of the Swift scraped the chains of a mine which, however, failed to explode. My father was in the engine-room when this occurred. He rarely spoke of his wartime experiences but on the one occasion when as a boy of nine I overheard him mention, almost casually (and certainly not very graphically) this particular incident to one of his friends, I can remember the strange feeling it evoked in me. It was as if I myself had been there. This impression was most vivid in my young mind. I remember that same night, after overhearing the account, I lay awake thinking of it. After a while it seemed to me my bedroom walls appeared to dissolve to give place to the interior of a ship. With my limited knowledge of any kind of vessel other than the paddle steamer to the Isle of Wight, or the small ferry-boat to Gosport, the mental picture was, naturally, restricted to their simple engine-rooms although the general impression of such seemed much magnified in this most vivid mental picture. Strangely, the massive wheels and pistons appeared to be noiseless as they moved all about me. In the midst of this scene I became aware of an ominous scraping noise. I heard it with bated breath. The intense feeling of apprehension it engendered was at length followed by one of great relief as this awesome sound died away.

For some years I was to relive in my imagination that scene with all its deep sensations. It was an experience which returned at intervals until I was about twelve years old. It ceased to trouble me though from the day when its realism came to a pitch during a very special treat I received. It happened like this.

One of my uncles, a Naval Officer, who was in command of a destroyer took me on board for the day when his ship was going on gunnery exercise.

A marvellous day it was, too. He collected me from home very early in the morning and drove me in his fascinating open Morris Cowley (which was an adventure in itself in those days) to Portsmouth Dockyard, where we boarded his ship. I remember how exciting it was to have lunch in the wardroom where, I guess, everyone treated me with the greatest attention and affection.

When we had reached the target area and all was ready for firing I recall how a steward was in charge of me while I clutched a rail to watch the practice. The destroyer was travelling very fast and the spray rose in great crested plumes ahead. Then the guns boomed. At first I only felt the excitement of it all. But then, as the firing continued, salvo after salvo, I found myself thinking of my father — and that engine room aboard HMS Swift. I could picture it well enough now because I had seen at first hand that very morning the engines of a destroyer during the tour I had been given round my uncle's ship.

There was that special smell of oil and steel everywhere and the great shudder of all those huge moving parts introduced a strange new world to me. As the guns crashed I seemed to be transported to that action in the Channel in April 1917. It was all so real. And all that din I was hearing now must have been so very like that which my father would have been hearing then. The strange thing in all this, however, was that I was not (at any rate consciously) *trying* to imagine the scene. Indeed the day had been far too exciting for me to think of anything but its present, vastly unusual, enjoyment. *It was rather as if the picture were being deliberately recreated for me by some force outside myself.* I felt an onlooker but deeply involved in it at the same time. Imagination can, of course, be very powerful when we are young. Imagined agonies can be especially real. In the midst of all the thrill and fun of that afternoon I was being reminded of something which must have had memorable significance for my father. As the vision gathered ever greater intensity and realism I felt my whole body pound with apprehension. The very deck under my feet threatened to open up to the violence of all that thunderous sound of guns and the thrashing menace of the waves. It was a breath-taking and almost overwhelming experience.

It was at the point when I felt most carried away by it all that the oppressive strain of apprehension began to pass from me. It did so as I remembered something else. Something my mother had told me once in explaining my Christian names. Apparently, on the morning after that action in the Channel the commander of HMS Swift sent for my father.

"News has been received" he told him "that a son has been born to you. Promise me something. When you name him will you call him 'Jack' after the sea and 'Dover' in memory of our Patrol? Do this because he brought us great luck last night."

And so it was to be. And the recollection of how my names originated did, in that experience aboard a destroyer twelve years after I was born, bring to me now a wonderful sense of relief. It was like having passed through a great danger safely. The tension lifted and was replaced by a marvellous feeling of gaiety — of gladness to be alive and to savour all the remaining delights of this day's high adventure to the full.

Of course, they say that those who sail the seas sometimes have more than an ordinary measure of superstition. What is probably nearer the truth is to say that their calling keeps them in surer touch with spiritual realities.

Is it pure fancy to believe that in the moment of birth there are spiritual powers released to protect us and help our future course? What angelic power enfolds us when we come from life in the womb to life in the world? Must we deny the ministry of angels? I certainly cannot. And when I think of what might have happened if I had been left fatherless, because that mine had exploded or enemy action had blasted the ship, I cannot see how my life could have taken the path it has. The captain of the Swift may have spoken truer words than he knew. And I? Well, I remain grateful to my guardian angel.

18

ANGELIC RESCUE

There have been other marked occasions in later life which have reinforced my belief in the care that is accorded us by 'guardian angels'.

During the Second World War I was one of those to be given the nickname of 'boffin'. At one time with a number of colleagues I had to verify the results of certain experiments we had conducted on a scale model of a warship. This entailed checks being made on the vessel itself which was then in Scapa Flow.

In order to reach her it was necessary to steam out on a small ship. This had to be boarded by clambering up a short rope ladder slung over the side.

We had purposely gone for these trials when a bout of severe weather was expected and already signs of the roughness to come were well evident. Not only was it raining hard but there was also a very strong wind blowing.

For those not accustomed to the gymnastic feat of boarding in this fashion such weather conditions are perilous enough. But to add to the difficulty we were encumbered with oilskins and sea boots and were carrying on our backs some fairly heavy items of scientific equipment.

I must say that the ascent of this ladder now swinging against the side of the ship, which was heaving quite strongly in the water, constituted for me a hazard made considerably worse because my spectacles (without which I could see very little) were not only dimmed by the salt spray but fitted somewhat too loosely. This, with the awkwardness of an unfamiliar south-wester perched on my head, made it imperative for me not to look too acutely downwards or they would have slipped from my face altogether. When it was my turn, as the last of the party to go aboard, I followed a colleague rather too closely up the ladder. For some reason he had ascended only a few rungs when he paused unexpectedly which momentarily threw me off my concentration. Almost blind because of the filthy state of my glasses, my hands numb with the intense cold, my whole being felt completely miserable and unsure. Somehow I knew that his heels had not left the next rung which my right hand was feeling for. Without thought I let go immediately as I imagined he would step on my fingers. In consequence I found myself swinging out sideways, clutching one side of the ladder only by my left hand.

The weight on my back and the constriction of all those heavy garments, made it impossible for me to heave myself square on and so seize the ladder again with my right hand. Now, to add to the discomfort of the whole operation came a new element — that of fear.

I could imagine, though I could not see it, the gurgling black water below me. I could not swim at all well and in any case the heavy clothing would have made it impossible. In the instant that followed I pictured myself being crushed by the ship's side if I did fall into the sea.

It was indeed a moment of peril. An enterprise which I had started upon with much enthusiasm and interest had suddenly turned into something of a nightmare. I felt completely hopeless since the more I struggled to gain that other hold the more unbearable became the strain on my left hand, arm and shoulder which were the only link with the swaying ladder.

I felt that I was but seconds away from fainting with the wrenching pain. A great fear now seized me as I realised the loss of my remaining hold was imminent. It could only have been a flashing moment in which I prayed for God's help. But the miracle happened.

Because of a lurching of the vessel or because those above me had clambered aboard and thereby the ladder had lost its tautness — whatever the mechanical cause may have been — I was swung back so that my right hand was able to close round the ladder once more.

But the mysterious thing was that there was nothing sudden or violent about this. I distinctly felt a strange pressure, quite gentle but decidely firm — for all the world like a push from a friendly hand. It acted against my right shoulder and restored my position and equilibrium. In that same instant a wonderful sense of peace and confidence flooded through me. I even felt tingling with warmth.

Within seconds I had climbed safely on board. Instantly I gave the most heartfelt silent thanks to God as I stood upon that deck.

The whole incident must have occupied less than half a minute (though it seemed far longer to me). Only one of the party seemed to have noticed it, "My word," he said, "I thought you were going to end up in the drink."

Almost involuntarily I replied: "I must thank my guardian angel that I didn't."

He grinned back as if I were joking.

Nevertheless, with that sensation as of an unseen but very real hand propelling me to safety vividly in mind, I certainly meant what I said.

19

AIR RAIDS AND PHENOMENA

It was also during the Second World War that I had other escapes from danger which were accompanied by certain phenomena.

My home was in Portsmouth — later to be recognised as the most bombed city in England. Night after night the German planes would either make a definite target of it or, if its citizens were spared a major attack, the Luftwaffe would save a bomb or two for them on the way back from raids on targets inland. In consequence one very rarely had a night of uninterrupted sleep. Perhaps this fact made most inhabitants a little blasé about the whole business and in the end most would only take shelter when things got really bad.

The experience I now record happened during a period when the enemy was using a great many incendiary bombs as well as high explosives.

Working as I did for the Admiralty meant that, like most Government staff, I had the opportunity of receiving some Air Raid Precaution drill. This was mainly in fire-fighting, and our office had its own trailer pump which we towed behind a mammoth old Ford saloon car.

Only a few days before this particular raid on Portsmouth my squad had been receiving some instruction in how to deal with fire-bombs. I never suspected that so soon afterwards I would be trying to put this tuition into real practice.

There was no cellar in our house but my father had constructed a quite comfortable air raid shelter in it by making a trapdoor in the floor boards of the dining room. Through this one could descend into the quite spacious foundations. On this occasion neither he nor I were in this shelter because soon after the warning sirens sounded we had heard some peculiar noises in the garden. They were unlike anything we had known hitherto during air raids, so we went outside to reconnoitre. Then we saw the reason for them. There were sparks and flames in neighbouring gardens and here and there small fires had started in them although, as yet, no houses appeared to be affected.

Overhead was the steady drone of aircraft and searchlights were fingering the sky. There was a desultory crump of anti-aircraft guns but activity was still only slight and it seemed clear that the main raid must be elsewhere that night. Then, suddenly, there were menacing whistling sounds which made us duck back quickly into the nearest safety of the back door of the house. This door opened into the kitchen.

We were not sure if anything had struck the house although we suspected it. So I returned to the garden and looked up at the back of the house. There was nothing untoward. I breathed a sigh of relief. I remember thinking what a lovely night it was. The moon and the stars were brilliant. But in the distance there were now great flashes and the ground under my feet trembled with explosions. Somewhere the city was getting it cruelly. Most of the sky glowed red and there was a strong smell of smoke.

Then, to my surprise, I realised that this odour was not just a general one but was rising very pungently just behind me. I had been so concerned with observing the rear of the main part of the house that I had given no thought to the scullery which jutted out into the garden as a kind of outhouse. There were no rooms above it. From its low roof was coming a hissing sound and a good deal of smoke.

However, as soon as I had realised that an incendiary bomb had struck the slates it pierced through them and fell inside the scullery.

In that moment I thought how lucky we were that it had not fallen on the main roof where it would have been impossible to do anything until it had burned its way through into a bedroom. By that time of course a fire would have started in the timbers of the roof, which would have been almost impossible to cope with.

Somewhat proud of the fact that I knew how to deal with incendiaries, and congratulating myself on my forethought in having a bucket of sand ready, I ran back through the kitchen door and made for the scullery. This was at the far end of the kitchen.

I must say I felt quite lighthearted about the whole matter as I went with my sand bucket at the ready. I found the scullery thick with smoke and the bomb burning merrily in the cat's basket. (The cat, I need hardly say, had made for a safe corner in the house at the first note of the air raid siren). I threw the bucket of sand over the smoking heap and stood triumphantly watching the result, thinking how fortunate it was that the floor in this part of the house was flag stones and not wood. Then, quite suddenly, my concentration was arrested by the strangest feeling. It was as if someone had pulled me by the right shoulder. And there was an urgent sounding voice — loud and distinct — saying: "*Your eyes, your eyes!*"

I swung round to see who on earth could be speaking to me — but there was no one! For a fleeting moment I seemed to be outside my own body. It was as if I were looking on the whole scene from a distance. Thus it never occurred to me to question the reality of this experience or to dismiss the tug on my shoulder and the imperative voice as being of no account.

The sense of impending danger was so strong that I felt compelled to turn back to the kitchen. I slammed shut the scullery door as it there were a devil behind it. In that same instant there was an explosion which shook the floor under me so that I had difficulty in remaining upright. the door which I was in the very act of closing rattled against the lock. I could feel it heave against my hand which was still on the knob.

Unknown to me when I had so confidently and almost gleefully tackled it that incendiary was of a new order. It was, I believe, the first time such types were dropped though they were to be common from then on. Unlike the earlier variety which only caused fires, this kind finally exploded as well in order to make dealing with it hazardous.

Had there not been that powerful sensation of another presence and the insistence of that warning voice I would have quite happily remained standing over the apparently harmless fire until I had witnessed its complete extinction. In that case I would have taken the blast of the anti-personnel incendiary full in my face. Heaven knows what injury would have resulted. At the least, and most likely, it would have blinded me. Only the shield of the door being closed at that precise moment saved me.

Many times I have reflected upon that night. What lingers is the sensation of being temporarily out of my body. But for that I think I would have been tempted to try to rationalise the strange jerk upon my shoulder and the voice which accompanied it. In that event, through my delaying to react immediately, disaster would have overtaken me.

Together with other experiences is it any wonder that I am sure that angels do seek to guard us?

There are, of course, certain facts to take into consideration. To begin with there was the accumulated fatigue of many nights of inadequate sleep due to regular enemy air activity. This tiredness was intensified by a week of night duty only just concluded. It is when the body and mind are near to exhaustion that the psychic faculties are usually heightened. The excitement of that night with all its physical stress was temporarily lulled by the easeful satisfaction of contemplating what I believed to be the successful tackling of that incendiary. Gazing so fixedly at it in the way I did, after casting over it the bucketful of sand, probably induced a degree of self-hypnosis.

The result of these combined circumstances would encourage the liberation of my spirit-soul. As I have suggested the spirit-soul has cognition of matters of which, in our ordinary state, we are not aware. It is also able to have communication directly with another spirit or spirits. Hence, a spirit with its greater knowledge (and desirous of communicating that knowledge) i.e. a guardian angel, might be the most satisfactory explanation of the sudden warning I received that night to remove myself before the bomb exploded.

Another 'lucky' escape during the War occurred a few months later. It happened on a Sunday night towards the end of April 1941. After attending Evensong at St Mark's Church, Portsmouth, I asked Dorothy (the girl who six years later was to become my wife) to take a walk along Southsea promenade. It had to be a fairly short expedition because the air raids had for some weeks past been almost a nightly occurrence and it was wisest therefore to take the bus home a full hour before the raid was likely to start.

I took Dorothy back to her home and then immediately set out for my own which was about ten minutes walk away. Even as I left her the siren warning wailed and the few people still about began to hurry to their homes or towards the nearest shelters. However, I reached the house without hearing a plane.

At this period it had become usual for the sirens to be sounded some time before any enemy activity could be heard. Unlike in the early days of the War one felt it unnecessary to seek shelter unless there was gunfire heard or the throb of planes in the distance. I was, therefore, in no hurry as I sat at the dining table on my own to eat a light supper which had been laid for me. My father had already eaten and gone to the shelter. An hour or two earlier he had seen my mother off to stay the night at a room which he rented for her in an outlying country district where she would be less disturbed and get much needed rest. The blackout curtains were already drawn and I had lighted the room with just a single table lamp by the fireplace. The subdued light encouraged reflection and I found myself thinking of the events of the evening.

The Church service had been a specially helpful one, while the walk afterwards in sight of the sea in the company of this very beautiful girl, whom I had only recently met, had been rather romantic.

Among my thoughts were those in which I began to hope more than ever that this wretched War would soon end. The strain of it, particularly on my mother, had begun to be apparent and this distressed me. Like everyone I was feeling the need of some uninterrupted sleep. During the day working hours were long with regular periods of night shifts. There were always, as well, the ARP duties at the office which, with its proximity to other Admiralty establishments, was considered a most likely target for bombing.

I should explain that everything had been arranged for me to go up to Oxford in Michaelmas 1939 to prepare for ordination. The outbreak of the War only a month before this term began changed all that. My work with the Admirality was immediately deemed vital to the War effort and I had, therefore, to continue with it. My training for the Ministry must be postponed until the War was over.

Meanwhile, I had to exercise patience. Like many others whose future plans were delayed I found how hard that was. In any case would one come out of all this alive? And, if so, at the end of hostilities would one be able to pursue one's former hopes? Would, indeed, the world be the same — and the old opportunities return?

And now to all these questionings an added one: having met this girl who already attracted me so much would the War end in such a way that we could marry when it was over? After all, it had been on long enough and the raids sufficiently prolonged and repeated to mean that there were already among our circle of friends and acquaintances those who bore the sorrows and losses of the conflict. The grimness of war had been brought home to nearly everyone. Life had become a big question mark and suffering of one kind or another almost universal.

It had been an emotional and exciting evening and as this flood of thoughts and reflections swirled within me I could not be bothered to prepare a hot drink but sat at the table and gave myself over to most heartfelt prayer.

I prayed that all would be well for my family; for this girl who had so enchanted me; and for myself that I might remain true to that vision granted me seven years earlier when, as I believed, God had called me to serve Him in the ministry of the Church of England.

And there was something else. During the evening service that Sunday night the vicar had preached what I felt was one of his finest sermons ever — and he was an extremely effective preacher always. His theme had been the Third Collect (for Aid against all Perils):

"Lighten our darkness, we beseech Thee, O Lord;
and by Thy great mercy defend us from all perils
and dangers of this night; for the love of Thy
only Son, our Saviour Jesus Christ. Amen."

To the normal congregation in peace-time this prayer may not have much significance. But at that time it was all too relevant and this particular sermon had given it even greater point. Not only, indeed, had the night become filled with the dread of great perils but there was the danger of spiritual darkness engulfing us all. The certainty of the loving concern of God was a need that rose deep from the human heart. The words of the Collect glowed with the certainty that God still cared — that His Son knew the anguish of our crazy world.

"Lighten our darkness" — the phrase went over and over in my mind. The words built themselves into a kind of banner headline that was declaring the only news that mattered amid our present madness and darkness. I found a great influx of inspiration and I felt spiritually uplifted. My own impatience and despondency about the future vanished completely. "Lighten our darkness, O Lord". Indeed He had lightened it for me! The word 'light' itself was invested with the most enriching and profound of meanings.

127

It was then that my reverie took a new turn.

I have noticed when my prayers are most deeply felt that I am often constrained after a while to open my eyes and gaze upwards. I did so now and found myself looking fixedly at the unlighted lamps over the table. They were suspended from an ornate, heavily moulded, ceiling rose.

Unacccountably I began to take in the detail of this for the first time in my life. I even took such stock of it that I was mentally comparing it with a smaller one I had seen in the home of my girl friend. I became almost hypnotised by it and found the intricate pattern of shadows cast upon the ceiling by the dim side light stimulated a sense of other worldness. I seemed to slip out of my physical body — completely absorbed. I presume I must have entered something approaching a trance condition.

My mind was now filled with the thought of God's transcendent power at work in all my hopes and affairs. It gave great elation. I felt transported to a world where all was peace and glory.

How long this sublime sensation lasted I do not know. Probably only seconds. But such experiences belong outside time and cannot be assessed by their duration. Then, abruptly, my reverie was broken. The ceiling rose lost its haze of subdued light and the pattern not only darkened but seemed to change its shape. The serenity which had emanated from it before faded and I thought I could see a fearsome visage taking form above me.

The elation and tranquillity died in an instant, and in its place, I experienced a most disturbing and horrible foreboding. Now there was no doubt it was a vile manifestation of a face of some supernatural kind filled with dire menace. I cannot convey in words any adequate description of its appearance. Up to that time I had never experienced the manifestation of an evil entity and the effect was so alarming that I felt physical nausea.

The previous warm glow of assurance and inner strength was replaced with a cold shivering down my spine and an awful sickening in the pit of my stomach. It was so alarming that I drew back from the table. But then there was another sensation which immediately followed. It was like a cloak wrapping me around with protection. Now I moved as if propelled by a strange invisible force which was jerking my whole body from within — almost like a puppet on a string — towards the kitchen. Seconds after reaching it, I could hear the sudden din of aircraft and rapid gun-fire. There was a terrible explosion followed by a seemingly endless falling of heavy debris all over the house.

My father called from the shelter and I reassured him that I was alright but that I thought the house had been badly damaged.

Together we went into the dining room. It was littered everywhere with broken glass and plaster. Looking up we saw there was a gaping hole in the ceiling and, lying on the dining table — the stout top of which had been split by the impact — was the massive ceiling rose. The chair in which I had been sitting only moments before was smothered with debris. Had I stayed less than half a minute longer at that table my skull must surely have been fractured — or worse.

My father and I went to examine the house for any further damage. Upstairs it appeared no great harm had been done after all. It was evidently one of those freaks of bomb blast that had only really affected the dining room.

I remember we said something about being very lucky, that bombs never fell again in the same place, and therefore we had been left off lightly.

The effects of my strange experience at the dining table had not yet worn off, though at the time I said nothing about it to my father. There were other things to consider in that hour. Nevertheless, I still seemed to be in the grip of some powerful influence. It had certainly saved me from a serious hurt already and now it seemed to compel me to suggest that we should reconnoitre the garden and examine the rear of the house. My father, on the other hand, was all for looking around the outside front of the house first. My counsel prevailed.

It was fortunate for us both that it did. For when we reached the garden there was a tremendous explosion which rocked the ground so violently that we clutched each other in order to remain upright. We were quite dazed by it and were certain that the front of the house had been struck.

However, on returning inside, we could see nothing wrong. The storm doors which we usually bolted during air raids were still intact. (It was only in the light of early dawn that we were to discover that this time the house had really caught it with most of the roof blown away). But at that moment, hearing a great commotion in the street, we unbolted these doors and stepped outside to behold a scene which remains indelible upon my memory.

There was a sheet of flame in the road and vehicles were grouped in front of our house. An ARP worker spoke to us at the gate. We could not make out for a while what he was saying or, rather, trying to say. Something to the effect that he could not find his mates. Had we seen them? We were later to realise that his whole squad, apart from himself, must have been wiped out by that last explosion and he was walking about half-stunned. What had happened that night was that a high explosive bomb had fallen in the road which had caused the first damage to our dining room. The bomb itself had struck the road and pierced the gas main. Firemen and rescue workers had arrived promptly to deal with matters and then, within minutes, a land mine fell almost on the same spot creating widespread damage and mortal injury. It was this latter which had annihilated a rescue squad and had wrecked our house and many others. Had we gone to the front instead of to the back of the house as my father proposed we must surely have perished. The force of my premonition of ill had made me insist on doing the opposite — and this saved us for the house being between had shielded us from the full blast of that mine.

When we were able to assess what damage had been done to our home we found most of the roof and every ceiling caved in. Plaster and glass were everywhere but the walls still stood firm. Either through delayed shock or through sheer thankfulness at having survived without injury (though our faces felt very sore with the blast for several days afterwards) we were almost in high spirits, even in jocular mood, as we salvaged our possessions and set about the task of finding somewhere else in the city to live.

However, there were occasions later (and even one soon after the war was over) when I suffered a nightmare in which the scenes of that night were most vividly re-enacted. That awesome feeling under the ceiling rose and the manifestation of that loathsome face; my sudden possession by a dominating spirit which urged me with overwhelming power to hasten from the room; the continuing presentiment of danger if we went outside to the front of the house; the rocking explosions and sickening crash of falling debris; the wild scene which met us when we did go outside into the road. All this would be repeated in so real a manner that I would wake up in extreme perspiration and think I could hear the heavy beat of bomber engines filling the air.

Then, on realising it was all a dream, I would think again of how we had been preserved and give thanks to God and His angels.

I am satisfied by reason of these and other experiences that the world of spirit is a fact. I am sure that both evil and good spirits have dealings with the life of this world. I believe one explanation of that forbidding apparition which manifested itself that particular night is that it was an evil entity which gathered delight from the savagery and destruction of war. Was it gloating over impending tragedy? And what of that extraordinary power that had seemed to manipulate me to safety in the nick of time — a power which I am convinced was not my own?

Can I view these preservations as mere coincidences — just lucky escapes? I cannot, because the compulsion of these premonitions to vacate a particular spot within seconds of a great danger befalling, were of such a peculiar nature that they convinced me that supernatural powers do desire to inform and, if possible, to preserve us.

The only other explanation which commends itself to me is that under certain conditions of stress one's spirit-soul is able to act as pure spirit and in consequence one might receive knowledge beyond the normal range which would then alert one of otherwise unknowable perils.

But, as I have said, the strong impression these phenomena gave me was that there are spiritual entities, of good or evil nature, who can affect our world.

20

WITNESS TO ANGELS

Practitioners of psychiatric medicine often have to carry such an enormous workload of patients that they may be tempted to judge anyone who professes to hear voices, see visions or to have experience of angels or of devils (particularly the latter!), to be exhibiting the usual signs of what is generally termed schizophrenia. In other words that all these pecularities arise from a disordered personality and signify mental sickness.

Even though they may be right in the majority of cases, who can deny that in some the experience is not hallucination but an authentic psychical or mystical one? That there are persons with more developed extra-sensory perceptions than most and yet are perfectly well-balanced is certain. Great figures of history as well as countless humble and sensible folk testify to this.

Throughout a ministry of over forty years many folk have given me their personal accounts of what they were convinced were angelic encounters which greatly blessed their lives. In most of them I recognise both the genuineness of their testimony and the wholesomeness of their mental and spiritual attitudes.

As witness to this I am quoting just three of the testimonies I have been so privileged to hear.

The first is from the lips of a very charming and lively middle-aged woman who is a most encouraging witness to the Christian faith as she heroically copes with a debilitating illness. She vouchsafed the following record after I had, according to my usual practice, reminded the congregation during a service of baptism of the reality of guardian aangels. "The Church" I had said "used to speak about them on such occasions but nowadays, to our great loss I believe, does so very rarely, if at all."

This remark prompted Marjorie W-, who was present, to tell me that for a couple of years she had felt that her own two Guardian Angels were pressing her to publicise the rôle of angels. She explained that her psychic experiences had brought her awareness of angelic presences who, she was convinced, had given her guidance and healing in times of danger, perplexity, deep sorrow and illness.

"In my experience" she explained, "one of my two Angels is always 'on duty' and they join forces in my moments of great need." Then she went on to say:

"What never ceases to amaze me is their split-second timing which is demonstrated almost every day of my life..."

Later she was to write an account for me of what she described as "the most wonderful example of this (angelic help) occurring in the early hours of 26th February 1968, when 'my Angels' woke me to witness my husband's passing."

This is her written story:

"My husband, Len, had been desperately ill for four years following two strokes caused by his long illness. In spite of this he would not give in and fought back with a tremendous will to live. However, his life on earth was very near its close at this time and that night the District Nurse and I were unable to move him in any way because of the weight of water in his unconscious body.

I had fallen asleep, fully dressed, whilst lying beside him on the bed and was awakened by movement. I turned and looked at my husband just in time to see his head apparently being lifted from the pillows and I watched while his eyes opened wide. He gazed straight ahead showing utter amazement and wonder. Then a smile lighted up his face and he was transfigured. All the marks of his illness and suffering were erased and he looked radiantly happy. I just broke into singing the Te Deum and the Magnificat — I could not help it.

I had glanced at the clock, and it showed seven minutes to four in the morning. The room was filled with light, a feeling of sublime joy, and a sense of awe and wonder. I think whoever came to call my husband must have acknowledged me because I know my face lighted up with a broad smile.

After two minutes his soul flew joyfully away with some of the unseen throng which I felt were present. Then his head was gently replaced upon the pillow, and he ceased breathing. I could not help singing;

'The strike is o'er, the battle done;
Now is the Victor's triumph won;
O let the song of praise be sung,
Alleluia.'

In the moment Len was called... he was healed. When I took the pillows away from his head and pulled down the covers I saw how complete was his healing. The black blisters had disappeared from his legs and the blackness gone from his feet and I moved him quite easily.

I went out into the kitchen still singing away, refilled my hot water bottle and made a pot of tea and took them back into the bedroom. I reclined on the bed and, as I recorded at the time: "...here I am writing it down as I drink the tea and keep glancing at this still figure, so lately torn with suffering..."

The room was filled with ministering angels. I kept looking at my husband and saying "Little pet, you look marvellous." His eyes were open wider than I had ever seen, because he had very bad sight and could scarcely see without his glasses. And his face held the rapture of transfiguration — and he appeared young again, no more than twenty or so.

What emerged so strongly from this experience was the tremendous power of God available to us from the spiritual world — of which we are only scratching the surface. It seems strange that our Church appears to have ignored angels for so long when one learns, in both the Old and the New Testament, of the important rôle they play in life. Particularly are they evident in the life of Jesus. It was the Angel Gabriel who told Mary she would bear a son and should call Him, Jesus. An Angel told Joseph to flee from Egypt with Mary and the Child to avoid King Herod's massacre of the children. Angels ministered to Jesus during His temptation in the Wilderness. They strengthened Him when He prayed in spiritual anguish in the Garden of Gethsemane where, soon after, He was betrayed and arrested.

Angels were seen at the empty tomb at Easter. We can well imagine there were many more unrecorded instances when Jesus knew angelic support.

It is the angels who give us messages from God and who are ever at hand. Never bossy or intrusive, but helping and strengthening us at every turn.

I have long been able to look beyond present difficulties knowing that everything works together for our good if only we trust in God's understanding love and the companionship of His angels.

One of the most important messages that my Guardian Angels gave me following my beloved husband's passing was that I should not dwell on his years of suffering or it would destroy me. That suffering was entirely finished with, and never to be thought of again with personal anguish.

I believe the angels are longing to break through into our consciousness, to let us know that they are toiling away on our behalf and will continue to do so until our life here is done...'

The second testimony concerns Harry, a retired fisherman, who had been with the fishing boats off the east coast of Scotland ever since he was a lad. During a holiday my wife and I took in the Black Isle, Harry told me how he had met an angel. He had been shipwrecked in abominable, icy weather and lay stranded on some rocks for eight hours. During that time he lost all feeling in his legs and began to wonder if he would ever be rescued.

Then, as his senses almost faded with the intense cold and pain, he saw his Angel. "Just like the pictures I knew as a child,' he said. "A beautiful figure in shining whiteness stood before me, and in that moment I knew all would turn out well."

And so it did, for he was rescued in the very nick of time. The same vision came to him as he lay in hospital while doctors were working vigorously on restoring circulation to his numbed lower body. He saw his Angel again. Once more it gave him peace and reassurance.

"I saw that angel," he declared "as clearly as anything in this world. I shall always remember the joy and the hope it gave me."

He was unable to return to full fishing work again because of the weakness left in his legs but he was to lead a life quite active in every other way and busied himself, and still does, at over seventy years of age, with repairing nets and making lobster creels.

He is a very religious man and a devout churchgoer, most openhearted and humorous, but in telling this matter of 'his Angel' he is deeply serious and patently sincere. His story is a classic example of how a strong belief in angels (in his case, he informed me, inculcated from childhood) predisposes the soul to apprehend their guardianship.

Similar experiences to his have been recorded in the lives of many persons of great faith who have been in circumstances of mortal danger from which they have been saved just when that possibility seemed most unlikely. They have been given the will, the courage, and the final ounce of strength, to hold on through the darkest hour till succour came. All this because, as they have earnestly declared, an angelic being appeared and assured them of deliverance.

The third testimony is that of a friend, Daniel, who gave us much help as a gardener. For many years he lived the disciplined life of a soldier and saw a good deal of action in various theatres of war. He had often exhibited to my wife and myself his remarkable gift of psychometry and always expressed his absorbing interest in psychic affairs.

In the last weeks of his life in hospital I mentioned I would be including his experience in this book. At this time his tall, strong frame was ravaged with cancer and, knowing his illness to be terminal, he said to me: "It's not much of a story, vicar, — not worth the mention."

Yet, of course, it is. All the more because of his humility when he first disclosed it to me.

It concerned an incident during his army service in India during World War II. He and a corporal driver were in a jeep on a narrow road going at some speed when a child suddenly crossed in front of them. The corporal breaked fiercely and unavoidably swerved into a deep roadside ditch causing the jeep to overturn. Daniel said he was flung in the air but in his flight felt very definitely that hands were supporting him beneath his armpits. He landed without losing consciousness on the grass verge and almost immediately got up to see how his companion had fared.

The corporal was under the vehicle, the red hot exhaust pipe was across his chest pinning him down. He was unconscious.

Without thought of the seeming impossibility of his action Daniel struggled to lift the vehicle in order to release his companion. He found that he was given some extraordinary strength to achieve this. "I realised that help came from beyond myself. I can only say that it was power given me from the spiritual world. I believe it was from my Guardian Angel."

Having dragged the corporal from the vehicle Daniel went in search of assistance along what was a rather lonely road.

Eventually, again (as he felt) with the encouragement and guidance of his Angel, he managed to find someone to convey a message to his headquarters.

In due course the rescue team arrived and Daniel and the corporal were taken to the barracks. The medical officer who first examined Daniel, now in a hospital bed, could scarcely believe what had happened. "I can't understand" he said, "how you moved after that accident, let alone raised that jeep to free the corporal, because your back is broken."

A while later he realised that Daniel must have been mobile immediately after the crash for him to have gone for help and, indeed, to have walked into the hospital primarily concerned for his corporal. The latter bore the serious burn and bruising across his chest from the hot exhaust pipe and it was consistent with him having been pinned under the vehicle.

Daniel assured me that he was convinced that throughout the affair he had been tended by his Guardian Angel. The invisible hands which supported him during the accident were, he declared, definite, reassuring and strong. His mind remained clear throughout and he had no physical pain until much later. He maintained that at no time did he feel alone and helpless, but that his brain continued to function clearly and even more precisely than it might have been expected to do in the circumstances. He was certain that he was not only being succoured but helpfully and confidently guided in what he must do.

Daniel was to spend six months in the Army hospital after the accident but the wonderful experience he had received of unseen ministration continued to sustain him through the long period of recuperation until his complete recovery — a recovery which he was sure his Guardian Angel had intimated to him.

To the end of his life Daniel was an active and energetic person whose faith in an angelic world, ready to support us if we would keep our faith and trust in it, remained clear and unequivocal. It was a faith which had begun through the teaching given him, like that of fisherman Harry and Marjorie W- in childhood.

21

AT DEATH'S PORTAL

A holiday in Scotland provided my wife and I with an introduction to a delightful lady who related to us the experience of her son. This had, she said, served to deepen her already strong belief in an after life. Many similar experiences to the one she disclosed have been recorded by others in recent times. They come about, one must surmise, because of the excellent progress of medical science which has made possible the 'bringing back to life' of those who, not so many years ago, would have been deemed beyond recovery.

Her son, George, in his middle years had undergone a very serious operation and, in the course of it, he 'died'. Up to that moment, he said, he had 'known' pain despite the anaesthetic. Now, it seemed, he was floating above his inert body and looking down at it. He was able to watch the course of the operation and noted details of the operating theatre.

When he 'died' however the pain immediately left him and he felt such a transport of joy that he did not wish to 'come back'.

In his words he saw what seemed to be a beautiful green-coloured scene. It intimated a transcendent beauty the detail of which he felt he was about to know more closely. But his 'death' was so brief that he did not have that exquisite pleasure.

During his 'death' he found himself surveying his physical body on the operating table and thinking that he did not wish to return to it, although at the same time he had strong thoughts of love towards his family. Then he heard one of the surgeons say: "My God, I think he has gone!" Next he saw the surgeon making a gesture; flinging out his right arm and calling for recovery action. Within seconds George felt himself drawn back into his body and again he 'felt' pain.

Afterwards he described to the doctor what he had heard, seen and felt during his brief period of 'death'. The surgeon was amazed at his account. "I would never have believed it" he said. "You were completely unconscious throughout — yet during the serious crisis in the operation what you say happened is absolutely true, even to my gestures."

This experience bears out the view that when the spirit-soul is disencumbered of the body-soul as in sleep (whether natural or artificially induced) and also, it is logical to believe, in its twin-brother death, it exercises its own special extra-sensory perceptions.

George's story also suggests that a kind of 'double' exists which is normally housed in the physical body but can escape from it under certain circumstances — and will certainly do so at death.

For George's mother her son's experience confirmed her belief that our departed loved ones are about us, unseen, but nevertheless caring for us, and specially supporting us in our time of death.

We may feel that this is an unwarranted conclusion to draw from George's particular psychic revelation. Nevertheless it does suggest that immediately after death there is a continued sense of attachment to this world and its activity. How long that absorption continues is, however, not attested because, of course, all such psychic experiences of death are necessarily of the briefest duration. But this kind of experience helps to underline that which Christian believers confidently accept, namely, the binding power of love which unites us forever with our dear ones in some unique and glorified way, beyond our present understanding.

There is another point which is worthy of reflection. George told of a scene, hazy of detail because there was insufficient time to gather more, but which nevertheless suggested a transcendent beauty in which the colour green predominated. Can we hazard a guess that this hue was an indication of lovely 'spiritual' countryside which his soul was able, fleetingly, to apprehend during the release of 'death'? We should bear in mind that George was a countryman at heart although for many years working in an English city. He had been reared in one of the loveliest parts of rural Scotland and remained deeply and longingly attached to it. The comfort received immediately after death must be of a nature which does not startle, distress or overwhelm the soul but, in the loving goodness and mercy of God, allows a gentle transition from its earthly existence.

A Priest and the Paranormal

For George we might well believe, therefore, that such peace and reassurance would take the form of green pastures. For city lovers there might well be a different type of scene vouchsafed to provide, in similar manner, some immediate and enjoyable familiarity. We go back again to our Lord's words from the Cross to the repentant thief crucified beside Him. "Today (i.e. immediately after the experience of death) thou shalt be with Me in Paradise." Paradise does have the meaning 'garden'. It suggests tranquillity, a beauty which provides repose for the soul immediately after the wrench of death. From the comfort of that first reassuring scene the soul thus derives the confidence to venture on in its newfound purely spiritual environment. There is, of course, another hypothesis to be gathered from George's experience. This is that the soul may long to re-acquaint itself with that locale of this world which meant much to it. Hence the fact that within moments of death departed persons have given intimations of their presence, through psychic experience, to near relatives (who sometimes are miles away) is a fairly common one.

George's mother was also the source of other psychic material which bears out my own conviction about death and the ministry of angels who are at hand when it comes.

On three or four occasions, she told me, she had seen 'the strange light' of approaching death in her family circle.

At the first of these she had been overawed by the appearance of a light of unearthly brilliance which descended upon the home of a relative on the night before the latter died.

On the second occasion during a dark wintry night her son, George, who was then only eight years old, asked if he could fetch his spinning top from the shed outdoors. She replied that as she was going out to collect coal she would also bring his top. The child insisted that he would accompany her as he knew exactly where he had left his toy. Together, therefore, they left the house through the back door. Once outside the child exclaimed "Oh, mummy, is granny's house on fire?" His mother also saw the brilliant and peculiar radiance. It was coming from the bedroom window of the nearby cottage where her mother was lying ill. It remained for quite a time and was almost too bright to gaze upon. The next day her mother died.

Of course we must remember the intense religious belief of that rural area and how the woman had been brought up with the conviction of the Angel of Death heralding a soul's departure. On the first occasion she had beheld such a light she had mentioned it to her minister.

He had shaken his head, telling her it was only her imagination. However, after the death had taken place (again in this instance on the following day) the minister agreed that she had indeed seen 'the light'. He had felt it best, however, not to alarm her at the time because he well knew what it foretold for her family.

Even allowing for a mental and psychical predisposition to the 'seeing' of the phenomenon it is striking to note that both the child and his mother witnessed it. Indeed, although it happened at so tender an age George, now middle-aged, has remembered it as a most vivid experience. Even though other memories of his childhood are very few he can still describe this particular experience as if it had occurred but yesterday.

As I have mentioned elsewhere 'the light' has on a number of occasions been observed by me at the bedside of the dying. It is a most comforting and uplifting experience. It deepens one's sense that the unseen world is making reassuring contact with oneself and also provides a peculiar rapport with the departing soul.

Again, like all psychic experience, it gives feelings which can never be more than hinted at in words. One feels one would most dearly wish to convey the beauty and inspiration of it to others so that they might share also in the ineffable peace which is bestowed in such elevating moments. Of one thing I am firmly convinced; that angelic beings do attend upon the dying Christian soul in the hour of death and that they minister to the person in the power, authority and love of their Master, Jesus Christ, who is the Resurrection and the Life.

22

ANIMALS

Extraordinary indeed are the powers with which the animal creation is endowed. Cats and dogs find their way home even though they have been transported many miles away. Birds and fish migrate over vast distances. The astounding homing instinct of pigeons remains a fascinating mystery. There is the ability of birds and certain animals to build their quarters with amazing skill, solving intricate constructional problems akin to those which man has taken centuries to encompass.

All these (and there are many more) remarkable matters are instinctive. There is no conscious intellectual effort behind them whereas man has to exercise his mental, as well as his physical, faculties to achieve survival. By that very fact the life-style of human beings has developed and progressed whilst the animal creation has remained on its instinctual level.

Clearly, therefore, God has endowed the lower creations with special faculties which allow them to live within their ordained limits without that effort of mental creativity which must generally precede the activities of mankind. Some would say, therefore, that these instinctive powers of the animal creation correspond to the extra-sensory perceptions of man since the latter also function in him (when they do) quite unconsciously i.e. instinctively.

Of course if such an equation is made for the instincts of animals with human ESP, it follows that as the latter are the property of man's spirit-soul therefore the animal creation must also possess a spirit-soul (as well, of course, of a body-soul).

Such reasoning naturally raises the question "Do animals possess souls like unto those of mankind and therefore survive death as pure spirits?"

142

Here the author would vouchsafe his opinion as one possible answer.

First, we should observe that these remarkable instincts of the lower creation are on a higher level than those of ourselves. On the other hand the extra-sensory perceptions of human beings vary much with one another in degree. They are in embryo (or remain as vestiges of what were dominant in a former race) in every man because they are the faculties of his spirit-soul, but some men have certainly exhibited them (and developed them) more than others. Possibly certain ages of man's history have had a higher incidence of their activity than others.

If the instincts (which are the occult activities) of the animal world could be shown to be prompted by individual creatures then those specimens would be of greater perspicacity and skill than man. But this is clearly not so. What we observe is a *general* spirit, evenly active within a species, and entirely instinctive in operation. It is a special gift from the Creator which works throughout that species for one purpose only — to ensure its survival and to maintain its place in the scale of creation.

As there is no sign of an individual, creative, free, spirit-soul at work in each creature of a species, we cannot attribute to the animal kingdom the proposition that individual animals possess spirit-souls which must, for that very reason, individually survive death.

But having said this I must go on to make a qualification in the case of those animals which have a close proximity to man and are the recipients of human love and care.

Here, I believe, we enter upon a new plane. By exercising his wisdom, love and protection, man can elevate the existence of an individual animal so that it acquires something extra to its species — a mysterious, peculiar 'something' rubs off, as it were, upon the domesticated animal and subtly alters its primitive nature.

It is that 'extra' which many people discern in their pets and which endows them, as they firmly believe, with individuality and personality. I cannot see that anyone should disagree with this even if he or she is not particularly fond of animals. It seems to me that it is a perfectly logical conclusion and borne out (for those who have the eyes to see and the hearts to feel) in the testimony of many who maintain real love and care for their pets.

It is just because I believe that there is this raising of the domesticated creature to a higher plane than its undomesticated cousin that

I can conduct without reserve (or theological misgiving!) spiritual healing for a pet.

I know from personal experience with three much loved animals which my wife and I have had at various times in our household that their aura responds - and surprisingly quickly - to the laying-on of hands with prayer.

Often I have combined this ministry with bringing my forehead close to that of the sick pet. The 'third eye', as it has been described, is an area situated in the centre of the forehead and regarded by some as the point of concentration in us of our psychic power. I have certainly found that this particular practice causes a headache which can be quite painful until I rivet my mind upon the healing power of Christ. It is as if one absorbs through that psychic 'eye' the suffering of the animal and that this must be counterbalanced by us through the exercise of faith (that supremely important faculty of the spirit-soul). Faith, that is, in the healing love of God which comes through seeking, and acknowledging, the presence of His unique Son, Jesus Christ.

I cite the following example as testimony to what I mean.

Some years ago our cat, Sheba, fell sick soon after our return from a holiday we had taken in Morocco. We think that perhaps from our footwear or outer clothing she picked up an unusual germ from that country where animals often roam free in squalid conditions. At any rate the germ was sufficiently peculiar to mystify the vet. After a day or two during which Sheba had maintained an abnormally high temperature there was cause for serious alarm. She just lay prone on a sofa in my study completely uncaring for any of her most favourite food so that she faded to a mere furry skeleton. By the fifth day the vet, who had tried two different drug injections without success, informed us that we should prepare for the fact that the cat could not survive and that, on the morrow, he would probably have to take her away to be 'put to sleep'.

At regular intervals during each day I had conducted the laying-on of hands for the animal and I had noted the increasing weakness of her aura.

On that last night I took recourse to following up my laying-on of hands with the holding of her tiny head against my forehead. The pain this caused me was so severe that I was compelled to cry out to the Lord for his help and mercy. The pain only passed as I concentrated upon the thought that our loving Creator was upholding me in my ministry.

It then came to me in a strange, almost intuitive, way that now I must agitate myself no longer. I had the clearest premonition that the cat would begin to get better from that moment. Indeed I upheld in my mind's eye her restoration — seeing her as whole and full of life roaming, as was her wont, in the garden.

Remarkable as was my own reaction, that of my wife, Dorothy, was, I think, even more so — and certainly provided an important spiritual lesson.

At the close of the same day she had knelt beside the stricken creature. Sheba's eyes stared back at her, unblinking. Her breathing was now scarcely perceptible. Dorothy began to pray the Lord's own prayer. Already she began to experience a sense of resignation about the future of the cat. When, however, she reached the words "Thy will be done..." she suddenly felt compelled to stop the prayer.

Afterwards she said it was as if for the first time she had become truly aware of both the great efficacy and the significance of the prayer. Spontaneously she cried out: "Lord, if You want Sheba, You must take her. If that is Your will — so be it. Now I must give up and leave everything to You."

In that moment she had grasped vividly what each of us must come to realise, and accept graciously and unreservedly, that God's Will and not our own, must be our prayer and only desire.

She rose from her knees after that and went to bed. That night both of us slept without the brooding anxiety of those preceding nights when our minds had been filled with worried thoughts of Sheba and during which, over and over again, we had let rise simple arrow prayers for her healing.

Dorothy confessed later that she had completely reconciled herself to accepting the death of Sheba and half-expected it to occur by the morning.

The following day I went downstairs to prepare as usual early morning tea and paused to look into my study. To my joy Sheba, for the first time since her illness, turned her head towards the door as I entered.

I hurried towards the sofa and gently stroked her head and again commended her to God's healing. She began to purr faintly. Then she stretched her body and very slowly struggled off the couch to the floor. I felt I must not help her other than by encouraging words and prayers. It was pitiful at first to see how she endeavoured to stand upright on her trembling legs, but there was a feeling of victory in the air as she moved to the short staircase from my study into the hall of the vicarage. Hardly daring to breathe, and praying earnestly all the while, I followed her slow unsteady movement towards the dining-room. Since it was her custom at this hour each day to go out I realised immediately that she wished me to open the door to the garden. Carefully and yet seeming to gather more stability as she went she made her way down the single step into the early morning sunshine and on to the dew laden grass.

I could contain myself no longer and exclaiming "Oh thank You, God, thank You God," I raced upstairs to Dorothy, calling out as I went: "Do you know Sheba got up and is now in the garden. She made it all on her own! I know she will be O.K."

Scarcely accepting the possibility of such news Dorothy quickly joined me as I returned to the garden. Sheba was sitting on the lawn and then began to move slowly across it. Sniffing the ground as she went she finally chose some grass to chew.

The miracle had happened. Within a few hours she was eating again and a day or two later was looking her normal self.

Dorothy had learned, as never before, the true manner of prayer — to ask only that God's Will be done in all things. I had been able to confirm my belief that pets, truly loved and cared for by human beings can thereby acquire a spirit-soul with which our own can have rapport. Therefore, I do believe they are pure spirits when death comes to them and must, for that reason, survive it.

Those who have read '*A Priest's Psychic Diary*' will know of experiences which have further testified to me that there is an individual spiritual side to our beloved pets. I recorded there the large white dog which appeared in a vision to me over the altar of my church when my wife and I were praying for our spaniel, Judy, when she was very ill and undergoing surgery. I like to think that this vision indicated that there are 'angelic' animals in the unseen world which are to the animal world what guardian angels are to ourselves.

During the period when I was praying often for Sheba I found that into the picture of Christ (which I endeavour to present to my mind during the ministry of spiritual healing) the image of a cat of exceptional beauty and regality often intruded. It appeared to be an altogether ethereal creature, shining, transcendent.

When one reflects upon St Paul's own belief that through Christ there emerges a new Creation, not just for humans but for *all* the physical world, we are not, I would suggest, moving into either fanciful or unscriptural speculation if we postulate the existence of spiritual counterparts to our animals.

Maybe there was something auto-suggestive about my repeated vision of an 'angelic' cat. Undoubtedly some would make that assessment but I can only record that my whole attention each time was upon the healing power of God and in upholding Sheba for His blessing. In the intensity of my experience I am wholly convinced that a transcendent creation watches not only over us humans, but over our pets as well. Is there not some logic then, in the idea of 'angelic animals' having a connection, or concern, for animals in this world?

PART TWO

Essays on the Paranormal

1

RELEASE OF THE SPIRIT-SOUL

In the first part of this book I have recounted a selection of the psychic experiences which I have known during over fifty years, and particularly those which have occurred in forty years of my ministry in the Church of England.

I regard them as the activity of my spirit-soul when a state of trance had released it from the encumbrance of my body-soul. Such trance, whole or partial, was variously induced by one or more of the following:

1) Prayer or meditation. Or both.

2) Intense mental concentration.

3) The abandonment of self through a sense of complete helplessness and inadequacy as, for example, when faced with a very perplexing pastoral problem or someone's plea for healing, with a consequent entire surrender of myself to the guidance and power of God.

4) Physical and/or mental fatigue.

All the extra-sensory perceptions I have described I attribute to the functioning of my spirit-soul in one or more of these circumstances.

I have also acknowledged my belief that the faculties of my spirit-soul have sometimes been stirred and influenced by spirits, either angelic or demonic. In other cases by the souls of departed persons, or by the souls of living persons who are acting under great emotional stress.

This raises the question whether there be a realm of spiritual beings. Here we must listen to the long history of religion which testifies that man has been assured of the reality of such a realm and of its important relationship with him.

The very origin of religion is that through his extra-sensory perceptions (i.e. faculties of his spirit-soul) man gained knowledge of the invisible realm.

Probably this was an evolutionary perception. Beginning with man's sense of a mystical union with the world of nature and then with his fellows (as he began to live in communities), and only finally with a suprasensory realm.

It is in this latter sense of what is called the 'numinous' that we must speak of the mysterious operation of 'revelation'. By this is meant that out of the spiritual world something mysteriously declares itself which lifts a little the veil between itself and this material world and thereby reveals some idea of its character to us.

In describing their own revelations the great ones of religion speak of hearing voices or receiving visions.

These seers agree that their peculiar knowledge of that invisible spiritual realm was gained by supernatural experience, i.e. through the faculties of their spirit-souls. To describe the manner of their illumination they tell of voices coming to them or of seeing strange things. Sometimes these spiritual experiences were both auditory and visionary. In describing them to others they had to do so in the only way any of us can ever describe anything, including that which is purely abstract, i.e. by using the material concepts and symbols which make up human language.

In consequence of their experiences these specially gifted and great souls felt themselves brought into a close relationship with that invisible world which had thus revealed itself to them. They recognised this relationship as being a vital one between man and his Creator. So compelling was this insight that they had an overwhelming urge to impart it to their fellows in order that they too might share its truth and know its great importance for their lives.

All this is signally observed in the Hebrews who stand out in history as a people uniquely endowed with religious sensitivity (i.e. a consciousness of God through the faculties of the spirit-soul) and possessing leaders of towering spiritual genius.

Those leaders urged their people to follow a moral and ethical path because their revelations had shown them that such is the way their Maker would have them live if they were to attain fulfilment and His blessing.

However, due to the impediment of sin which is universal in human nature they found that keeping a moral law which counsels perfection is impossible. Consequently they sought an escape from this predicament by contriving an elaborate system of ritual law (including sacrifice) which it would be possible (however irksome) to observe.

This contains the idea that through it man propitiates his Creator for his failure to achieve moral and spiritual perfection. Thereby he believed his harmonious relationship with God could be restored.

The Hebrews had settled for this ritual law although their greatest prophets constantly inveighed against the hollowness of thinking that its observance could ever supersede the moral and spiritual law or even be held in the balance against the breaking of it.

For Saul, a most ardent Jew of the university city of Tarsus, Christianity was to provide 'the Way' which solved his own nagging dilemma of earnestly seeking spiritual perfection yet never achieving it because of sin. His meticulous observance of the ritual laws of his religion was powerless to ease his mind in its quest for peace with God. Indeed it only made him more and more spiritually restless.

However, he hoped to salve his conscience by throwing himself wholeheartedly into a fanatical persecution of Christians because he saw them as enemies of his beloved Judaism — and therefore of God Himself.

That persecution was the tinder which sparked off his extraordinary experience on the Damascus Road.

To understand why this happened we must try to appreciate the intense strain of his anguished conscience in its long search for spiritual answers and relief. This culminated in the tremendous impact made upon him by the amazingly courageous and dedicated witness given to Christ by those whom he persecuted and, supremely, of St Stephen whose nobly borne martyrdom he had not only ordered but had personally watched.

As so often happens after profound and lengthy mental and spiritual torment the sufferer slips suddenly into a trance condition when the strain has become intolerable. A vision then occurs to the spirit-soul which lifts the burden and brings relief from the continuing nightmare of inner tension.

This was what occurred to Saul on his journey to Damascus. The strange light which blinded him for a time and the voice of Jesus which spoke to him in that visionary experience convinced him of the truth of Christianity. It assured him of its power to change his life from one of interior discontent (by his failure to find peace with God because of sin) into one of hopeful confidence through what Jesus Christ had done in delivering him and all mankind from the tyranny of sin and the ineffectiveness of the Law to deal with it.

It was like release from bondage when he realised that by exercising his spirit-soul's faculty of faith he attained a mystical union with the sinless Christ, and through that union was freed from sin's hitherto unconquerable grip upon him.

The Spirit of Jesus which had thus taken possession of his soul was turning him into a new creature because the unique power of Christ's Life, Death, Resurrection, Ascension and Bequest of His Spirit, had completely reconciled him to God.

So he knew now a wonderful release from that sense of guilt which had always dogged and agonised him. Not by good works, not by slavery to ritual laws, was he to be saved (i.e. restored to harmony with God), but simply and only by faith — faith in Jesus Christ Whom he now realised was both the Lord and the Saviour of all humanity. This was the conversion point of his life and the making of him into Saint Paul.

While not asserting that our own goal must be to attain the heights of the great mystics this writer would nevertheless urge that we accept their disclosures to us of the nature of the spiritual realm, and that a measure of mysticism is not only possible for everyone but natural and necessary to religion.

The simple path to follow is to seek first a period of quiet and to relax one's physical body as much as possible. Deep, steady breathing and a comfortable posture can greatly help. Then to concentrate the mind upon realising the Presence of Christ. This is best done through meditation upon His Life and Teaching as given in the New Testament. We shall then be exercising the spirit-soul's faculty of faith by means of our Christ-centred imagination. There will ensue a gradual disencumbrance of our spirit-soul from our body-soul. A state of trance is produced when absorption in the thoughts and attitudes of Jesus is complete, i.e. when the mind has excluded all other thoughts and attitudes. The soul is now possessed by the Spirit of Christ and the trance controlled only by Him.

With this release of the spirit-soul there is sometimes vouchsafed a special perception of a transcendent realm accompanied by ecstasy. But such an experience is neither to be sought for its own sake nor to be judged as necessary proof of true mystical experience. For here all is of God and what He grants or withholds in that experience is according to His good Will for us.

It must remain sufficient for us to believe that through the exercise of our faith we are brought into the Presence of Christ and that this mystical union with Him enriches our souls with His sublime Spirit. When we return to the matters of this world from that Jesus-inspired trance we shall find that they are transfigured. Nothing will be able to daunt or overcome our spiritual peace. Problems, difficulties and sorrows may indeed still afflict us but the serenity and power which Christ has bestowed upon us in that mystical experience will uphold, guide and heal us, so that we shall be able to deal with them effectively.

Like St Paul we shall have discovered that by exercising faith in Christ we receive the gift of His unconquerable and eternal Spirit.

2

WORSHIP: THE VEHICLE OF ESP

As already mentioned the faculties of the spirit-soul or extra-sensory perceptions released in an *uncontrolled* trance produce hallucination. On the other hand the *controlled* trance of hypnosis, whether self-induced or otherwise, always has some relevance to reality and therefore encourages the extra-sensory perceptions to be purposefully employed.

Controlled trance, however, has varying value according to the nature of the object or idea upon which the subject has concentrated. Thus the dowsing-rod can have certain practical value. The object of Nature such as a flower, a landscape, etc. can produce an exhilarating and often poetic type of transport. Contraptions like the ouija board can bring contact with elemental, and often harmful, spiritual entities.

The hypnotist who controls a trance can, according to his will, produce good or harmful results in his subject, but in any event erodes something of the latter's precious freedom of will.

The most sublime, and potentially beneficial, controlled trance is that which is produced by prayer (par excellence, by Christian prayer). However, the ecstatic condition which sometimes results, can only be fruitful of worthy and practical results if that which induced it was a contemplation of the highest spiritual values, i.e. goodness, truth and beauty.

But these must be removed from the vagueness of pure abstractions by introducing mental pictures which enshrine precise examples of these qualities. Hence the importance of meditation upon the life and teaching of Jesus. These become the inspirational directive for good works and of unselfish service to others.

Man's nature desires mystical experience and to pray with conviction. The Church, besides enjoining personal and private devotions, provides such deep spiritual experience through her 'acts' of corporate prayer and worship. These not only witness to the majesty, dominion and glory of God but declare with thanksgiving the mystical unity with Christ of those who believe in Jesus as God's unique Son.

Under hypnosis the spirit-soul of a person will accept the orders and ideas which are dictated by the hypnotist and then instruct the body-soul to fulfil them.

The 'mechanics' of Christian worship are similar to those of hypnosis. But the effect is more deep-rooted and of far greater consequence. The absorption of those taking part in the acts of worship offered in churches should produce in them a condition of trance. This is of a controlled kind because such worship commands attention to the reality of this world since the themes which govern church services are found in the mission and message of the historic Jesus and in those theological doctrines which the Church (out of love for Him and in her quest to understand the relevance of His life for all mankind) has conceived.

Obviously the greater the attention a person gives to an act of worship the deeper is the trance induced in him. The 'orders and ideas' he receives during it control his spirit-soul so that he then goes from a church service into the life of the world outside with their inspiration at work in him. He will therefore perform, spontaneously and effectively, that loving and selfless service towards his fellows which Christ commands.

So a church service should not only inculcate the mystical union between Christ and the believer but ensure that this is made relevant to the world in which all men live

Prominent and most potent in Christian worship is the service of Holy Communion. (Sometimes called the Mass or the Lord's Supper).

In this we can perceive the superlative religious genius and foresight of Jesus.

He lived nearly two thousand years ago. We have His story in the New Testament and a glorious story it is but unlike His disciples we have not seen or touched Him in the flesh. Our need, therefore, of something material to be the focus which will hold our spiritual experience to the reality of this physical world is great indeed. Such objectivity Christ has given us, superbly and yet so simply. Because, during His last night on earth, He took things quite common to life's sustenance which were lying before Him on the supper table. He took bread, blessed and broke it, and giving it to His disciples said:

"This is My body which is given for you."

Then, at the conclusion of the meal, taking the cup of wine He said:

"Drink all of you of this. This is My blood of the New Covenant which is shed for you and for many."

The symbolism of His words and actions were not fully comprehended by His disciples in that hour. His command that they should continue henceforth "to do this in remembrance of Me" when they met around the supper table was to remain a mystery to them until a particular experience of two of the disciples made it clear.

To understand what happened we must pause to consider the Resurrection of Jesus which has long been the centre of controversy. Christians will agree on *the historical fact* of the Resurrection yet differ in their views of its *mode* and its *nature*. Some would say that His body was resuscitated, others that it was His spiritual body which was seen or a transmutation of His physical body. And there are those who regard the Resurrection as purely a subjective or visionary experience (a psychical occurrence) of the disciples.

Among the recorded appearances of the Risen Christ is the one when He appeared to two disciples who had left Jerusalem to go to the village of Emmaus on the very day that the tomb of Jesus had been found empty by some women (who had visited it in order to preserve His corpse with specially prepared spices).

They had become so sure that Jesus was the long awaited Messiah, but the unbelievable had happened. He had died a felon's death by crucifixion and this had devastated their high hopes of Him. It plunged them into a turmoil of doubt, perplexity, disappointment and unutterable grief. For how could one who had been treated so ignominiously be the glorious Messiah who would save Israel? True there had come the strange rumour that day that Jesus had risen from the dead and had appeared to certain women of their company. Nevertheless that was still only rumour and their despondency remained, agonising and desolating.

Then something happened. We are told that as the two disciples journeyed they fell in with a stranger who asked the reason for their evident dejection and agitation. They explained to him how they believed that Jesus was the Messiah but now His shameful death made this seem incongruous.

Then the stranger proceeded to give them an exposition of the Scriptures of the Old Testament which disclosed that what had happened to Jesus far from denying the genuineness of His Messiahship actually proclaimed and fulfilled it. I believe the stranger's discourse must have gone along the following lines:

"Israel believed she was a people especially chosen by God to bring the knowledge of Him to the whole earth. By her own faithfulness to God's Will she would prove a light to lighten the Gentiles. Her long history of being conquered and persecuted by her neighbours and mighty empires showed that she was ordained to be the Suffering Servant of God in this task.

But Israel had failed in her high calling. She, too, proved a faithless, sinful people. Hope, therefore, must rest in a truly faithful remnant of persons in her midst who would themselves perfectly fulfil her God-appointed rôle. This remnant would be the Servant of God inevitably suffering great tribulation from the evil of the world it was elected to save.

In the final analysis, however, such a wholly faithful remnant had not been found. None in Israel were innocent of transgressing God's Commandments and His Will.

So God Himself had come to the rescue. In His completely faithful and unique Son, Jesus of Nazareth, He had given the world the needed Representative, Perfect Man. The Faithful Remnant *and* the Suffering Servant were to be found in His Person. Jesus was both Messiah and Suffering Servant of God."

This sublime concept was an amazing revelation to the two disciples. It actually behoved the Messiah to suffer at the hands of sinful men and to be put to death by them! As irrefutable testimony the stranger quoted the relevant prophecies of Isaiah.

When they heard this the disciples said that their hearts began "to burn within them". That is, the fire of hope was being kindled. But there was more to come.

As it was getting late they asked this stranger to stay in their lodgings. According to custom they invited him to say the usual prayers of grace and blessing for the evening meal.

Then it happened. As the stranger broke the bread and uttered the prayers everything fell into place. The gospel says "their eyes were opened, and they knew Him (Jesus)."

159

Let us try to understand their condition. The extreme physical and nervous tension which they had suffered in the days immediately before and after their Master's Crucifixion, to say nothing of the devastating effect of that first Good Friday, together with their desperate search for understanding had made them peculiarly open to a profound spiritual experience. Their rapt attention to the stranger's words and all their pent-up emotions had induced a state of trance. Now, after the dark night of their souls they were to be vouchsafed a vision. In the stranger's breaking of bread and the familiar prayers the memory of Jesus, and particularly of all He had said and done on the night of that Last Supper with them, became vividly clear. Through their released extra-sensory perceptions they knew — not just believed but *knew* without any doubt — that their Master had conquered death and was here and now wonderfully present with them.

As they watched the stranger they could see, with the faculty of their spirit-souls, Jesus Himself performing the blessing of bread and wine and saying, in effect:

"Partake. For these are as My life given for you, body broken and blood outpoured, that your sins may be forgiven. By doing this you are recalling Me into your midst. Here I am present with you again, bringing you once more into fellowship with Myself."

All doubt was gone. Sorrow turned into unimaginable joy. Certainty of His presence became a glorious blazing conviction. The story of those women who had gone early that day to the sepulchre to find it empty was *true*, Jesus had risen indeed from death! Here, in their meal of fellowship and in the prayers, the stranger had been the focal instument of revealing the Risen Christ in all His glory to them.

On other occasions the Risen Christ made Himself known to His disciples. For forty days the phenomena of His Resurrection was experienced until His Ascension into the realm of pure spirit from whence His promised Presence could be known — no longer confined to one place at one time but everywhere and always to every believer who called upon Him in faith and love.

But His disciples found that the special wonder of that simple meal was repeated every time they met for it. And so that meal became a sacrament — an outward and visible sign to them of their Lord's spiritual Presence among them, ever strengthening their souls with the blessed assurance of His continuing care.

160

Moreover, Christ had spoken to them of His life being given to inaugurate a new covenant between man and God. Under the old covenant man had tried to maintain a ritual system which would excuse him for his failure to make a perfect moral and spiritual response to his Creator. By offering to God the sacrifice of animals man believed that God would forgive his sins and he would be restored to Divine favour.

Jesus underlined on the night of the Last Supper that sacrifice could not be a proxy matter achieved by the slaughter of unwilling and unwitting animals. Sacrifice for human sin could only be effected through the free offering of a perfect human life which would inaugurate a new type of humanity no more under the dominion of sin and its concomitant of death.

Such perfect voluntary sacrifice Jesus, unique Son of God, True Representative Man, alone could make.

He had constantly offered His life to God's Will while on earth and now His willingly accepted death at the hands of men who, because of that universal defect of sin did not recognise God when He was in their midst, would set the final seal on the consistency and constancy of His life style. His total self-offering would be a once-for-all atoning sacrifice for the sins of all mankind.

By faith in Him and what He had done man would be brought into that new creation which He had begun. This is the very Kingdom of God, where God rules completely and where sin and death are no more.

And so the disciples discovered that each celebration of that Supper, memorially repeated at their Lord's Command, not only gave them awareness of His Presence but also the glorious certainty of their adoption by Him into that new type of humanity which under God He had brought into being in this world and which conferred on them absolution from sin and an undying life.

Hence the believing fellowship of the Church is the light in this world which beckons all men to Jesus Christ as their Saviour and their hope of eternal life. And her sacrament of Holy Communion a continuing means of receiving in themselves His victorious life, which assures them of a transformation into a transcendent realm.

That the Church has largely been failing in the task of providing man with a profound spiritual experience is evident. Her acts of worship are not as effective as they should be in the world today.

161

This is one of the reasons for the decline in churchgoing and the decrease in the number of converts.

It is to her abounding credit that she admits this. Hence her attempts to provide so-called relevance to the world by inventing new patterns of worship and updating the language of the traditional services, particularly of Holy Communion. However, these efforts have not proved all that great an encouragement to evangelism. Indeed they have robbed them even more of mystical power and caused much controversy among the faithful. For one thing the new services are the product of several minds coming to a compromise rather than of one superbly inspired and visionary soul. Also a measure of 'special language' is not to be despised if men are to be lifted into a transcendent realm.

But the really important fact is that changes in language and setting cannot in themselves arouse a deep spiritual experience. What is most required is that the priest who conducts the church service must project the thoughts of its prayers and the truth of its symbolic actions through the conscientious exercise of the faculties of his spirit-soul. Only then can the act of worship really come to life.

Personally I find great difficulty in concentrating as I should if there is more than one server or assistant priest taking part in the conduct of the service when I am celebrating the Holy Communion. Their movements and the change of voices in the reading of prayers and scripture tend to distract so that for me the celebration is jerky and unrounded. Of course this is a personal reaction. It doubtless indicates a weakness on my part since many other priests evidently feel the reverse.

I believe the aim of the celebrant should be to concentrate so fully upon the meaning of the service that as he goes step by step through it he will achieve a greater and greater liberation of his spirit-soul. When he reaches the act of consecration of the Bread and Wine he will be aware, by extra-sensory perception, of the Presence of Christ and of union with Him.

He *wills* that the members of his congregation may also enter that mystical union. His spirit-soul reaches out to 'touch' theirs so that he and they become 'one in Christ'.

By the faculty of faith and creative imagination the service has led the celebrant and his people into the significance of the Last Supper of the Lord. All that it symbolises and all it bequeathes to those who love Jesus become the possession of the worshippers. They share the experience of the priest and receive the refreshing power of the Spirit of Christ.

How important it is, therefore, that the thoughts provided by every prayer and action of the Holy Communion should have real meaning for the celebrant as he utters them. Mechanical, unimaginative, perfunctory, hurried execution of the sacrament is bound to circumscribe its spiritual power, inhibit the extra-sensory perception of the priest and so fail to elevate his people.

Spirit-soul must communicate with spirit-soul and that cannot be truly done unless the attention given to the service by the celebrant is so great he attains an 'out of the body' experience in which he is able to 'perceive' the Presence of Christ and so communicates the joy and beauty of this to the communicants.

In this matter the Church has been somewhat hampered by the doctrine that the validity of the sacrament is not impaired by the short-comings, however great, of the priest who performs it. Certainly the sacrament is dependent upon the faith of those who share in it but its efficacy can be limited if sloth of spirit prevails.

Happily, in mystical union, the spirit-soul of the weaker brother is helped by that of the stronger. Nevertheless it is obvious that while the worshippers must play their part by fully concentrating upon the service they cannot be caught up entirely in Holy Communion if the one who is leading them is not himself completely immersed in it.

The joyful wonder is that where Christian worship is deep and united the stranger present, who may not understand the service or even speak the language in which it is rendered, will also be drawn into it at the deep level of his spirit-soul (if he so wills) and will receive spiritual elevation.

What is true of the Holy Communion is true for every church service and every corporate prayer that is uttered therein if these are to confer real blessing and inspiration on everyone concerned.

Many member of the Church of England very rarely come to church services yet there is a strong desire by them that death should be dignified by Christians rites. It is in the funeral service, therefore, that the priest has a golden opportunity not only to bring Christian consolation and hope to the mourners but to draw them into the joy of a truly profound spiritual experience.

Hence the fact that funeral services are sometimes remote, uncomforting, and unfeeling affairs taken by clergy who themselves appear to regard them as meaningless to those who attend (simply because they are not numbered among regular churchoers) is a sad indictment of the Church. For in this she is failing to recognise that *every* funeral service must be made relevant and uplifting through the faith and concentration of the minister who conducts it.

Some clergy complain that the Prayer Book Funeral Service itself is not very helpful but that is no excuse why they cannot enliven the essence of it and so make it more personal — and thus more real to all concerned. It does not have to be something so slavishly tied to the book, so completely set in all its prayers and phrases that there is no room to manoeuvre the feelings of those who deeply mourn into the way of a satisfying and consoling experience.

For my part I like to preface the service by reminding those present that they are about to share in a very deep experience of the spirit; that these moments are, in a sense, eternal and made especially beautiful by the deep feelings they have in their hearts. (Feelings at such a time of those who mourn enshrine, of course, so much and go beyond the power of words to describe). They must be assured that God uses our deep inarticulate feelings (which He knows completely) for prayer. Indeed that they are our true prayers, ranging out into the world of spirit to carry our affection. An initial statement along these lines goes a long way to gain real attention to the service and to instill the realisation that it is not a routine formula but something uniquely personal, to be truly shared and is wholly meaningful.

Using Christ's parable of the seed which must die to fulfil itself (elaborated upon by St Paul in his letter to the church at Corinth) I underline that the death of the seed produces the glory of a new creation. (If there are flowers given in memory of the departed these serve as a ready example and will have special personal significance to those who gave them).

Though Christianity cannot tell us much about life beyond death because the glory of it transcends our present capacity of understanding, nevertheless in one of His parables (which a clergyman friend described to me as an account of 'five minutes after death') Jesus has given us some clues about it. The story of Dives and Lazarus implies that beyond death we shall recognise others, retain our power of memory, and know a great consolation. It is surely helpful to the inculcation of a profound spiritual experience in the service if the clergyman can introduce, through the prayers or otherwise, these comforting truths of the after life.

3

THE AURA — IN LIFE
AND IN DEATH

Mention of 'the aura' can cause disquiet in some Church circles. It arouses the suspicion that the speaker must have surrendered orthodox beliefs for Spiritualist ones.

But the fact is that many who exercise a regular ministry of the laying-on of hands become well aware of the physical reality of the aura.

The experiments of Dr Walter Kilner in 1917 at St Thomas's Hospital, London, (in which he looked first through a specially dyed screen, and then at his patient) showed the aura as an emanation which radiated from the human body for a distance of six to twelve inches. He stated that it was affected in colour and density not only by the condition of the patient's health but by his or her mood.

No further research followed upon Dr Kilner's initial discovery until about twenty-five years later when a Russian electrician, Semyon Davidovich Kirlian, and his scientist wife, Valentina, developed a system by which they observed (statically at first and later, as their apparatus improved, in moving action) the auras of a variety of substances and plant life. Their so-called 'Kirlian photography' showed the changes which occur in the strength and activity of the aura of living things and even of inanimate objects.

Such experiments go some way to suggest that the idea of the 16th century philosopher Paracelsus (as of many mystics and psychically gifted people) could be right. Namely, that there is within the physical form a spiritual one which endows the former with its life and energy (and probably its shape as well, because this ethereal body has a similar 'outline image' to the physical one).

Because the aura is a physical manifestation it will be considered as a property of the body-soul but it is certainly affected by mental and spiritual attitudes and should be regarded, therefore, as having its origin and support in the spirit-soul.

I realise that the following description of my own experience of the aura must be largely subjective but I try to be as objective as possible.

The aura reveals itself to me as an influence (probably electrical) which rises from the person and to which I find myself sensitive only when, after deep prayer, I am giving the laying-on of hands. Usually I become aware of heat and vibration (often of both). During the trance condition of prayer a cold, or negative, sensation may be vouchsafed at first. This is generally so in cases where the person attended is very depressed or emotionally distraught, or has been taking drugs (maybe for medical reasons, e.g. to allay pain or nervous tension).

However, by continued concentration this coldness usually gives place to the positive reaction of heat and/or vibration.

Usually during the laying-on of hands I find that it is not necessary to touch the person because the aura can be felt a few inches and even several feet away, especially as the depth of prayer (and so, of trance) increases during the ministration.

Intuitively I begin to sense that the aura requires soothing, as it were, while my prayer thoughts (whether spoken or silent) are guiding the patient and myself into maintaining a faith union with the Presence of Christ. Consequently, after a while, I feel impelled to 'stroke' the aura in a calming manner with my hands. Sometimes I become aware of 'trouble spots' where I know I must exercise even greater concentration and '*will*' them to wholeness and harmony with the rest of the aura.

The active physical aspect of the laying-on of hands, therefore, appears to generate in the aura of the subject a sense of tranquillity and strength where before there was raggedness and lack of vitality or (as I often sense it to be) a *negative* quality which feels cold and lifeless.

I have noted that the aura has a degree of resilience or sponginess once it has come through.

Intuitively I sense that any undue pressure upon it by my hands would be unnatural. Indeed I would go further and say that there is such a peculiar restraint or control imposed on my being that I believe it would not only be inadvisable but even impossible to 'break through' the barrier of the aura with my hands during the period in which prayer is maintained. Towards the close of ministration the field of the person's aura often seems to expand so that in many cases I can still feel its heat and vibration even when my hands are stretched apart at arm's length. What appears to occur is that at some mysterious point there is what I can only describe as *a release* which permits the aura to be fully liberated. The result produces in me an exalted state of such remarkable lightness that the transport of it is, quite literally, like floating on air. I feel so caught up, as it were, that my body seems levitated, emptied of all substance and to have become like a hollow tube which, however, is pulsing with a peculiar and most exhilarating power.

All through this experience I sense another Presence with me and controlling me. It conveys an ineffable peace and ecstatic assurance. The whole matter is one which defies adequate description but it is certainly most beautiful.

When the session ends I will, quite involuntarily, rub my hands gently but firmly over each other as if washing them. I believe that this action, which I must emphasise is an automatic one, effects something which I have not yet been able to diagnose. Maybe it removes any negative charge (evil?) from them and could originate in some ancient ritual of spiritual cleansing of which, however, I have no knowledge. Most likely, as it seems to me, it is simply instinctive.

We have all experienced, of course, how some persons can instil confidence in us while others leave us more depressed than we were or, at best, unchanged. We observe this as some quality in the personality.

Thus the doctor who has a reassuring bedside manner can go a long way to make us more cheerful and less distressed even before he has diagnosed and prescribed. What happens is that our weakened aura receives vitality from one person but just the opposite from another.

Here there is no laying-on of hands and it might be argued, therefore, that such a practice would be unnecessary if we would but exercise a ministry of 'will-power' to project healing.

The healer should recognise if he takes such a view that a very high degree of spirituality indeed would need to be achieved in order to develop his own aura perfectly. His spirit-soul would then be acting upon the spirit-soul of the patient in direct communication — what one might term a purely angelic function. The fact is, of course, that we require some help from the natural world in order to focus our attention on Christ and on the supernatural. Doubtless this is why our Lord, in His complete understanding of our human situation, exercised the laying-on of hands and commended its practice in order that the use of this physical action might serve as a focus for stimulating spiritual perception and thus deepening prayer.

It is likewise with the elements of bread and wine in Holy Communion, and of water in Baptism. The Church recognises these helps to 'the infirmity of faith' and speaks of the sacramental principle. We might note, in passing, that even the words of prayer perform the same function because they are thought-forms derived from the physical world. They serve us as vehicles of spiritual insight and communication because our human nature demands material realities to arouse spiritual ones.

An accompanying purpose of the ministration of the laying-on of hands is that its physical action roots our prayers for the sick very surely into the reality of this world. We realise that the sick person is, like ourselves, temporarily inhabiting a physical body. Of course we desire his or her *spiritual* healing but we also know that the physical body must react to that healing. We should always pray, therefore, that the body *and* the spirit may be healed. During the ministration prayer causes the sense perceptions to retire so that the deeper it becomes the more free is the spirit-soul. Thereby extra-sensory powers may be liberated and an ecstatic condition can ensue. It is important, therefore, that the healer holds fast all the while not only to the thought of Christ but to the particular need of the sufferer. The laying-on of hands provides 'the anchor' which keeps the healer's own exalted spiritual state firmly grounded upon the purpose of bringing to the patient the healing he or she needs and which flows from the healer's faith union with Christ.

There must also be a vicarious element in the healer's work because there can be situations wherein the faith of the sick person is very weak or even entirely lacking. The healer must, therefore, by creative imagination, exercise not only compassionate understanding for the afflicted but also faith on their behalf. There is a New Testament illustration of this in the healing of the paralysed young man who was let down on a litter through the roof of a house where Jesus was, having been borne there by his friends. Maybe the paralytic was brought to Jesus without any desire on his own part. Perhaps he did not think there was any point. He may have felt completely hopeless about himself and therefore wholly indifferent to the whole thing. We note, however, that Jesus seeing the faith not of the youth but *of his friends* was enabled to heal.

I cannot claim always to *see* the aura of all who come to me for the laying-on of hands — and certainly not with the immediacy which apparently some clairvoyants have. During prayer for the healing Presence of Christ, however, I am almost always able to *feel* it.

There have also been occasions when I have been privileged to see, during the laying-on of hands, what I can only call 'the transfiguration' of the sufferer. This has certainly occurred, with some regularity, where death is imminent. Taking the hand of those who are in final coma, while praying for their happy and tranquil passage into the unseen world, I have frequently observed, towards the end of my prayers, a peculiar radiance about the person's face and form. This has its own special 'life' about it. Some kind of energy also appears to be transmitted which affects my own being. I have not yet been able to analyse this clearly enough to be able to say whether I am receiving it from the dying person or am myself imparting it to him or her.

If it be coming from myself I am certain that I am acting simply as a channel of that energy. I surmise that the special power of the spiritual world is at work. Most likely the dying person and myself are being uniquely involved in the ministry of those angels who are responsible for guiding, reassuring and welcoming the departing soul through its exodus (death) into the new condition of post-mortem life. Perhaps the angels find it of help to them when they perform their ministry in this world to have human agents co-operating with them. In the case of the death-bed I have found on numerous occasions that the aura of the dying person is extremely beautiful (one might say fascinating) and appears to dissolve all the marks of age or the ravages of pain to present a delicate loveliness of countenance, serene and expectant. This effect of the aura lingers for a while after death.

I would also add that I may receive an intuition when death is imminent. If the dying person has relatives or friends present I will excuse myself shortly before the end so that they may be alone with their dear one for that sacred moment. Invariably, after commending the soul to God's loving care and mercy, death comes within a few minutes of my departure from the bedside, (although I feel sure that generally the immortal soul has already entered eternity before the fact of clinical death).

During that commendation I mark the forehead of the dying with the sign of the cross and hold my other hand a few inches above the stomach. I have noted that then I appear to be in contact with a subtle energy which communicates itself to my palm.

I find myself intuitively urged to 'hold' this emanation gently for a little while and then, equally gently, sweep my hand aside at the close of the prayer. I am convinced that this strange force flowing upward from the dying body is a kind of umbilical cord connecting it with its spiritual counterpart. I cannot say I have actually seen this 'cord' because I am usually constrained to close my eyes in prayer but I do most surely feel it to be there. The instinctive movement of my hand suggests to me that this cord is gently broken and physical death will shortly follow.

Hence I am led to believe that there is what has been called 'the silver cord' which links our spiritual body with the physical one. When it breaks (or surrenders its peculiar energy or life-force) death comes as really a 'new birth' into the spiritual world. I consider that the aura, although a physical manifestation, is actually a product of the spiritual body.

If there be a long period of unconsciousness or coma before death I am sure that the spirit-soul, being almost completely liberated from the body-soul, can communicate with loved ones and others at a psychic level and may also continue to do so for a period after death, whether the recipient of that communication is truly aware of it or not.

Among a number of experiences in which I have been persuaded of the temporary ability of a dying person to act on the physical level to make contact with the living I would cite the following:

I had been called out after midnight to be at the bedside in hospital of a very dear friend, Marjorie. I arrived to find her husband sitting, grief-stricken, at her side. It was evident that our friend was close to death and after simple prayers, in which the husband tearfully joined, I commended her soul to God. Under my hands the sense of her spiritual 'cord' was very marked. When the pulsation from it had subsided to a faint tremor I left her to be alone with her husband for the final moment.

Returning to my car, in which my wife was waiting (she had been visiting Marjorie in the hospital over the previous weeks but now felt too distraught to see her this night) I started up the car saying that our friend's death could only be minutes away.

However, for the first time ever (and never since) the automatic gears seemed not to engage properly, producing a strange uneven movement in the vehicle. Several times I re-started the car and re-engaged the gear. Each time the same peculiar response. All the while in my mind's eye I was haunted by the image of Marjorie as I had left her, drained of colour, terribly sunken of cheek and with skeletal arms, most cruelly ravaged by her wasting illness.

But on the fifth attempt to commence the car I had a sudden vision of Marjorie looking very cheerful and smiling. It forcibly reminded me of happy occasions in the past when she had visited my wife and I. She seemed to be saying: "Look at me now. I am so happy."

I found myself replying mentally "Hello — how lovely to see you." The picture of her was so vivid and appeared to be set in a golden brilliance, overcoming the murky darkness of the night.

Almost directly after my salutation the vision faded and this time the car moved normally.

I am fully convinced that during this incident our friend had joined us. In order to remove my mind from its sad reflection she had arrested my attention through the mechanics of the car and then, having been recognised in her radiant state of release, she allowed the motor to perform naturally. On reaching home a telephone call came from our friend's daughter. She informed us of her mother's death only minutes after I had left her bedside, coinciding with my return to where my car was parked.

I believe that death having released her spirit-soul she had been able to work momentarily in the physical world upon the functioning of my car.* Once recognised and given proof of her new joyful condition she was content.

---

* One of the powers of pure spirit must be a unique understanding of matter.

4

THE AURA AND MOOD

Dr Kilner declared that his experiments showed that mood can affect the aura.

Now although it is true we can allow our mood to be swayed by physical elements (e.g. the weather), by our surroundings or by our particular circumstances, nevertheless our control over these things is within our own will. And the will is the great attribute of the soul. It is a breakdown of that control which drives men to some extreme when, as we say "things get too much" for them. Mood must ultimately be conceived as coming from the will which is the spiritual nature of man, i.e. it issues from his soul.

Among the most powerful moods of man is that of faith. If his prevailing attitude (mood) is one of complete trust in the eternal goodness, mercy and loving kindness of his Creator towards him then he receives in fullest measure (because of his willing 'openness' to it) these refreshing blessings of God. They bestow confidence, equanimity, inner happiness and assurance. And all this despite the slings and arrows which, like all his fellows, he will sustain during his mortal life.

He *knows* whatever happens that he is counted by God as an individual in His sight and is eternally loved by Him. The physical aspect of his life thus becomes 'swallowed up' by the spiritual through the continuous stream of true life which God supplies to those who place their trust in Him.

Thus faith in God endows our experiences of the joy and beauty of earthly life with deeper, more exciting and precious significance. Likewise the anguishes and adversities of life have conferred upon them a spiritual illumination which elevates them with the comforting knowledge that they are totally shared by God, fully known and understood by Him.

The aura of one whose life is supported by this faith is strong and buoyant. It mysteriously communicates blessing to others even though neither he nor they may be really conscious of this influence.

It is faith in the beneficent Source of Life-giving — the God whom Jesus Christ reveals to men — which nourishes the spiritual body. Over and over again in the laying-on of hands I have consciously felt the influx of new vitality into the auras of those to whom I minister and also in myself.

I cannot say that I am always immediately aware of this. When the person has come to me dulled by drugs, or wholly wrapped up in his or her own feeling of rejection, completely introverted, depressed, disconsolate, it can be many minutes before this particular phenomenon of revitalising of the aura is actually sensed by me. Indeed there are cases when I have had to see the person on several occasions before such a vital breakthrough has been felt in any positive degree. Nevertheless I believe that even in those apparently barren first encounters the stirring of new life has begun — otherwise it is hardly likely that such people would return, as they generally do, for further ministration of this kind.

The cycle and pattern of healing is clear. I *must* begin with acknowledging afresh in my own self the power of that new life which Christ's Spiritual presence imparts. This realisation must start by an act of faith, (which is the inner assurance of the actual reality of what is not perceived through the natural senses). Meditation upon an event in Christ's earthly life or upon His teaching is, for me, imperative in this exercise.

I usually conduct this with my eyes closed to minimise distraction, and while standing beside the person who will have been asked to relax in an easy chair. (Helping such relaxation by appropriate suggestion is essential). Of course patients may be in bed in which case kneeling beside them and holding one of their hands is often most appropriate and helpful.

The meditation causes my spirit-soul to become partially free of the body-soul and this promotes sensitivity of an extra-sensory kind. It is this sensitivity which then moves me to give the laying-on of hands. It also enables me to 'feel' the aura and, in some cases, to 'see' it. I place the words 'feel' and 'see' in inverted commas because I am quite sure that without prior meditation and prayer

I would *not* be aware at all of the aura. In other words I realise that the power to influence the person's aura and so to promote healing, does not come from my own self. I am purely a channel of that power which springs from the creative source of life, God Himself, Who, through His unique Son Jesus Christ, has ordained that His loving relationship with all His human creatures shall be made known to them. I am also aware that there is an interaction of my spirit-soul with that of the sufferer. This is added proof of the spiritual link of all souls because of the life-source we have in common, and issuing eternally from our Creator.

Disturbances in that harmonious interplay of soul with soul caused by so many human factors (disagreements, hatred, selfishness, distrust, arrogance and so on) are overcome and our differences reconciled when we exercise, in sincerity, our faith in Jesus Christ.

I have said that it is an important factor to prepare the patient's state of mind and ensure his relaxation but of course there are cases where time, distance, or the particular condition of the person, makes this impossible. Then there is the value of absent healing. This is best continued by the healer stating a regular time to the patient (and his loved ones) when he will be praying for him. It is also aided by giving the sick person a simple prayer to use, following upon the Lord's Prayer.

I will often suggest that he should stand in his room and while describing a circle about himself with his outstretched arms, repeat something like the following "'At this hour I know that I and others are being prayed for and I would link myself in sympathy with them", and then: "Lord Jesus, in Whom I have all my trust, surround me with the circle of Thy divine protection, and may Thy holy angels dwell in my home".

Of course if the sick person is bed-ridden, or otherwise incapable of making the circle around himself, it is sufficient to visualise this in his imagination. The only point of the procedure is to give a focus for concentration upon the prayer.

It is also good that the sick person regularly uses a simple commendation prayer just before sleep, e.g. "Into Thy hands I commend my spirit". First thing on waking to say: "Lord Jesus (or Heavenly Father) I thank Thee for Thy healing of me through last night. Help me to remember Thou art with me through this new day".

5

SPIRITUAL HEALING

The priest who realises he is called to the ministry of healing (though, of course, *all* priests should recognise it is an area of their vocation) will find that the demand upon his faith is tremendous.

There will be many times when the laying-on of his hands and praying with the sick strengthen his faith profoundly. But there will be most testing occasions, too, when he recognises his own great need of spiritual refreshment and the strengthening of personal faith.

The joyful occasions are when he is dealing with those who are among the believers, those who already have the confident assurance of a deep and daily trust in the loving presence of God. Then indeed the healing ministry is one of pure transport. But much more often he will find that those to whom he would bring the comfort of God's love are without faith, or have any hope that healing can come to them. Then it is that he has to become, as it were, faith for them. He should try to gather at least one or two believers who deeply care (and, if possible, know the sick person) who will also pray supportingly. In this there is the precedent of Jesus Who explained that *seeing the faith of others* He could heal one who probably had no faith at all.

Although I shall use the words 'spiritual healing' and 'healer' for brevity it should be understood that we acknowledge that *all* healing is from the source of life — God Himself.

So the healer does not heal but is used as a channel or agent of God's power — a power which the Christian believes comes when he recollects that he is in the Presence of Christ. Spiritual healing, therefore, is better defined as Divine Healing or Christ's Healing.

On many occasions I have found that folk who seek healing do not know how to relax. Most seem never to have known real serenity and composure over a number of years, in some cases even from puberty itself. Little wonder they have become, in the course of time, subject to various ills which are therefore likely to be purely psychosomatic in origin.

Because of the their deep rooted inner stress they must be brought into a tranquil state before their auras will 'come through' and be felt by me.

That is why I consider it most important to allow people to talk as freely as one can encourage them to do about their work, their interests, their families and friends. Indeed any topic which comes naturally into the conversation after my general opening questions which are designed to put them at ease and to establish confidence between us. This ensures they become much less introverted. Usually only then will I seek the full details of their trouble.

Hence I do not greatly care for public services of healing because the large number attending them makes it impossible for the healer to give that element of absolute attention to the individual which I find is so important if what follows is to be helpful and enduring.

Spiritual healing is certainly not easy. It is not just a matter of the healer having exceptional faith or possessing a special gift. Of the healer it demands giving complete attention to everyone who comes to him coupled with the acceptance that all healing is of God and that the issue of all things is in His Will.

I believe it is helpful if the healer seeks to become aware of the aura of his patient. To do so he must prolong or deepen, as the case may be, the state of trance which his own praying induces in him.

This is particularly important for discovering the need or not of exorcism which is betrayed by a cold, repellent aura. But much more usual is the fact that drugs, which may have been taken as medication, tend to 'deaden' the aura and so only after some while will it begin to 'surface' and the healer's hands become sensible of it. Always the healer should be endeavouring to encourage this liberation of the aura. He will find that this needs, besides his full concentration, the most thoughtful understanding of the patient's anxiety, and an appropriate direction of mind to the sick one through spoken prayers. Such intelligent ministration can only be built up by listening to the patient and asking him questions beforehand.

The tense person holds in or withdraws his aura into his body so that it seems non-existent. When relaxation takes place it is released and although at first probably uneven it can, after further concentration by the healer, be soothed to a more lively and settled condition.

On the physical level the healer will find himself helped in this purpose of enlivening the aura, by gently and steadily 'stroking' it. Usually he will 'sense' a natural placing of his hands for this — generally a few inches above the patient's head, or laying one hand on the forehead and the other at the back of the head.

It is sufficient to remind the patient that we live, move and have all our being in the loving goodness of God. his imagination should be pictorially assisted by the healer to accept that he is in the presence of the glorified Christ and that angels are ready to minister to him.

The healer will discover that as the meditation takes complete hold upon his own self he becomes aware that a peculiar power flows through him. It elevates him with a wondrous ecstasy. He realises that he is now being controlled by the Lord Jesus. The aura of the patient will then come through — strongly in some cases, while in others unevenly at first but soon to gather intensity.

The aura, although linked to the physical form is spiritual in origin. If it weakens, the body will show signs of illness. Physical conditions, as well as spiritual ones, may alter the vivacity of the aura, e.g. drugs taken, extremes of heat or cold, hunger or over-indulgence.*

It is clear, therefore, that the aura is inextricably linked to both the body-soul and spirit-soul. As a quality of the soul it receives its power and possibility of renewal from that creative and re-creative source of all life which religious people call God.

If our desire is for evil intent or if we are beset by despondency or despair then our intake is of a negative nature (anti-God) which unless there is a change of heart (i.e. a new direction of our will) leads to the malfunction of the aura and thus impairment of our spiritual body with the probability that physical disorder will manifest itself in due course.

---

* It is a great help, therefore, if the venue for this ministration is warm, physically comfortable and cheerful.

6

FURTHER THOUGHTS ON HEALING

Among the faculties of the spirit-soul is that of healing because in possessing power over matter it can influence the physical body.

This is exemplified in the work of 'faith healers'. Emile Coué, who died in 1926, was using this principle when he began his famous practice of healing by suggestion. He sought to influence the subconscious mind of his patients with thoughts of well-being. Beginning with the premise that thought always tries to express itself in fact, he went on to say that when we stop to consider the possibility of our thoughts entering reality we start to sift and analyse them for their practicality.

It is these acts of reasoning and evaluation which produce doubt and so prevent some of our thoughts being externally expressed.

Coué sought, therefore, to damp down the critical faculties in order to eliminate the obstructive element of doubt. He did this by telling his patients to repeat, just before they fell asleep and immediately they awakened, the phrase: "Every day and in every way I am getting better and better".

At those particular times of a reduced state of consciousness in our daily cycle the reasoning activity of our minds is at a low ebb. Hence the thought of well-being can be given straight to the subconscious without the interference of reason. There it can arouse the healing power of the sick individual's own spirit-soul.

We may remark that in the case of sophisticated man his process of ratiocination is strongly influenced by the scientific views of his society. Simple people in primitive communities on the other hand do not engage in doubt to that degree and readily accept by faith what their religion teaches and their leaders tell them. Hence the extraordinary powers of healing exhibited among them.

When we are asleep our conscious mind ceases but on the other hand our subconscious is very active as witness the much dreaming which takes place throughout the course of sleep although usually little of this is remembered unless we are suddenly awakened or have been tense and troubled during the day, making sleep fitful and restless. Here, then, is one source of keeping healthy — to go to bed with the thought of increasing well-being. This will go on feeding the spirit-soul and so control the functions of the body for its good.

It is for this reason that I tell those who are deeply concerned about a sick member of the family that they can bring a helpful measure of healing if they will wait until the patient is asleep and then quietly whisper close to his or her ear a few times — always slowly, deliberately and with earnest emphasis — the thought of whatever healing is required.

In particular I know many parents who have been grateful for this advice. It is very effective in assisting to overcome the afflictions of stammering and bed-wetting. The parent will wait until the child is asleep or just about to be and speak gently and soothingly of their love for the child. As many troubles are due to a child's anxiety, nervousness or sense of insecurity, the reassurance of love, protection and tenderness towards it during the susceptible state of sleep is of high importance and provides much therapeutic power.

It is worth reminding parents that besides using bed-time prayers they can inculcate into young children while they are sleeping the strength and support of the Christian faith by whispering to them such phrases as "God is caring for you. Jesus and His angels are watching over you".

Coupled with the daytime encouragement of telling them the stories of Jesus, such assurances work away deep within the child's soul inculcating the comfort and hope of the Christian faith.

It may well be that much later that seed of implanted faith thus deeply embedded will prove the anchor which will hold a storm-tossed adult life from being wrecked. And this could be so even though, through all the years between from infancy, the pursuit and practice of the religious life has been neglected.

Where patients have faith in Jesus Christ the healer can greatly fortify them by this practice of 'whispered healing'. The healer knows that faith in Jesus Christ brings his soul into a mystical union with God and with the soul of the sick one. When he conveys by whisper the assertion of the Presence of the Healing Christ he is implanting afresh in the subconscious mind of the patient the inspiration of that wondrous truth which will then stimulate the latter's spirit-soul faculties to take over the work of healing.

Clearly the same principle applies when dealing with a sick person who is fully awake though the practice may certainly be much more difficult. In this case the healer must counteract doubt (i.e. lack, or weakness, of faith) by endeavouring to build up the patient's confidence.

He will do this by thoroughly stimulating the imagination with a simple but precise picture of Christ's Presence so that the sick person can reflect upon it, gather trust and create a climate of faith. Always we have to remember that it is by arousing faith that the doubt is dispelled.

The greater the faith the less doubt to hinder the operation of the spirit-soul's healing faculty.

Perhaps it is well to state the obvious which is that both external and internal things have to be considered in the cure of many illnesses.

Clearly the external ones of hygiene, proper diet, fresh air and exercise, etc. are very important. Christianity certainly does not teach us to despise our bodies by neglecting their proper needs but stresses that, as temples of the spirit, they should be cared for and respected for the holy vessels they are.

But there is also the vital necessity of maintaining the internal qualities of peace, security, lack of tension and conflict in the mind, and keeping love in the heart. If we carry within us a mental boxing-ring we cannot know real health for this depends upon the mind's tranquillity.

In this present age so many are afflicted with psychological illnesses caused by various stresses and strains. They arise from domestic upsets, economic troubles, disrupted personal relationships and such like. It is only the strength of religion which can relieve these anguishes and restore calm to the inner being. In this the Christian faith is without equal.

Tranquillising drugs can at best only mask the disquiet of the soul by dulling the nervous system. They should only be used as a short term measure otherwise the patient becomes addicted to them as a crutch for making life just tolerable. They keep under the worst outward ravages of inner disorientation and frustration but cannot remove the actual causes of them.

It is a misconception that the purpose of Christianity is to make us good, moral people. That is a *by-product* of our faith.

What the Christian faith does is to make us *whole* persons, i.e. those whose mind, body and spirit are harmoniously integrated. In short, to make us healthy.

7

MIRACLES

How often have I been asked "Do miracles happen?" For answer the reader must forgive a simple examination of what the Christian believes is the nature of God. It is a necessary preliminary.

Astronomers predicate that billions of years ago creation was an infinitely concentrated mass. As a result of what is called 'the big bang' it exploded to shower its particles through space. One of these produced our earth and, through much evolutionary change, life upon it. Still that process goes on so that worlds in space are ever being born, while some are dying or are already dead. But what made that concentrated mass in the first place? What was its source — the very origin of creation?

Science provides a clue. It tells us that when matter is destroyed it produces energy. Sometimes that energy, thus released, can be of awesome intensity as the fearsome results of nuclear fission demonstrate.

While matter can be transformed into energy the reverse order, changing energy into matter, does not appear a possibility to us. But supposing *before* Creation, i.e. before that concentrated mass exploded, there existed the special condition or power which made the transformation of energy into matter possible?

In other words before creation did there exist an almighty energy?

This is, in fact, what Christians believe and what they read into the Bible story of the creation in the book of Genesis. That story may meet with scorn from twentieth century man who, armed with the findings of modern science, regards it as pure folklore and therefore unworthy of serious consideration. But the plain truth is that the writers of Genesis were not concerned with recording

182

factual history or making a precise scientific analysis of how the
world and life upon it began even if that had been possible for
them. They were concerned with a different level of understanding
— a simple basic philosophy which would enable man to realise
his dependence upon his Creator — namely, that God had made
the world *and* that He continues to be concerned in sustaining it.

Genesis states that God had made the world out of nothing.
Actually it says "In the beginning all was *without form and void*
...."

That, of course, is another way of saying that *before* creation
there was no matter since matter has form and fills space.

But there was God: "In the beginning God ..."
And God for the Christian *is* the Source of Energy — the life
power which makes and sustains all created things, animate and
inanimate. The believer goes further and identifies that this Almighty
Energy has Will — constructive, ordered, unchanging Will. So the
Christian declares that God is omnipotent, i.e. He has all power.

It is that definition, however, which leads to a confusion of thought
for many. To say God has all power does not mean that He can
do anything. That would signify He is able to do things which are
against His nature, i.e. contrary to His Will. Obviously that cannot
be. Indeed it would be an insecure, uncertain, impossible world
for us if the known laws of Nature could be arbitrarily suspended
by God. Just because the essence fo Nature *is* law we are able to
examine it and make it yield, bit by bit, its secrets. Hence we can
use, if we are wise, the knowledge we have gained to promote our
well-being and advancement upon the earth. Without an ordered
universe that would not be possible.

Upon the unchanging laws of God's creation we depend and
must rejoice that God is not capricious, as we so often allow
ourselves to be.

It follows that if the laws of Nature (i.e. of God) are unchanging
we must accept them or court disaster if we defy them, whether
with conscious purpose or not.

Thus a child who climbs a tree may fall from it to break a limb
or worse. The mother cannot blame God for that result or expect
that He should have suspended the law of gravity in this instance
to ensure her child's protection.

Nevertheless, we realise we do not yet know *all* God's natural laws.
Maybe some will forever elude the grasp of human understanding

183

or discovery. Nor do we apprehend all God's power. Indeed there must always be a great gap in our knowledge of Him for He is infinitely greater and wiser than ourselves.

This area of absolute mystery, totally beyond human ability to comprehend, includes that experience which we term miraculous.

That child falling from the tree must normally hit the ground. But if the parent is there at the time to catch him he will be saved from harm, not because gravity is ceasing to operate but simply because a new power has been introduced into the situation.

Likewise a miracle does not mean an occurrence which is contrary to the laws of Nature (which would make nonsense of God) but it is what happens when an additional, mysterious energy comes into action and creates a new condition for the working of the natural laws.

Those laws have not been broken, reversed or superseded, but an extra force has been brought to bear upon them in a given situation. And that extra force — as does all energy — flows from God. It is a transcendent, transforming power which effects an alteration of (or exception to) the normally expected result.

It could well be that science will discover further fields of energy than those known to it at present. Perhaps among them one which comes from the human psyche itself and which could produce, in the matter of healing, what now we could only call miracles. It would be a matter, of course, not only of discovering that special field of energy but of learning its purpose and understanding its laws. But like all the fields of energy now known to us it would still be God's energy.

In the case of unusual healings we must realise that not all are miracles. Most will result from the loving care of others and because of profound faith. These encourage the natural restoring of life by God. Few indeed are miracles in the true sense. Miracles are those rare healings or incidents which are unique, incomprehensible and immediate.

They are produced only by the closest union of the soul of man with His Creator's Will for him.

Hence the miracles of Jesus Christ who intimately knew His Heavenly Father and perfectly fulfilled His Will. Through that perfect union of Himself with God He was able to bring into action that additional mysterious energy which, in His unaltering nature, God provides but can only do so where there is such complete communion with Himself. Thereby a special condition is created which does not break any natural laws but transcends their activity to produce an entirely original condition.

Reflection upon this matter should draw us to the conclusion that a true miracle is the unique life of Christ. This remains the greatest miracle the world has known and, because His risen life dwells in every believer, it is an unceasing one.

8

THE NEW CREATION

Jesus Christ expressed the fact that there is a direct connection between the soul and God. He showed this explicitly in the manner of His life and implicitly by the way He prayed to the Father.

His earthly life was a pure mystical state of being, i.e. an unbroken union of His soul (in its totality of spirit-soul and body-soul) with the Spirit of God.

Because His spirit-soul dominated His body-soul He could exercise the powers of pure spirit. Hence those phenomena of His visions and voices which are chronicled in the New Testament. Hence also the activity of His spirit-soul in the telepathic knowledge, the clairvoyance, the prophecy, the premonitions, the Transfiguration, and — not least — the profound simplicity of His teaching. We must also add to this list His healing miracles which were examples of the domination of His spirit-soul over matter. (We might also include the 'Nature miracles' like the stilling of the tempest, the walking on water and the feeding of a multitude with a small hamper of provisions, if we do not accept that these can have other quite 'natural' explanations).

As has been said the spirit-soul has faculties which, because of sin, are only rudiments of those which were in 'original' man i.e. before the 'Fall' when he came under the domination of matter.

Because of the sinless nature of Christ His spirit-soul and His body-soul worked in the harmony of one undivided soul and produced the perfection of the powers of original or true Man. He was indeed the second Adam Who to our rescue came.

In this world which is dominated by matter His perfect state of mystical union with the Creator meant that His own experience of death (which, like change and decay, disease and suffering is the result of sin) *introduced an entirely new type, or order, of creation upon this planet.* i.e. one in which the soul, in its completeness of body-soul and spirit-soul, could be known through the normal sense perceptions of His disciples in what is called 'the body of His Resurrection' or 'Risen Life'. It revealed the truth that because His spirit-soul had complete mastery over His body-soul He was not under the domination of matter and therefore victorious over sin and death.

Thus He demonstrated that it is not just the spirit-soul which is immortal but that the 'Christ Life' incorporates the body-soul as well into that immortality.

In the Resurrection of Jesus we have the sign of the 'new creation'. It is not that this present creation is passing away in the sense that it is ultimately to be destroyed but rather that all of it may be made new. In other words there is envisaged a transformation of the old order wherein not matter but spirit holds complete domination.

However, it was only a foretaste of the new creation which was given in the Resurrection of Christ for He could not remain within the old order of this present world with the limitation it imposes of matter. Hence the necessity of His 'Ascension' into that realm where the new creation prevails and in which the souls of men are made perfect — the life of Heaven.

So, when He appeared in His Resurrection Body to the heart-broken, grief-stricken Mary in the garden, where at first she mistook Him for the gardener, He bade her not 'to cling' to Him. This admonition does not require the ingenious explanation of some who maintain that Mary would have received some kind of shock if she had touched Him. It meant that she must not allow herself to be ensnared into believing that what was all-important was His (apparent) physical presence and this world of matter. She must learn to reach out *beyond* her sense perceptions.

In that farewell to His disciples when He accorded them the last manifestation of His Resurrection Body in the guise of matter, He promised He would not leave them on their own. From the vantage of the new creation, i.e. from Heaven, where all matter, space and time are transcended, He would bestow the powers of His Spirit to those who loved Him and who desired, because of that love, to continue to perform His will in the world. In His glorified state His influence could transcend the order of this world. Henceforth

He could be everywhere, and ever present, to all who believe in Him.

For those who follow Him, and keep faith with Him, there is the promise of the foretaste of the new creation while in this life. The only manner in which one can speak of this (since language is confined to the concepts of the sense perceptions) is to describe the union of Christ with those who love Him as a 'mystical' one. His Spirit is in communion with their own and influencing them to obey His Will. So the Scriptures present this spiritual experience as one in which believers are 'in Christ' and 'He in them'.

This mystical union fulfils itself by issuing into the present world in thoughts and deeds of goodness and truth, beauty and love. These then are the inspired outcome of a man's fellowship with the Spirit of Jesus or Holy Spirit. It is by such fruits that the Christian signifies his love for the Lord of Life. Moreover, this new type of life so distinct from that which constitutes the 'natural' and selfish life of man (which is not Christ-centred) bears within it reassuring glimpses here and now of the glory which shall be known transcendently and completely when the last experience of earthly life has been undergone.

That last experience, death, comes, then, then not as an enemy but as a friend. For the Christian has all along been preparing himself for it by a constant 'dying' to himself through the discipline of his natural appetites and by a willingness to relinquish his own life and desires for the service and well-being of others according to the pattern of Christ. The grave thus becomes the way through to the complete victory of the spirit-soul over the domination of the body-soul as the power of sin is finally broken. The Risen and Glorified Christ will shepherd him to the wonder of the new creation wherein his spirit-soul will be clothed with a 'new' body which will consummate his immortality in the life of Heaven.

9

THE SEANCE

The cult of Spiritualism believes that communication with the dead is achieved through certain peculiarly endowed persons called 'mediums'. At a meeting for this purpose (a seance) the medium enters a state of trance. Whilst the medium's body-soul is thus practically dormant a discarnate spirit (called a 'control') takes over the communicative powers of the medium and thereby, as it is believed, delivers to the seeker information from the world of departed spirits.

In this belief Spiritualism is certainly not modern for the literature of antiquity contains plenty of reference to the practice of necromancy, or conjuration of the dead.

The Bible mentions it with strong condemnation although, in all fairness, this disapproval appears to be less against the actual practice as against the idolatrous associations which had become attached to it. In the twenty-eighth chapter of the First Book of Samuel there is a classic example of a seance in the meeting of Saul, King of Israel, with the Witch of Endor. That encounter is most instructive and worth reflecting upon in detail. The Witch of Endor is described as a woman 'with a familiar spirit' (i.e. a 'control'). In other words she was a medium.

We should remember that Saul had publicly denounced the practice of conjuring the dead for the purpose of gaining occult information from them. He had actually promulgated a law to forbid it and had carried out a severe pogrom of its practitioners, driving 'those that had familiar spirits, and the wizards, out of the land'.

Clearly, however, he still had a secret hankering for the seance and its possibilities. Thus, in a time of deep personal anxiety over

A Priest and the Paranormal

the imminent invasion of his kingdom by the Philistines, he thought
he could obtain some advice by consulting a medium.

At that time the Witch of Endor was evidently a medium of
considerable reputation and so Saul went to her. As it would not
do for him to be known as breaking his own edict he came well
disguised.

Of one thing he was quite sure that if anyone knew the answer
to his military dilemma it would be the prophet Samuel. The latter
had been his great friend, a most highly esteemed counsellor —
the very man indeed who had obtained for him the kingship of
Israel.

But Samuel had recently died. However, Saul felt that the Witch
of Endor would be able to contact his departed friend and through
her mediumship obtain from him the answers he needed.

At first the Witch was afraid to comply. She reminded her
visitor that it would be dangerous for her to break the King's law,
forbidding seances. However, Saul manages to persuade her and
she enquires of him who he wishes to contact.

"Bring me up Samuel." he replies.
It is here we should note the Witch's exceptional telepathic power.
(And it is telepathy, I believe, which has such a strong part to play
in the work of mediums).

In trance this heightened extra-sensory faculty of hers is able to
penetrate Saul's disguise.

In trepidation, as she thus perceives his true identity, she cries out:
"Why hast thou deceived me for *thou* art Saul?"

The King immediately seeks to allay her fears, assuring her that
no harm will come to her if only she will exercise her ability to
conjure for him the departed Samuel.

Then she continues the seance and declares that she sees "a god
coming up out of the earth.'

In passing we may note that this apparition is not seen by
Saul himself for he has to ask her for a description of it. It is
evident, therefore, that her psychic awareness is not shared by her
client.

When she describes the form of the spirit which she has contacted
Saul knows it must be that of Samuel. In deepest reverence he
prostrates himself. But Saul finds that the message the departed
prophet gives is highly unsatisfactory from his point of view and
very discouraging.

190

In fact the departed Samuel is obviously very annoyed and utters the rebuke:

"Why has thou disquieted me by bringing me up?"

He then indicates that if, as Saul himself admits, the Lord had departed from him and refused to provide him with advice through dreams or the counsels of wise men, then he can expect nothing but disaster.

We may conclude that whereas there *may* come to us personal intimations from the unseen world of the spirit by means of our *own* psychic experience (which include dreams and visions) it is not fitting or profitable for us to *seek* them through mediums or by any occult practices, or even through prayers in which we importune God for them. Such intimations, if and when they come, are purely in the province of the Holy Spirit of God. Indeed it is often (as I have myself discovered, and have learned likewise from many others) that revelations concerning our departed loved ones only truly come to us when they are *unsought* and when our own hearts and minds are at peace, not restless, not anxious, not straining to pierce the present veil that hides them from us. All we need to bear in mind is that unceasing spiritual fellowship of love which binds us eternally to each other. We do not love our dear ones less if they go to live in some distant part of the earth where we are unlikely to meet them physically again. Likewise love abides when our beloved ones pass through death and are hid from our present sight.

Their love for us is now a transcendent love which needs not the physical but only the spiritual bond — a bond, indeed, which will know its full glory when we also have shed our earthly frames and thus can rejoice completely with them in a perfect union of the spirit.

Nowadays we have greater enlightenment upon the mysterious, often murky, realm of the subconscious mind. We also realise how highly suggestible our minds are. The pronounced psychic gift of a medium is that of telepathy. Thus the Witch of Endor perceived the true identity of her client and had rapport with his guilty conscience as he sought her help contrary to his own edict.

The Witch and King Saul were mutually wide open at the deep level of their subconscious mind to whatever pre-conceptions and thoughts they formed — the Witch with her hardly subdued fear of performing an illegal action and Saul who knew his own shameful duplicity.

Recognising the effect of this interplay of two disturbed minds during that seance we must come to the conclusion that 'the message' received would have been coloured by it.

We are well aware of how the content of a verbal message passed from one person to a series of others often becomes changed during its relay so that the final recipient may receive an inaccurate, sometimes even contrary, report. Now if that is true where conscious minds have been at work we can appreciate that where subconscious minds are concerned there can arise vague, jumbled, or half true messages which become even more adulterated when the conscious mind has to sort them out and try to interpret them through the filter of our reasoning process.

We should realise that in the condition of trance which mediums require for a seance that they can then telepathically pick up memories long forgotten but nevertheless still stored away in the client's subconscious mind waiting to be tapped. Nor should we ignore the possibility that the medium may acquire knowledge from the mind or minds of others not immediately involved in the seance. Moreover, the subconscious mind of the medium may also tend to colour and interpret information received. This is no wise imputes fraudulence on the part of the medium for, most likely, he or she cannot sift with *total* accuracy that information or know precisely from whence it comes.

I recall the only personal interview I have had with a medium who was a middle-aged woman of high reputation in her field. The seance had actually been arranged though a mutual friend of the medium and myself.

I was shown into a room where the daylight had been subdued by drawn curtains and the medium asked me to sit in an easy chair. She sat opposite me in a high-backed one beside a table. At one period she rested her forearms on the latter and bade me be as relaxed as possible. Actually I found that I could think of nothing very relevant. Vaguely I sensed that she was able to read my mind and so, for that very reason I suppose, I allowed my mind to become more or less blank. Even her opening questions did not elict from me much more than the briefest, and rather non-committal, replies.

Perhaps she thought I was unco-operative for she grew, I felt, a little impatient and asked me not to leave my mind so blank.

One or two statements came from her after this and she spoke of me having a brother who had died a while ago. At that moment I had indeed been remembering my brother because I half-wondered if she would be able to tell me something about him. Actually he had died about nine years before but she did not quote that figure and seemed to think his death was fairly recent. Possibly she could not receive telepathically this exact knowledge from me because I had not worked out the number of years for myself at that juncture. She did state (accurately) that my brother had been a Naval Officer who had served in the Second World War and that he had two children and that his widow was working very successfully and very hard to support them. She indicated that he was very happy in the life of the spirit world but no more than that. I could not help but think at the time that much of what she told me was being telepathically gathered from myself.

Indeed as the seance progressed I began to have a peculiar and increasing sense of having thought drawn up, as it were, from the very depths of my being and then being passed from me.

I have to add that though the medium spoke of my brother's happiness in the world of the spirit that statement gave me no special heart-warming. Whereas a psychical experience in which my wife and I saw my brother, who had died several years earlier, was a wonderful and much treasured blessing. It occurred one night in an old manor house close to the village church after we had been asleep for a few hours. He appeared to both of us, radiating happiness and reassurance, at the foot of the bed and seemed to be in his naval uniform because we could see the officer markings on his sleeve. This appearance certainly did not happen when I was reflecting upon him but when I was going through a very testing period of my life. It left a great and lasting impression and holding for both of us an intriguing psychic atmosphere.

After this, breathing very deeply, the medium really did enter a deep trance. At last she 'came through'. In a heavy masculine Scottish accent she announced that a departed doctor known to me was speaking.

His message was that I must take great care of my throat as I had a special weaknesss in that organ.

Now it is very true that as a child and into my early teens I repeatedly suffered with tonsilitis. Every cold I caught would seriously affect my throat causing the greatest discomfort and was so weakening that many days at school were lost.

Finally so bad did this repeated illness become that our family doctor announced in my presence that one more such bad throat and the removal of my tonsils must be considered.

This statement came as a great shock to me. The very thought of hospitals and operations, (although I knew absolutely nothing of either at that time) chilled me so much that I am sure it provided a psychological fright which somehow saved me from a repeat of serious throat trouble from that day on — and I still have my tonsils!

However, through the years that doctor's words have remained indelibly embedded in the back of my mind so that I still become somewhat anxious when I catch a cold as to whether it will affect my throat and therefore hinder my work. Prior to my sitting with the medium I had actually only just recovered from a cold which had resulted in a degree of hoarseness and so made the services in my Church rather painful to conduct. The throat problem was therefore still on my mind.

I surmise that she had telepathically received my thoughts in this matter. Nor can I help coming to the conclusion that she had also read from my subconscious mind the unhappy trauma occasioned by the doctor's ultimatum those many years ago. Perhaps this guess is all the more likely when it is remembered that the family physician at that time in my youth was a gruff-voiced Scot.

To sum up. I certainly do *not* close the door upon the possibility of messages being received by us from the departed. Indeed I would go further and say that because they are pure spirits their powers must far excel the mere delivery of messages. I have many dear friends who are convinced that their beloved dead have made themselves known at seances to them. Knowing them so well I cannot doubt them. Some are fully assured of the claims of Spiritualism while still remaining staunch churchgoers of their various denominations. I must also say that some of their individual cases appear strongly to support the view they take.

Nevertheless I have deep reservations about the propriety of asking the departed to afford us material proof, as it were, of their personal survival or of satisfying our curiosity about conditions in the spiritual world. Any ghostly appearances they may make to us must be for some very worthy reason in accordance with the holy Will of God and in order to advance His Kingdom in our own souls here on earth.

Their bliss is that of the spiritual realm, indescribable in our material terms, with its greater light of God. Their company is that of other good departed souls who understand as they do the spiritual world, and of the angels. How selfish of us, therefore, if we demand their attention for less than the highest purposes!

For my own part I have had experiences which have assured me of the continued love and interest of dear ones, both family and friends, who have entered the unseen world. But all these have been revelations entirely unsought by me. They have just 'happened' without any conscious or deliberate attempt on my part to communicate with the dead — or even to desire such communication. I must admit, however, that they have occurred at those moment in my life when I have been under a particular emotional stress or deeply concerned in some pastoral problem.

These experiences have not been in the nature of precise messages informing me of the state of dear ones in the next world but rather intimations from them of a continued loving and caring nature which have provided great comfort to me in my troubled condition.

At such times I have been aware of what I can only describe as their 'presence' in some transcendent, unexplainable way (though it is also true that I have had psychic experiences in which I have 'seen' loved ones). In the depth of my being I am made as sure of their intangible presence as I would be of any material reality which comes through the senses.

It is this very fact which has conveyed not only consolation and cheer but a veritable influx of new life because these experiences have given added assurance of the supreme powers of the spiritual realm and the knowledge that my burden is understood and also shared by it. It is only a by-product, as it were, that there issues from these experiences the knowledge that the departed loved ones are in a condition of blissful energy.

10

REVELATION OF THE BEYOND

Some may take issue with the previous chapter, protesting they are certain that messages from their beloved dead have come to them through mediums. Let me hasten to say, therefore, that I do not doubt mediums can, on occasions, contact the spirit world, though their communications often seem somewhat trivial. They *might* be from lying spirits masquerading mischievously as the departed loved one, or the information supplied *might* simply have been gained telepathically from the sitter.

It is noteworthy that mediums and those who consult them always assume that it must be some other person who is being contacted and not an interchange within their own souls. We should not overlook that none of us can distinguish completely what may rise up out of our subconscious mind. This does not impute fraudulence on the part of the mediums. The fact is that, however sincere, they cannot be *absolutely* certain of the source of every message received. They *can* be deceived. In the trance state the powers of a medium's spirit-soul begin to act. It should not, therefore, be surprising that clairvoyant knowledge may be vouchsafed because the soul of the medium is then working almost as pure spirit. The results may well appear remarkable but that does not require us to believe that departed souls have always provided them.

We should also remember that during public and private seances a great deal of emotion is usually generated. In consequence minds may be in a highly suggestible state, anxious to ensure that the seance shall be successful in gaining something which, on the face of it, will prove that contact has been made with the departed.

My own psychical experiences and those of many friends have

convinced me that rapport with souls beyond the veil of death does occur, but in every case these experiences were *unsought*. When they happened, unexpectedly, they were entirely natural, not 'spooky', alarming or distressing, but rather the reverse — comforting, uplifting, sublime, affording hope and reassurance (and never banal). They were really beyond the power of full description.

They are bestowed as a free and unmerited gift of God. The initiative is taken not by us but by our departed loved ones. They, not us, do the contacting. We might also ask ourselves whether, from our own knowledge of departed loved ones, they would be at ease in the peculiar surroundings of a public (or even private) meeting when imparting to us their messages of comfort and guidance.

Inevitably, if men believe in survival after death there will always be some among them who will seek communication with those who have died and will endeavour to chart the mysterious realm beyond the grave.

That exercise is only natural. One could argue that it is the rational, proper and adventurous response of human beings. After all we are endowed by God with inquisitiveness which in other spheres has advanced our frontiers of knowledge and thereby enhanced civilization. One should not condemn, therefore, those who are genuinely seeking to widen our spiritual understanding in this particular regard, nor erect unnecessary barriers against their research. Perhaps there could, in fact, be few more worthwhile activities than revealing to mankind the reality of life after death other than *only* by the eye of Christian faith. It might disperse the fears and forebodings (and often bizarre beliefs) which beset so many over the business of dying and about conditions in the immediate hereafter.

Therefore, I do not say that mediums *cannot* contact the spirit realm but that their communications must be of variable value. I would certainly say that mediums might well be helpful in the cure of hauntings by identifying the earthbound departed souls causing them.

Also I have no doubt that a good case can be made for some of the tenets of what is generally called Spiritualism. Most of them are covered by the Christian belief in the Communion of Saints and the Ministry of Angels. Certainly one should distinguish between the enlightened activity of Spiritualist Churches and that gross practice of spirit-raising condemned in the Old Testament, rife as it was with superstition as well as deceit.

197

Are we able then to urge what one might call a *Christian* Spiritualism? I believe we can because the New Testament itself provides an example of *'speaking with the dead'* during the life of Jesus Himself.

I refer to the Gospel record of His Transfiguration which, therefore, merits close study.

First, let us see what it did for the disciple, Peter.

In the Greek New Testament the word used for our Lord's Transfiguration is *metamorphosis*. Literally this means a change of form. But whereas in ancient legends concerning this phenomenon the change was usually from a human being into an animal (or some strange mixture of animals) in the case of Jesus it was a change in which His physical body apparently became radiant, luminous. Indeed it attained such brilliance that it dazzled the beholder.

In "The Mission and Message of Jesus" Dr H.D.A. Major classes those narratives of the New Testament which deal with the Baptism, the Temptation, the Transfiguration and the Resurrection fo Jesus, as being accounts of visionary experiences, i.e. of a psychical nature.

Perhaps then only Peter of the three disciples present actually enjoyed the vision of his Master's Transfiguration. Besides beholding Jesus assume a glorified appearance he sees Him talking to those two great personalities of the Old Testament — Moses and Elijah.

Then Peter experiences an overwhelming sense of the Presence of God. This is the meaning of the cloud which overshadows the group. The ancient people of Israel always used the symbol of a luminous cloud (the Shekinah) to express the Divine Presence. From the cloud (i.e. from God) the Divine Voice (the Bath-Qol) proclaims: "This is my beloved Son: hear ye Him."

A while before, at Caeasarea Philippi, Peter had declared his conviction that Jesus was the long awaited Messiah. Jesus meets this confession by telling his disciples that they must keep His Messiahship secret. They must tell no man of it. And he goes on to express to them what His Messiahship must involve. He must suffer many things, be repudiated and die an ignominious death.

Peter is utterly perplexed and deeply grieved by this pronouncement, which ran completely counter to the popular conception (which he shared) of the Messiah as being a glorious, all powerful and triumphant Being.

The notion that his beloved Jesus would meet the fate He had predicted was so alien and inconceivable that it incurred in him an agonising test of his faith in his Master. Through witnessing the Transfiguration Peter was reassured, however, that Jesus was after all the Messiah. The details of that visionary experience, culminating in the testimony of the Divine Voice, ratified his belief in our Lord. Now he could begin to reconcile the apparent anomaly that God's Anointed could be One Who should suffer in the manner that Jesus had declared.

A vision is the outcome of a psychical state which may be induced by the strain of a deep fear or anxiety. Though Peter had still a long way to go (and it was a way which was to include his denial of Jesus when He was arrested and brought to trial) before he could fully understand the implications of Messiahship, yet the Transfiguration gave him the immediate comfort he needed. Because of it he was enabled to surmount the intense anguish he had been enduring since His Master's shattering pronouncement.

The account of the Transfiguration, as given in St Luke's Gospel, affirms the myrtyrdom which Jesus will accomplish at Jerusalem. The subject of His conversation with the illustrious prophets, Moses and Elijah, is about this very fact. Such confirmation of the Messiah's destiny would be of immense spiritual consolation to Peter.

Temporarily at any rate Peter's mind was set at rest, therefore, by the transcendent testimony he had received through his vision of the Transfiguration. It was to be a spiritual experience he would hold dear forever.

We can observe in Peter's witness of the Transfiguration a parallel with the unsought and unexpected psychical experiences which occur sometimes in our own lives. These console our downcast spirit. They provide a mysterious inspiration which renews our hope and vitality so that our forebodings, questionings and anxieties are overcome, not by altering the facts of them or by immediately solving them, but by illumining us with a deeper meaning for our lives.

They enrich us with the certainty that we are not bearing our particular burden alone and that, despite our present temper, God is in control. Thus we are carried along — and through — our periods of trial and despondency.

Besides the help that the Transfiguration gave Peter concerning Messiahship it gave him insight into *his Master's relationship with those who had entered the unseen world.*.

The significant words in the Gospel narrative are:

"As He (Jesus) was praying, there talked with Him two men, which were Moses and Elijah, who appeared in glory."

It is clear, therefore, that Jesus was not praying *to* Moses and Elijah or seeking their aid. *He was not trying to make contact with them.* He was praying, as always, to His Heavenly Father for spiritual support. He had experienced the extremity of loneliness when, in trying to explain the meaning of Messiahship to His disciples they had obstinately remonstrated that it could not possibly involve His suffering, and certainly not His rejection by the world of men. How devasting for Him such a refusal to accept His insight must have been if those whom He had called to be His disciples could not, or would not, accept it. In contemplation of His own sense of loneliness He may have thought of how those great figures of the past, Moses and Elijah, had also endured spiritual dereliction and despondency. Moses had often protested that God had given him an impossible task to do in leading His people. Elijah had even sat down under the juniper tree and prayed God to take away his life for he could see nothing but darkness ahead.

Then, in the midst of His spiritual anguish, Jesus became aware that *He was actually being sustained by the company of those two illustrious spirits*. Moses and Elijah not only showed they completely understood His loneliness but predicted what lay ahead for Him. The Gospel says: "They spoke with Him of His death and departure which He should accomplish at Jerusalem."

We should note the significance of that word 'departure'. In the original Greek text it is *'exodos'*. This literally means 'the way out' or 'the way through'. It immediately reminds us of the Exodus i.e. the escape of the Children of Israel from their hard bondage in Egypt into the Promised Land. That great achievement in the history of God's people had been led by Moses.

So *while* Jesus was engaged in prayerful communion with God He is assured that, despite the present depressing appearance of things, He is not alone but in the heartening company of other great souls. Not only so but His mission is to be accomplished — the glorious one of leading His followers triumphantly *out of* death, which is revealed as the Exodus or 'the way through' to 'the Promised Land' (i.e. God's perfect and eternal Kingdom).

Hence if we would have a Christian Spiritualism it means that when we go simply, sincerely and trustingly, to our Heavenly Father in prayer we can be assured that we have the sustaining help of the spiritual world of departed faithful souls. In that supporting company, with Christ leading, we shall be taken all the way through this life on earth and also, at last, through death itself to our eternal home.

It is in complete confidence of this truth that we have our present peace and the sure promise of future fulfilment. We need no other (and ought to expect no other) assurance than this which is so amply confirmed by our Lord in His Transfiguration.

There is something more to be learned. Peter was so transported with joy by his witness of the Transfiguration that he desired it would never end. He suggested therefore that three tabernacles (wayside shrines) should be erected, one to Jesus, one to Moses and one to Elijah, in order to prolong the ecstasy of the experience.

But the vision passed and the next day his Master takes him and two other disciples down the mountain to the village below where immediately the pressing claims of this world are presented to them in the need of a sick boy to be healed. Thus Jesus taught the all important lesson that they could not expect to linger in the delight and transport of psychic revelation. That is also true for ourselves. However ecstatic our own special experience may be it is not meant to become our preoccupation so that we begin to exclude the reality and responsible claims of this world.

We could also note that the Transfiguration was witnessed because Peter's eyes were heavy but, nevertheless, he remained awake. In other words he had fallen into a state of trance whereby the extra-sensory perceptions of his spirit-soul were liberated, which enabled him to apprehend psychically the Transfiguration of his Master. The statement that he remained awake is no contradiction because those who experience psychic phenomena usually express the fact that during it they feel more alive and fulfilled than they have ever been in the ordinary wakeful state. It is the typical result of pure trance.

11

SOME THOUGHTS ON
THE AFTER LIFE

What life after death may be like is an absorbing topic. Particularly
for those who have realised in some deep spiritual experience that
death is a way through to another realm.

We may view rather cautiously, and even with incredulity, those
detailed descriptions of the hereafter which some sensitives have
provided and which emphasise a similarity of that life and its
conditions with those in this world. Yet to give them their due
they usually acknowledge that their insights are confined to life
immediately, or at any rate for not a distant future, after death. There
are certain clues which Jesus has given. All of them are concerned
with that same fact i.e. of life *immediately* following death, and in
essence they lend some support to 'materialistic' notions.

From the Cross He comforts the dying penitent thief who is
crucified at His side. The latter has recognised Jesus as one who
will assuredly pass through death to the glory of a very real and
special kingdom. To that man Christ declares "To-day (this very
day) you shall be with Me in Paradise."

Paradise is certainly a 'materialistic' word. It indicates a state
of bliss but it also evokes the idea of a garden and particularly of
the Garden of Eden where once man enjoyed a perfect relationship
with His Creator.

Now a garden intimates not only beauty but a condition of
constant growth. It certainly does not suggest something static but
that which is full of radiant life and peculiar energy.

The suggestion is, therefore, that *immediately* after death the
penitent thief would find himself in surroundings which would not

be so startlingly different as to be bewildering or off-putting to him but rather those which were in some measure both familiar and readily understandable, albeit of serene beauty and relaxing peace.

Clearly, after the awful physical agony and mental torment of his barbaric execution he would require above all else the balm of such tranquillity in order to adjust to his new sphere of life where the physical was finally set aside.

Moreover, he was assured that though, like all men, his passing through death would be an individual experience he would not in actual fact have to manage that strange journey alone. He recognised intuitively the purity and goodness of Christ's nature (so opposite to his own coarseness) as the tokens of a unique and exalted Kingship. It was that recognition which accorded him the company of Christ as He also passed through death to His Heavenly Kingdom. It is a recognition each of us must likewise make.

Now we know there was a 'resting' period for Christ of approximately three days from the time of His death on Good Friday afternoon until His Resurrection on Easter morning. In that period He, too, would have the spiritual recuperation of Paradise after the physical and spiritual testing of the cross.

Paradise, because it also refers us to when original man knew the true balance of body-soul and spirit-soul, speaks of another joy — the glorious ending of the body-soul's domination over the spirit-soul. That domination occurred when original man chose to follow his own will and not that of his Creator as expressed by the Fall when he was sent from the Garden of Eden.

That is to say those limitations which are the inheritance of man because of his physical nature will, when death comes, be done away. The soul will then be fully capable of its peculiar spiritual powers — extra-sensory ones which remain weak while it abides in this world because of the domination of the body-soul.

After death the soul can then acquire knowledge of what it wills to know, perfect communication with other souls if the latter are willing. Hence the interchange or communion of souls will have none of all those hazards known to us on earth, such as misjudgement, falsity, misapprehension, delusion or other deviation.

And the soul will know perfectly not only other souls but all the truth about its own self also.

Of course we should accept that the condition of life after death remains a mystery to us since it must be of a different order from our life on earth by the very reason that it no longer has the physical element of expression.

We use the words infinity and eternity to describe that purely spiritual life but what do those words mean?

It is wrong to think of infinity as unlimited space and eternity as unending time. Time and space are concepts we employ in our present life because of the confines of the material world and because we have bodies which are subject to change and decay. They are useful and sensible concepts for earthly life but they mean nothing for a wholly spiritual existence. The best we can say is that time and space take on a new meaning or are transcended in the spiritual realm. The terms 'eternity' and 'infinity' are intended to indicate that utterly mysterious change which death accords.

Our Christian faith, however, assures us that even here and now we have eternal life abiding in us. This is so because by faith attachment to the Spirit of Christ our spirit is in communion with His.

In some lives, now and then, a psychic experience may arise which provides a transcendental apprehension of the purely spiritual realm, but when it comes to describing it our language is always inadequate. Music, perhaps, above all the arts, can most satisfyingly indicate something of the beauty and the wonder such transporting experiences vouchsafe.

The Christian conceives life after death as but *another mode of living*, and recognises that Jesus had really conquered death before He met it on the Cross. This was so because His whole unique life had been a constant dying to self, a life given to God and perfectly dedicated to others, thus demonstrating that God's nature, in relationship to His human creation, is one of unselfish and ceaseless love.

We might allow ourselves to speculate upon what happens to some human souls which have passed through the experience of death. Having shed the flesh body they might still continue to have a strong desire for material existence. As death has left them with their purely spiritual nature they act as pure spirits, a condition which provides them with a thorough knowledge of matter. Through that knowledge maybe they achieve 'the compromise' of living within a *new system of matter* which is an unknown mutation of matter as we know it here (perhaps always unknowable to us in this present life).

This would provide a 'body' suitable for their existence. Maybe on another planet, where this rarer form of matter applies? On the other hand we might conjecture that for souls which have clung too hard and exclusively to the things of this world and whose relationships with others has been selfish and shallow will have formed a coarser mutation. To suit a grosser order of planet?

Some folk may doubtless make this their interpretation of our Lord's words in St John's Gospel: "In my Father's house there are many mansions (dwelling places)." If they do they should bear in mind that He goes on to say: "I go to prepare a place for you that where I am you may be also, and there may your joy be *complete.*"

Actually the 'many mansions' are properly understood to signify temporary resting places. We might compare them with the idea of the estaminets set up for soldiers in war time. There they would go for recuperation after the stress of a battle. So the many mansions picture could indicate spheres of temporary resting for the post mortem soul, perhaps differing according to its need. But more likely they should be thought of as representing ongoing stages prepared for it by God in the life of pure spirit.

The hope of the Christian is, of course, for perfect knowledge of God and to enjoy Him forever. That is the joy of Heaven. Then shall we fully comprehend that truth which Christ came to reveal to us — that the living God is the loving Father. In that glorious hope we can travel day by day in peace and confidence no matter what befalls.

We should also note the reply of Jesus to those inquiring about the Resurrection life. He made it clear that human relationships as we know them here would not exist in the heavenly realm but we would be as the angels, i.e. pure spirits with all which this suggests of full spiritual powers and perceptions;.

While the creative power of God is ever fashioning us physically from our conception to the end of our days through cellular changes, at the same time His creative power is continuously at work upon our growth in a spiritual sense i.e. forming character and personality through the many choices presented to us on earth and by the decisions we make regarding them.

Our human souls are created to work in and through our physical bodies. Each is necessary to the whole of our personality. That is why the Christian rejoices in the hope that his immortal soul will continue to indwell a body after death. Not indeed a body of earthly matter but one which transcends it and will be the proper vehicle for his consummation and perfect felicity.

Insight into this is provided by the Ascension of Jesus Christ. St Luke records the last appearance on earth of Christ's Resurrection Body and says that *then* He ascended into heaven.

Concerning the precise nature of Christ's disappearance at the Ascension we need not be involved here. Suffice it to say that by it an amazing truth had been revealed to mankind. Namely, that Christ had taken His perfect humanity into the purely spiritual realm. Those who witnessed the Ascension were convinced that in this extraordinary happening God was declaring that while hitherto the humanity of Jesus was, like their own, limited by matter, space and time, now it was transcending all those limitations.

Therefore those who had faith in Jesus Christ were also 'let in' on this wondrous transformation. Their own humanity would, in due course, likewise be taken up (ascend) into the purely spiritual realm wherein the physical is transcended. Thus Christians are assured that their souls will pass through death into the world of spirit not as shades or ghosts but to live positively in a new kind of body — a glorified body like unto their Master's.

And this amazing longed-for delight would come about because of their faith attachment to Jesus Who had inaugurated this new state for them.

Christ's Resurrection Body could only appear in one place at one time as in its various appearances to His disciples. Now His influence or Spirit (Holy Spirit) could be known for always and everywhere.

The full truth of this was realised by the disciples when they assembled in one place awaiting the Promise which Jesus had made at His Ascension ten days before, namely, that He would not leave them alone but would bequeath them His eternal Spirit.

That Promise was fulfilled on the first day of Pentecost (generally called Whit Sunday in the Church's calendar). On that day in a unique and powerful happening the disciples became imbued with Christ's Spirit. This fired them with courageous enthusiasm and driving energy to witness their joyful conviction of the lordship of Christ over all the world. They were to do so against all the hazards and dangers of a mainly hostile world even to martyrdom. So was the Church of Jesus Christ born and in the continuing power of Christ's Holy Spirit it maintains that witness of the first disciples.

The question is sometimes asked: "Will life after death be one worth living?" The Christian would say it depends upon the kind of life lived here on earth. Is it one in which love of God and love of neighbour figured?

Here Jesus' parable of the Good Samaritan portrays that quality of true life which He called eternal. It is found whenever we offer ourselves in loving service to others in their troubles even though they may sometimes be strangers or even enemies to us.

Death may raise the question of Heaven and Hell in the hereafter but it ought to be said that these are states of the mind and soul known in this present life also.

Hell is that condition wherein our souls feel the deepest loneliness and abandonment. The worst of such spiritual agony is shown in Jesus' cry of dereliction whilst dying on the cross: "My God why hast Thou forsaken me?" Then it was He experienced the cruellest torment of all in the sense of the temporary loss of God's presence.

Whenever we plumb the deepest depths of misery then we are 'in hell'. Nevertheless faith in Christ assures us that even there our Lord is with us, sharing our anguish and assuring us of ultimate victory over it.

Heaven is the very opposite of hell. Again it is a condition we can know on earth although only fully realised after death. It is the joy of happy conscience, of being at one with what we know is God's will for us, of being able to express our spiritual powers and so reach complete fulfilment.

Through the years many have told me of their own experiences wherein they receive intimations of the continuing life of their departed loved ones.

These gave them much consolation and unforgettable reassurance but were always unsought, which is as it should be.

Indeed it seems that this kind of revelation rarely, if ever, comes to people when they are beside themselves with grief or are purposely seeking some proof of their loved one's life in the unseen world.

On the contrary if this kind of perception arises at all it is when the mind is quiet and composed and there is no conscious desire for such experience.

Throughout the ages saints and seers have declared the efficacy of 'interior quiet' for acquiring the wisdom and revitalising life of God. They agree that such stillness is only achieved by overcoming worldly distractions and in surrendering the agony of personal tribulation and affliction.

In fact all must be set aside so that the restlessness of the soul may cease and its waiting upon God become the one and only desire. Then the 'power' which is in silence comes.

To become truly silent is certainly not easy. It takes practice and patience because for a good deal of this life we are prone to a confusion of fears, prejudices, imaginings, yearnings and half-processed thoughts as well as the cares and distractions of worldly things.

It is as if we carry around a mental boxing-ring in which a spiritual contest is nearly always going on to disturb our serenity.

But calm we must become if we are ever to apprehend spiritual reality. Jesus advised that we enter the 'inner chamber' in order to pray and bade us not to be anxious over anything. He meant that the secret room of our mind must be emptied of all distressing turmoil, all vain clutter, so that the great business of prayer could begin. Through the power of silence we rest in God and receive the manifold blessings of His Presence.

No wonder Whittier wrote:
"Breathe through the heats of our desire
Thy coolness and Thy balm;
Let sense be dumb, let flesh retire;
Speak through the earthquake, wind and fire,
O still small voice of calm!"

It is in the sublimity of that peace during which we reflect upon, and remember with love and gratitude, our departed dear ones, that we can rest completely assured of being spiritually united with them.

This is the highest communion of all for us to hold with those beyond death's veil. More important and enduring (because we can exercise it whenever we will) than any psychic manifestations which, in any case, many folk may never be vouchsafed.

It would be wrong to conclude this chapter without the observation that death cannot immediately change our character or personality. Five minutes after death we are the same persons in this respect.

12

HYPNOSIS

We realise that we are beings who are bound to our bodies and yet often have a desire to be free from them. Indeed this is something more than a mere desire. It is a kind of instinct which tells us that we are not really creatures who are completely fettered to our bodies.

So it is a natural urge to endeavour, at any rate at times, to escape from our immediate physical limitations.

The most common form this takes is the escapism of entertainment e.g. drama, poetry, music and all the arts. These diversions are harmless and can be stimulating and recuperative and often uplifting. But there are other means which may appear most immediate and positive such as drugs or hypnosis.

We must dismiss the use of drugs because they do not in fact achieve a worthwhile or genuine out-of-the-body experience. What they do provide is the unreality of hallucination due to the release of an entirely uncontrolled spirit-soul and, if persisted in, they cause an almost irretrievable deterioration of the health of the body. Drug addicts sink into a euphoria which disengages the subconscious to bring disorder and irrationality into their unfortunate lives.

Let us then consider hypnosiss. This is an artificial sleep which may be either self-induced or effected by another person.

SELF-INDUCED HYPNOSIS

By staring concentratedly at an object e.g. a crystal ball, candleflame, swinging pendulum or, if we are of a sufficiently poetic frame, at a flower or leaf, etc — indeed anything we care to choose so long as our attention is focused upon it, we can enter a condition of hypnotic trance. Some persons find this exercise easier than others do and some may give up the attempt through sheer boredom. Some find they attain trance through the dulling effect of soporific music or a steady rhythmic drum beat.

However, the drawback and limitation of this kind of trance is that it tends to leave the mind empty. Although it may release our extra-sensory perceptions these are liable, therefore, to be uncontrolled. They can give no real benefit apart, perhaps, for a degree of tranquillity in some persons (but not in all). Moreover, there is a strong likelihood of drawing upon untoward suggestions from the subconscious which can upset any such serenity. There is also the possibility of influence coming from a lower realm of the spiritual world i.e. from mischievous entities.

In this latter case we can include the distressing results which, in all too many instances, accompany the use of ouija boards. These I have examined elsewhere in this book.

There are areas where self-induced hypnosis can perform a useful purpose. Such include those of hylomancy (or psychometry) and divination.

In the former a person enters into trance while holding an object of which he has no prior foreknowledge. The object serves to tie his trance to this world and, as the spirit-soul is released from the domination of the body-soul, extra-sensory perception operates providing the practitioner with information concerning the possessor (who may be living or dead) of the object and the significance it has, or had, for him or her. A dear friend, now dead, was singularly gifted in this and able to make most interesting and, as far as we could discover, accurate readings of the owners and origins of various objects, such as brooches, watches, etc, which we gave him to handle.

In divination the diviner may employ a hazel rod, pendulum, or similar to tell where water or mineral deposits exist under ground. In this case the rod acts as the material object which holds the trance state rooted to this world so that extra-sensory perception informs the diviner of the knowledge he wishes to acquire. It follows that, for the more advanced adepts of this practice, the rod can be dispensed with and the necessary concentration for trance made simply through the outstretched hands.

The author himself, though not greatly skilled because of lack of practice (but even more because of disinterest!) has experimented in this field in a minor way and felt the bending of the forked hazel twig to indicate the running water of an underground stream in his garden. The sensation is as if some magnetic force is straining the twig downwards. But this reaction did not appear to him to be produced mechanically or automatically. It required a good deal of concentration and a very positive wish to discover water before he had any success. One must suppose that experts in both hylomancy and divination achieve results only after long practice, so that while their manner may give the impression that there is no great concentration required of them and that they simply exercise some special gift which they have developed the reverse is actually true. The state of trance must always demand some measure of concentration even for the most psychically gifted.

It is important to realise that when the spirit-soul obtains partial freedom from the body-soul through normal sleep or through the artificial sleep of trance it is liable to produce phenomena which can be unpredictable and arbitrary and often give rise to great confusion. Of course this is not generally so for healthy people who sleep normally. Yet even for them there can occasionally arise disturbing and exhausting nightmares — usually caused by over-indulgence or by prolonged worry about some personal problem.

In the case of highly nervous individuals sleep may never bring the healing and refreshment which it should. Recourse therefore is made to pills to promote relaxation and deep sleep. Potions can bring this about but equally they may not give genuinely restful sleep because the agitation of such persons had, in the course of time, penetrated to the deepest level of the subconscious. There, though the upper activity of the brain is stilled, the neurosis continues to work busily throughout unconsciousness.

HYPNOSIS BY ANOTHER PERSON

Of course if we place ourselves in the hands of a practitioner of hypnosis we shall have our wills guided and controlled by him. Thereby hypnotherapy has its healing power which is especially effective in psychosomatic illnesses and sometimes of purely physical complaints as well.

What occurs is that the will, being directed by positive and healing suggestions, releases the healing faculties of the spirit-soul which then affect the body-soul for its restoration.

In our normal wakeful state the material impressions we gain from the world around us are conveyed to the brain where, by means of the soul, our sense perceptions are appropriately released. When we are hypnotised this procedure is reversed. What happens is that the hypnotist suggests a certain impression which then governs the particular sense perception. Thus a hypnotised person can have his senses so played upon that he can experience heat for cold and vice versa; he can believe a rose smells like an onion, etc. In other words by the suggestions made to him his sense perceptions can be regulated and ordered or purposely misdirected. Under hypnosis it is therefore possible to have the subject's sense perceptions reduced to the point where there are no physical reactions to pain or, on the other hand, so abnormally heightening them that there is hypersensitivity. Thus a person can be operated upon without the need of an anaesthetic or, conversely, react most painfully to the slightest pinprick.

What we observe in this type of hypnotic trance is that the subject remains in touch with the material world. He is not transported to some mystical state which lifts him out of the physical realm altogether. Whatever guidance he is given either mentally or physically still anchors him to this world and the sense perceptions remain operating even though these are manipulated or deviated.

What takes place between the hypnotist and the hypnotised is that the latter has his spirit-soul freed from the natural domination of his body-soul and therefore the extra-sensory faculties of the spirit-soul may operate. The will, however, of the hypnotised person is at the behest of the hypnotist who can dictate its intention. In consequence a moral objection to hypnotism can be levelled since it is possible (despite popular opinion) for the hypnotised to be made to perform acts which are contrary to his character. Theologically we accept that God Himself does not force His will upon His human creatures but respects their free-will as essential to His love for them and of their freely given reciprocal response to that love.

Moreover, in every human being sin resides which means that the practitioner of hypnosis (however well meaning, learned and responsible) has introduced the frailty of human ignorance in his direct dealings thus with another human soul.

It can be argued, of course, that the general good achieved by the hypnotherapist should be taken into account and balanced against the infringement made upon the free-will of his patient. Nevertheless the point needs to be made that herein man is doing, even with the best motives, what is contrary to God's own nature i.e. the usurpation of the human will. God achieves His purpose only through the persuasion of His divine love as is completely manifested in the person of Jesus Christ. There is in Him no element of force, no dictation, no question of "because this is good for you, therefore I am doing it".

So we come to the question: "If hypnosis has valuable properties can we place it in a Christian context?" The simple answer is "Yes" — because hypnotic trance is allied to the experience of deep and sustained prayer. Freud was right in believing that hypnosis is a mystical condition although he was unable to explain it.

It would seem right, therefore, that the hypnotist should realise the mystical element in his work and consequently seek the control of the Spirit of Jesus in what he is doing. Thereby the danger of sin is eliminated because "in Christ" there is no sin, its power over human creation has been broken.

We will, therefore, consider mysticism in the next chapter.

I give the following simple personal illustration of how involuntary self-hypnosis may provide a degree of extra-sensory perception.

After a rather gruelling morning and early afternoon which made me feel very fatigued I came home and asked my wife to telephone my secretary for some information. The latter's housekeeper answered the call and said "could it wait" because they were about to watch the Derby race on television. Neither my wife nor I have much interest in these matters and, indeed, did not realise it was Derby Day.

As we understood from the housekeeper that the Queen's horse was running my wife suggested that for a little fun, even at this eleventh hour, we might place a bet upon it at the nearby betting shop. Feeling so tired I said that I could not be bothered, adding that I was not conversant with the procedure in such premises.

However, we turned on the television to watch the race. After a few minutes my eyes became heavy and I had difficulty in remaining awake. The commentator was speaking about the various horses and mentioned the Queen's horse. Quite suddenly the picture on the screen seemed to me to blot out and and in its place I saw what looked like the banner headline of a newspaper. I could not decipher this clearly but said to my wife I knew that the favourite would not win the race. Then the headline became clear: "Troy wins!"

A Priest and the Paranormal

"Dorothy, I have just had a premonition" I said "The winner will be Troy in any case"

"If you are so certain" she replied "why not go now and place a bet on it?"

"I'm all in" I said, "and it's probably too late now to do so."

Then I hesitated because the headline had faded. "I'm not sure" I went on "if it is Troy ... but, (and suddenly the headline came back and was even clearer this time), oh yes, now I see it again. It *is* Troy. *Troy wins.*"

Shortly after this the race was run and Troy came in first. What I must say is that I had not paid the slightest attention to newspaper comments as I have no interest in racing. The first mention of the name Troy was when I heard the horse listed on the TV screen that afternoon.

I believe what had happened was that my fatigue had incurred in me a partial state of trance causing the liberation of my spirit-soul which was then able to exercise a clairvoyant faculty and thus apprehend some way into the near future. The headline I had 'seen' was probably the one to be printed in the evening paper later.

Note

To divine subterranean water and minerals is not really a spiritual or occult practice but a physical one for the following reason.

Various elements in the earth produce a constant radiation which passes upward into the air above. These rays are actually essential to the health of all living organisms. But certain deposits (such as water, oil, coal, metals) being good conductors, divert their path and prevent them from travelling directly upward.

Consequently in those areas which thus lack those rays life is seriously affected, causing vegetation to be sparse and impairing the health of creatures, including humans, who would live there.

When the diviner walks over such barren regions his nervous system is sensitive to the absence of those important rays and in consequence his body is peculiarly agitated. The divining rod or pendulum he carries emphasises this reaction in his hands and thus indicates the presence of water and minerals below ground.

Hence divination is really a mechanical matter in the first instance. Unfortunately if it be much practiced the diviner will inevitably become prone to entering a trance condition because of the great concentration required.

For those, therefore, who strongly develop the art and spend many hours at it there is the danger of becoming so absorbed in the activity that their ordinary consciousness is largely set aside. They live more and more on the level of the subconsciouss. Because such extremists in divination are in trance they will be able to exercise their spirit-soul activities for a variety of other uses e.g. diagnosing disease, solving complex mathematic problems, finding hidden treasure and lost people, and even tracing criminals. This is usually done by suspending a pendulum above the human body or over a map of the area concerned.

Again there is the warning that excessive and protracted concentration on achieving this type of mysticism will debilitate the body and adversely affect the mind.

13

MYSTICISM

The mystical experience of the soul is contained in 'possession' (which is its communication with the Devil), in hypnosis (its communication with the hypnotist) and in religion (its communication with God).

In all these states the soul is partially freed from the body because it is the sense perceptions which inhibit the communion of spirit with spirit.

Eastern religions believe that the happiness of the soul comes when it is released from the body. Christianity, however, is concerned with the *whole* person achieving perfection i.e. spirit-soul and body-soul functioning in harmony as one individual soul.

Because religions other than the Christian one are preoccupied with the experience of the spirit-soul when it has been disencumbered of the senses they remain satisfied with the peculiar ecstasy which this exercise affords.

Their devotees are lifted into a suprasensory world whence may come visions of transcendent quality. But the result of these is to nurture the soul away from the plight of the material world and encourage no dealings with it. Life in this world and the senses generally is deemed to be an existence of endless suffering from which it is best to escape into the haven of these 'out-of-the-body' experiences. Such religions, therefore, do not encourage social activity and see no virtue in any endeavours to improve the material lot of mankind. The ecstatic experience is for them the goal and through it the soul's absorption, as it is thus conceived, into the God-head or Divine Essence.

The means to attain this mystical union is by trance attained through a monotonous recitation of prayers, special breathing exer-

cises and postures, often also by mortification of the body and even
in some cases by the use of drugs. In passing it should be noted
that the breathing exercises may restrict the supply of oxygen to
the brain and therefore produce hallucinations (even as drugs do)
which are often mistaken for genuine visions.

Such religions with their promise of ecstasy hold a fascination
for many Western folk in our time and the 'gurus' who expound
them are eagerly heard. However, such converts generally discover
that their exploration of Eastern religions (or a hotch-potch of
them sometimes mingled with snatches of European philosophies)
does not long avail. This is partly because the native temperament,
climate and long centuries of life style of lands such as India are
dissimilar to those of the West, but mainly because all these cults
have one great flaw: they seek experience of the spirit-soul by the
utter denial of the body-soul.

Only Christianity offers the complete mystic path to God in which
the totality of the soul shall achieve perfection i.e. spirit-soul *and*
body-soul in harmony as the true undivided soul. Only Christ of
all the Revealers of Spiritual Truth has, through His Life, Death,
Resurrection, Ascension and Gift of His Spirit, restored to humanity
full union with God. That union Christ has shown to be one of
love wherein man is always cared for by God in the completeness
of his personality: i.e. body, mind and spirit.

It is important, therefore, to consider Christian mysticism in
some detail. One of its greatest exponents, St John of the Cross,
said:

"The Father uttered one word. That word is His Son, and He
utters it forever in everlasting silence, and in silence the soul has
to hear it."

This is the key to the mystic path, for it is always in the strange
power of silence that the soul begins its journey towards God.
Only when truly tranquil within ourselves can we give undivided
attention to this great work of hearing what God has to disclose
to us in the Person of His Unique Son, Jesus Christ. Then do we
have communion with our Creator.

Prayer made in the Name (i.e. in the Spirit) of Jesus Christ
achieves that communion and has, as it were, steps in its upward
progress.

It begins, as already said, with a period of stillness and inner quiet
during which recollection is made of the awesome enterprise upon

which the soul is embarking All earthly concerns which distract full attention to this single purpose are resolutely set aside. Gradually this concentration brings an absorption into the abstractions of that piece of Christian truth upon which the mind of the mystic has proposed to dwell. (The sayings of Jesus in St John's Gospel provide mystics with much fruit for meditation).

Thus the mystic is drawn away from consciousness of the material world and of his or her physical body. When withdrawal of the senses is complete the mystical experience has begun. The spirit-soul is released from the domination of the body-soul which then becomes quiescent.

God and the spirit-soul are now approaching. The latter is more and more attracted to union with God.

It is at this stage that the mystic suffers the 'dark night' as it has been called. This is the agony caused by the soul's realisation of a gulf which separates it from union with the All Holy God — a gulf caused by recognising its own imperfection or sin.

It is the agony of the lover crying out to know the Beloved more perfectly but aware that his fallen nature must keep him from the joy of that union.

Endeavouring to counter this anguish the mystic resolves to deepen personal discipleship with Christ and to overcome any besetting sins. (As there is now a state of trance these determinations to live a holier life act upon the will in a similar manner to thoughts injected under hypnosis so that after emerging from the mystical experience a purer manner of life is in fact followed for the soul has been refreshed by the Spirit of Christ).

Notwithstanding its high intention the soul remains inconsolable over the universal impediment of sin until its travail of being 'locked out' is at last ended by the glorious comprehension of the Gospel truth that Jesus Christ has overcome the power of sin.

This doctrine, previously accepted by faith, is now comprehended not just intellectually or emotionally but as a very real fact, sublimely beautiful, supremely true. It is as if the soul has actually absorbed the very essence of the mystery of Christ's Death and Passion with complete spiritual insight and overwhelming illumination.

The transport which the soul then experiences as the barrier of sin crumbles away may produce ecstasies in which the sense perceptions have no part for they have ceased to operate.

Consequently, as St Augustine has described, in such a condition the mystic "will see nothing although his eyes may be open nor will he hear the voices of those around. The soul is more withdrawn from the bodily sense than it is in sleep, but to a lesser degree than in death." With body and soul thus rent apart the body can become rigid and may even be levitated as the soul is raised above all earthly concerns. Various other bodily changes may also take place, e.g. in the pulse rate and the temperature.

In this ecstatic condition which is really one of profound trance there may occur visions and voices, clairvoyance, prophecy, indeed the whole range of extra-sensory perceptions.

This state of the spirit-soul's liberation from the body-soul is regarded by the mystics of religions other than Christianity as the ultimate goal of the mystic way. By shedding the trammels of the body and thus escaping from suffering (believed to be the world's curse) the mystic considers he has been temporarily absorbed into the Divine Essence. After this the soul returns downwards, as it were, to the earth plane and back into the body. It is accepted that only at death can the soul be lost finally in the Divine Essence. These earthly transports meantime are the promise of that goal.

But for the Christian mystic this ecstatic state is counted as of little or no value. The soul is not content and knows that it must go on seeking God. It perceives with awesome clarity that the body *cannot* be left outside union with God because it is an inseparable element of the personality, containing the special experience of this physical world in which God has placed it.

This second dark night is, therefore, the agony of the soul realising that flesh and blood cannot inherit the Kingdom of God.

Something, therefore, must be effected in the body itself which will provide the way to transcend this physical barrier with its last great enemy, death, which together with the other inheritance of matter i.e. fatigue, suffering, decay, etc. bind our physical bodies.

The first dark night ended with the revelation of Christ having overcome sin. The second dark night ends with the glorious knowledge that He has also conquered death by the unique power of His Resurrection.

Once again what Christ has effected for mankind is perceived in a sublime mystical experience which grants absolute proof of what has hitherto been the soul's acceptance by faith alone.

The mystic's goal, therefore, is the soul's abandonment in love to the Spirit of Christ for what He has done for mankind. Thus united with the Son the soul is brought into a communion with God like that of Christ's with the Father. The mystical union with Jesus has thereby transformed the soul and because of that transformation it is granted knowledge of the 'new creation' wherein matter totally serves the spirit. Such perfection of the mystic way is attained only by the great and dedicated masters of it who are inspired by their consuming faith in Christ and their burning love of Him.

St John of the Cross describes it as 'spiritual marriage'. In this state the mystic can perform the ordinary tasks of this life and, at the same time, have sublime communion with God.

It is an exercise of the total soul — body-soul and spirit-soul in true harmony — which is only interrupted by the unconsciousness of sleep.

Hence the blessed experience of the Christian mystic bears testimony to the truth upon which Christianity is built i.e. that through faith in Christ (which means accepting that He has revealed the truth about God's relationship with us) we partake of His own eternal and perfect nature.

We realise that because of what our Lord Jesus Christ has done for us death does not rob us of 'our body' so that we exist in the hereafter only as immortal spirit but that we shall be clothed, through God's wondrous and mysterious working, with a new kind of body (born, as it were, of our spiritual and physical experience on earth) like unto Christ's glorious body through which our personality shall be fulfilled in the life of Heaven.

During earthly life every believer has the promise, and maybe at times, the foretaste, of that new creation. After death he will know it as eternal reality. Among those foretastes can be included certain psychic experiences which indicate the potential of the soul when it transcends the senses.

We can note that the mentally disturbed often become morbidly conscious of sin. So do drug addicts in some of their experiences. This is because the spirit-soul has been separated from the rationality of the body-soul. There is in both cases an inability, it seems, to accept that God offers His forgiveness and redeeming love to them.

The mystics, too, as has been already observed, perceive the flaw of sin to an exceptional degree but their spiritual experience of its conquest by Christ elevates their natural lives, serving as an inspiration for them to live effectively and tranquilly.

The spiritual experiences of the schizophrenic or the drug addict have no such beneficial outcome. They seem only to remove from them more and more the ability to live normally. Their lives are often clouded with depression when the experience ends. Rational attitudes become seriously eroded in this false kind of mysticism.

Those who have close contact with the drug-addicted will know how fascinating some of their tales of heightened perception can be. Indeed these are often touched with an exquisite appreciation of beauty. However, the result is always the same. After the experience there follows further enfeeblement of the will and of the reasoning faculties.

There ensues an increasing desire for more drugs which will take them out of what now constitutes the pain of ordinary life onto the plane of a spiritual existence which is really hallucinatory.

Eventually every material thing, even food, is repulsive to them in contrast with that which is presented to them by the world beyond the senses. The end can only be that their bodies become emaciated and their minds damaged.

Suicide may often be the only way out if the supply of drugs ceases or becomes more difficult to purchase. Premature death is likely to occur because of the ravages of the drugs upon the constitution or there may often be accidental overdoses taken. Unless a cure can be effected early the prospect is bleak indeed.

14

A SPECULATION

If we accept that spiritual beings other than ourselves do exist we may come to conclusions such as these:-

(1) Believe that on other planets in this amazing universe finite beings live. Maybe they, too, have bodies of matter — though of what kind we might not comprehend since it could be of a nature totally foreign to us. Perhaps it would be impossible for us ever to know while we are in our present space/time/matter environment with its limited spheres of understanding.

(2) That beings of purely spiritual nature evolved at some stage in creation and that from one strand of them our own human stock arose.
It could then be likely that those pure spirits would still be ready to influence us because they recognise their degree of common spirituality with us.

They would be to us, who gather information through our five senses which require matter to stimulate them, unseen and mainly unapprehended. Nevertheless, by perceptive powers which transcend the senses (our sub-angelic, extra-sensory ones) we may sometimes, however feebly, acquire an inkling of their presence and of their concern for us.

This is a theory which many would say is no theory to them but a positive acceptance reinforced by the psychic phenomena they have experienced. Of course the long history of religious experience states this belief in what the Church describes as the Ministry of Angels.

(3) It is a reasonable assumption that after the transformation which death brings to them some human souls may continue to have influence upon our present lives. This, of course, is widely accepted and is agreeable to the teaching of the Christian Church which speaks of 'one Church above, beneath'. This is the Communion of Saints i.e. the eternal and unbroken fellowship of all who have endeavoured to become true children of God through their desire to be filled with the Spirit of Jesus.

(4) As God is One and He is Love there must exist where His will is obeyed a single, reciprocal, interpenetrating power (His Holy Spirit) which energises all His created beings, thereby containing them in a condition of benign influence upon each other and constituting that perfect harmony we call the Kingdom of God, i.e. where God reigns completely. Conversely, we have to recognise that our freedom of will means we can love the Divine Will or spurn it, accept it or defy it.

This must mean evil influence can be energised not only by man but by spiritual beings who we call demons or devils. All the spirits, even as we do, possess the power of will so that they can choose to obey God or to disobey Him.

Hence the devils are virtually at war with the angels. That war is assured of ultimate vanquishment of evil by good as signified and foreshadowed by Christ's victory over sin and death.

If we believe in the unity of God as a principle of His nature we must believe that His creation is a universe and not a multiverse.

It follows that the Divine Will is for *all* created things to have a right relationship with each other. The fact that complete communication and harmony do not prevail among human beings is the grievous result of their contra-desire to the Will of God. That contra-desire is called 'sin'. It indicates the 'fallen' state pictorially presented in the Bible's Book of Genesis by the story of Adam and Eve whose decision to be as gods in their earthly domain meant denying their Creator's sovereignty over all. As a consequence they were cast out of Eden. In other words their hitherto perfect communion with God had been shattered by their own wayward will. Because they had chosen the order of matter above that of spirit they and their descendants (ourselves) must abide with the limitations of matter, the order of which, as we know, is change, suffering, decay and death.

15

THE NATURE OF ANGELS

We are limited because we are subject to the properties of matter. If we are tired, sick, hungry, suffer extremes of heat or cold, we know we lose the capacity to exert all our powers. If many demands are made upon us most of us know that we can only deal properly with one of them at a time. Any profound knowledge we acquire has to come through sustained and concentrated effort, which often means we must exclude from our attention other fields of study.

This dominance of the body-soul cannot be better illustrated than when we are wracked with severe physical pain. Then it is that our one desire is to have relief from it. Little else, if anything, can hold our attention.

We are unable to bring immediately to mind all we have learned over the years or clearly recall all our memories. However, in the trance condition induced by hypnosis the subconscious mind, which stores up all this acquired knowledge as well as every incident in our lives, can be made to convey some of them up to our conscious mind. Likewise in that trance state our senses can be manipulated. Such facts indicate our cousinship, as it were, with the pure spirits.

The angels do not have our human frailty because as pure spirits they are not subject to the inhibiting properties of matter. They do not know fatigue or sickness. They are not forgetful and can turn their intelligence to whatever they wish so that no field of knowledge is beyond them and all of it is instantly and completely understood. Hence, if they so desire, they know not only the spiritual realm but all about the material one as well — possibly through their communion with us.

But although their knowledge is so boundless there is an area which remains beyond their ken. This is the one which depends upon our use of God-given free-will when making the choices which shape our courses. The angels cannot know which way a human soul will decide to go during its earthly existence. Indeed they observe the principle of free-will (which is theirs also) and will not influence another spirit unless the latter freely and willingly desires it.

Therefore, although angels can immediately pass their thoughts to other spirits they can only do this if those others wish to receive them.

Likewise with ourselves who are also spirits, albeit of a lesser order. The angels can communicate with us if they will, but only as we desire this of them and are ready and willing to give them our attention.

So the assistance which the angelic world can afford us is circumscribed by our own attitude towards it. If we refuse to accept that it has any possible bearing on our lives or deny the very existence of it then clearly the angels cannot influence us. If we turn our backs to them they cannot and will not force their protection, guidance or superior wisdom upon us.

In the matter of their guardianship of us we must realise that they have, as already said, a full understanding of matter and so they have the power to control it and even to transform it. By their ability to effect changes in matter it is possible for them to afford us safety in time of danger and succour in illness, albeit always according to the will of God whom they constantly and freely obey. And God, in His infinite wisdom and love orders everything for our ultimate good, even our mistakes, in a manner which passes understanding for He alone knows all there is to know.

As free spirits we have, of course, our own thoughts which prompt our relationships with our fellows for their good or otherwise. Since the pure spirits include evil angels (or devils) as well as good ones and all have similar powers, it follows that we can receive some thoughts from these pure spirits (according to the tendencies of our personality) which may issue in either good or evil as the case may be.

On the one hand the angels can assist us in acquiring richer understanding and increased joy of spirit granting us moments of true revelation and inspiration by acting upon us through the mighty working of our imagination.

They may communicate with us in our dreams when we have committed ourselves to the peace of God and emptied ourselves of ill-will prior to sleep. They may also come to us during earnest prayer. For at such times our spirit-soul is almost body free and we are most like unto pure spirits.

On the other hand the devils may insinuate their destructive notions in the same manner if we sleep with hearts filled with malice and unforgiveness or when we surrender our daily thoughts to resentment and intemperate desires.

It must be remembered that if our minds dwell deeply and prolongedly upon any particular subject whether good or bad such concentration produces a condition wherein our spirit-soul becomes free to act as almost pure spirit.

It follows that then we are more than ever open to the influence of angels or devils.

It is through the creative power of our imagination that God and His angels, and the Devil and his angels come to us. Imagination is the channel for all spiritual communication. The power of the pure spirits to affect our character — according as we permit or encourage them by our desires — is no mean power. It can heal or it can wound. It can make for love or for hate, for good or for evil, for illumination or for continued ignorance, for fuller life or for destructive debasement.

By the cultivation of our general attitudes and interests we receive the added blessing of the Angels of Light over whom Jesus Christ is Lord or the mischief and desolation of the Demons of Darkness over whom Satan still rules although his ultimate power is broken by Christ's victory over him.

It is a choice we can consciously make by believing in the reality of the spiritual world. Day by day that is a momentous choice for us.

We have, of course, our own thoughts which prompt our behaviour with our fellows for their good or otherwise. Since the pure spirits include evil angels or devils as well as good ones — and all have similar powers — it follows that we can receive some thoughts from them which are good or evil as the case may be.

The angels progress from the complete knowledge of themselves to that of other spirits. Through that completed knowledge of spirit they reach their sublime knowledge of God who is Spirit and the Creator of all spirits.

As humans our path to God is different. Only through our experience of matter are we able to gather some notion of spiritual reality. The vehicle of matter which colours our thoughts (be they philosophic, scientific, artistic or religious) is the one by which, whilst we are on earth, we arrive at some comprehension of the nature of God. Hence for the Christian the potency of the Sacraments of the Church which actually convey spiritual reality under the cover of bread and wine and water, as likewise do her prayers and liturgical worship. All spiritual abstractions must be expressed in words which in turn relate to our material world.

Now although our understanding of spiritual reality (which must include our knowledge of God) is limited by reason of our physical make-up there does come to some ardent souls a recognition and revelation of God which is virtually angelic. They acquire it through the mystical experience — something considered in greater detail in another chapter.

16

THE ANGELS AND OURSELVES

At one time the Church believed that our first ancestors existed in a paradisal state, i.e. in perfect harmony with the Creator. Literal proof of this was regarded as having been given in the Bible story of Adam and Eve in the Garden of Eden.

Today that story is assumed to be pure parable, invented by the ancients to explain the origin of sin and the existence of free-will. Hence modern theologians do not maintain that it was a wrong choice made by our remote forbears which led to their 'fall' from an original state of perfection and that, in consequence, the succeeding generations have been affected by 'sin' due to that Fall. Instead they hold that humanity has always had an innate yearning for perfection implanted in it by God which it has never yet known how to attain in reality.

Having had an early scientific training I find this latter interpretation personally satisfying, but can the possibility of Paradise in pre-history be definitely ruled out? It is significant that ancient civilizations, which do not appear to have had contact with each other, have legends about a perfection which prevailed in our earliest ancestors and their world.

Despite imaginative embellishment by historic man the basic concept in these tales of a condition in which matter was entirely subservient to the spirit could be true. In such cases we can postulate angelic precursors of ourselves who left their impress on our folk consciousness, and that this early race of beings fulfilled perfectly the will of the Creator.

We may further speculate that eventually the realm of matter became too oppressive for some of them to wish to continue within it. Maybe they were fearful of losing their purity as spirit. In consequence these perfect archetypes of mankind vacated the material realm and left no trace (save a faint memory in the human race). Dominating matter, they are not subject like ourselves to its properties.

Perhaps there was a mechanical upset in creation (for example a 'collision of worlds') which caused some part of the universe to begin again, including this planet. Then new life came to it which required the long toil of the evolutionary process to produce the present continuing creation. And this life contained the defect of sin. That is, it was now under the domination of the properties of matter.

It is natural to ask where might those angelic creatures be now? Most likely, I believe, they inhabit an unseen, eternal, and wholly spiritual realm which has a mysterious and intimate relationship with our visible, impermanent and material world. Some therefore, may act as 'guardian' angels who have a caring influence upon our lives through communication with us at the level of our spirit-soul.

I have often heard the dying speak of seeing not only their departed loved ones at their side but also strange 'beautiful people' who appear to be greeting and comforting them. Even unreligious souls have revealed this to me on their death-beds. Since the spirit-soul is near its complete liberation as death approaches, it is reasonable to assume that its awareness, by extra-sensory perception, of the presence of guardian angels would be especially acute at that time.

Some angels may dwell on other planets where they continue their dominion over an order of matter less oppressive in its properties than our own. In such case it would not be too fanciful to suppose that at some stage in our history angels may visit this earth for a signal purpose. Doubtless that would be to herald the winding-up of the creative process as we know it. This would be the prelude to something mysterious and entirely different replacing it or, more correctly, transforming it.

In that case the prophetic vision of Christianity which perceives a 'Second Coming' of Christ in glory with His angels could be literally fulfilled, even though the spiritualised interpretation of this event is certainly true, namely, that He has already come the 'second' time by bequeathing His Spirit to those who believe in Him and love Him.

The end of the world should not be conceived as a cataclysmic oblivion but as a consummation of the creative process. We must envisage a transformation whereby the present domination of matter, space and time will be changed into an order in which the spirit will be entirely freed of that domination and will be in perfect and eternal control.

It may be fruitful when hypothesising on the subject of spiritual beings to remind ourselves that there is nothing which possesses absolute density. Our bodies, like all matter, are whirling complexes of atoms held together by energy into forms which make us visible and identifiable. When, however, the density of any matter is greatly reduced it becomes invisible to us.

We can, therefore, postulate spiritual entities (some good and some evil in nature) whose 'density' is so refined (to the degree of infinity?) or of such a peculiar character that our sense perceptions cannot comprehend them. The only means by which we could 'know' them would be those which transcend the five senses, namely, the extra-sensory perceptions of our spirit-soul.

Most likely, I believe, spiritual entities are all around us. Though in the ordinary course of our lives we cannot be 'aware' of them they can, *if they will*, make themselves known to us. This could be the case when, for some reason or other, our minds are deeply preoccupied. Then they can alert our attention at the level of our partially liberated spirit-soul. Perhaps also, by utilising energy, they can change their 'density' and so make us become, albeit dimly, aware of their presence through our natural senses. Maybe that energy is taken from ourselves, which would account for the lowering in body temperature which always seems to accompany manifestations of spiritual entities.

In this matter of our realising the presence of the angels the initiative lies always *with them* as superior beings. If we have completely rejected the possibility of their existence they will not force themselves upon the citadel of our souls. Such a course would be alien because for them the will (which is a purely spiritual faculty), be it that of a human being or of another angel, must remain inviolate.

Jesus Christ was, I believe, one of these pre-existent angelic beings. Out of compassion for us who are His 'brother' angels (albeit 'fallen') He chose to experience our life on this planet. That life of His was a fully human one in as much as He knew to the uttermost the testing and limitation of the properties of this physical world including birth and death. But throughout it

He remained entirely 'sinless' by reason of His origin and because of His perfect obedience to the Will of the Creator. His purpose in dwelling on earth was to inform us of our own potentiality as beings who could be restored to 'angelhood'.

This change in our status He achieved by experiencing that principle of sin in the world and in our nature which ever besets and spoils us. By completely overcoming it on earth He offered us the way of deliverance from its power. That way means accepting *by faith in Him* what He had done in breaking its grip upon humanity. Further, we must lovingly acknowledge His spiritual direction, as manifested in His life and teaching, in all things. Thus we would receive the assistance of His victorious and eternal Spirit and, after death, be raised up to the glory of His own angelic nature through the power of His Resurrection.

We can ask with hope in our hearts and with a sense of high adventure ahead whether our extra-sensory powers, beginning with faith, will provide the means which will move humanity away from self-destruction onto a higher and happier path. May not prayer, better understood, bring us such wonderful communication with the resources of the spiritual realm that man will then go forward into a wonderful new age? Will faith in Christ prove the only way for such mastery of the body-soul as will transform the present nature of man and so make of him 'true' (i.e. perfect) man — able to control matter, always and only, for good?

There is nothing we ourselves can do to win (or to deserve) participation in the 'new' creation which Christ has begun. Only by the exercise of our faith in Him, in what He has done and in the validity of His teaching, can we be heirs with Him of that realm where He reigns. There sin can inhibit us no more, and life is eternal, boundless, perfect and free.

When the state of trance frees our spirit-soul from our body-soul we act as pure spirit. Our extra-sensory perceptions function more efficiently making known to us that which is otherwise hidden from us by the restriction of the five senses. We are ourselves then approaching the level of the life of the angels who are uninhibited by the binding laws of matter. In this condition we can conceive that our communion with them would be enhanced and their influence upon us much increased. Because of this basic spirituality which we have in common with the angels it seems likely that after death some human souls may not only join the company of the angels but actually become as they are and hence perform their type of activity in the realm of spirit including the rôle of guardian angels ministering to us on earth.

That man once possessed near angelic faculties (that is, those which are not circumscribed by physical conditions) in greater measure than he normally exhibits today is suggested by something that a fellow clergyman, whom my wife and I met during a working holiday, told us.

He had worked as a missionary in the educational sphere and explained that members of a tribe among whom he had lived for many years could communicate instantly across great distances with the inhabitants of other villages, telepathically and clairvoyantly. However, with the growing encroachment of the white man into their region these people gradually lost their highly developed psychic gifts.

Sometime after the last world war he returned to this region and spoke to one of their chiefs about this, and asked the cause of their diminished powers. He was told that when it was seen how superior the white man was with his technical marvels of radio, motor cars, aircraft and medicine, the tribe had realised how insignificant its own achievements were. In a vivid phrase they explained that, on recognising this, "their spirit left them".

This lends support to the belief that early man was indeed but a little lower than the angels in the sense that he was endowed like them with the ability to communicate without spoken language simply by thought transference — one person's spirit-soul immediately making itself known to another's spirit-soul *at will*.

Man's increasing sophistication and his over concentrated concern for the cultivation and enrichment of his material existence has weakened his psychic powers. But, however vestigial, they still remain as faculties of his spirit-soul and provide him with extra-sensory perception. They can be revived and developed by a manner of life which is spiritually orientated and where the claims of the body-soul are strictly controlled. If we are governed by Christian belief these spirit-soul faculties of ours can bring a great and far-reaching good. Herein lies the tremendous power of true prayer which activates the spirit-soul and, in turn, influences the body-soul to produce harmony in the whole personality.

Thus as the Psalmist described shall we truly become but "a little lower than the angels".

17

THE ASCENSION OF
JESUS CHRIST

We know that all created things whether animate or inanimate are composed of the material elements of this earth. All are made of the same stuff! But the forms this matter takes differ in a fascinating multitude of ways — all due to the creative energy of God Who works upon matter to produce that variety.

Though we realise there is a creative force at work upon us as it were from *outside*, we also realise that this same force is active *within* us.

Thus, while that creativity of God is ever fashioning us from our conception to the end of our years by transforming our physical bodies through cellular changes, at the same time that creative power is at work upon our spiritual growth by means of the continuing and great range of choices presented to us and the decisions we make regarding them.

Having this influence upon our personality we recognise that this creative power (God) has the quality of a Person also. The unique Person of Jesus Christ reveals the Person of God.

When we say God created man in His own image we mean that in every individual His Spirit dwells. For we are not created and then left bereft of God's constant concern. He is ever desiring to manifest something of Himself through and in us. We are, as it were, sparks owing our individual finite light to Him Who is the full and infinite light. Hence the true purpose of life is to allow our immortal souls to reflect the Will of God.

We have to accept that our souls were created to work through the levels of body-soul and spirit-soul. This is why the Christian

233

believes that his immortal soul must continue to indwell a body after death — not indeed a body of this world's matter but one transcending matter which will be the perfect vehicle for its consummation and felicity. By the exercise of faith the believer enters into a mystical relationship with Jesus. It is a communion so intimate and interpenetrating that it is described as Christ living in him and he in Christ.

Thereby the believer enters into the perfected humanity of Jesus and becomes heir to the victory which his Lord has won over all that inhibits or destroys a human being's potential i.e. sin and death.

St Luke (in his Gospel and in his Acts of the Apostles) describes the last appearance on earth of Christ's Resurrection Body and then says he ascended into heaven. Concerning the precise nature of that final disappearance there is no need to get involved in here. Suffice it that quite clearly Luke psychically received in the Lord's Ascension an amazing insight. Namely, that Christ had taken His perfect humanity into the purely spiritual realm.

Those who shared in witnessing the Ascension became convinced that in an extraordinary fiat God was thus declaring that although hitherto the humanity of Jesus (albeit uniquely sinless) was like their own, limited by matter, space and time, yet now all those limiting factors were ended for Him. His perfect life of communion with God could be recognised as Divine and His divinity seen as humanity raised to the n'th degree.

This meant that believers were also let in on this wondrous transformation of the material and all that matter makes of the human condition. Their own humanity will in due course be taken up into the purely spiritual realm. Thus they were assured their souls will pass through death into that realm not as shades or ghosts but to exist in a new kind of glorified body like unto their Master's. This amazing delight would come about because of their faith attachment to Jesus Who had inaugurated this new state for human souls.

The lesson of the Ascension is that Jesus was no longer confined to that extraordinary transmutation of His physical body called His Resurrection Body which could still only be known at one time and at one place, but henceforth His Spirit or Influence could be known everywhere and for all time in the hearts of believers.

That fact was ratified in the experience of Pentecost when, assembled in the Upper Room, His first disciples were empowered by His

Spirit (or Holy Spirit of God) in an unforgettable and dramatic psychic manifestation. The result of that experience was to fire them with unconquerable enthusiasm to make the Lord Jesus known to whom, and wherever, they could. So the Church as the community of first believers moved forward with missionary zeal to work for a brotherhood which in time would encompass the world with the glory of faith in Jesus Christ.

18

THE GREAT COMMANDMENT

Goodness, Truth and Beauty are often quoted among the attributes of God. They reach their highest in us, therefore, when we heartily desire His Holy Spirit.

In St John's Gospel Jesus declares that He is the Way, the Truth and the Life. This means that by allowing Christ's Spirit to control our own spirit we will acquire clear insight into what constitutes goodness, truth and beauty in our lives.

The theme is developed further in the same Gospel for Jesus says that He and the Father are one, meaning that a complete unity of will pertains between them. Therefore those who 'see' Jesus (i.e. recognise Christ's unique relationship with God as Son to the Father and thereby revealing God's relationship to them) come to the knowledge of God.

But *how* do we know God?

We do so through the variety of experiences in our lives wherein our souls receive their highest joys — and, if seen aright, these can mean within pain as well as pleasure.

We give high place, therefore, to the whole range of the interactions of human love as portrayed in family life and friendships and wherever our contact with others produces a sense of gratitude and compassion. Nor would we limit the field to those alone, for we realise the debt we owe to all which in ages past and present has contributed to the world's vast and ever increasing treasure house of goodness, truth and beauty as exampled in human lives and in the arts which adorn and inspire life for us. Amazingly, sorrows and frustrations and testings of every kind as well as the manifold joys and satisfactions of life can be accepted gracefully as blessings upon us in the complex, mysterious working of God. This is so because the Son of God accepted in Himself all the facts of suffering, of human ill-will, and the limitations and frustrations associated with the physical body. He did so with entire trust in God's complete understanding and sharing of them. That trust was vindicated, after the apparent defeat of His goodness by the forces of evil on the Cross, in the victory of His glorious Resurrection accorded Him by God.

Christ revealed that God relates to us in eternal love and said that we should in turn love God with all our heart, mind and strength.

But *how* can we fulfil that great commandment?

Jesus supplies the answer by declaring that we can only love God if we are prepared to love our neighbours as though they were ourselves.

To do so demands a serious and sustained effort of the will until it becomes a veritable part of our nature, for Christian loving is concerned chiefly with the state of the will rather than of the affections.

We can discern from the teaching of Jesus four principles we must adopt if we are to fulfil the command of love.

(1) We must think about others in a truly positive way — never a negative one. We should see them and ourselves as on a pilgrimage together through this world, all of us having the potential to move onward to our fulfilment in God's purpose. (Incidentally this *positive* way of viewing everyone as a beloved child of God even as ourselves highlights the importance of 'seeing' a sick person as 'well' when we pray for them).

(2) We must endeavour to put aside our instinctive attitude of regarding folk as either those who are useful to us or (as far as we can see) those who are not. It means thinking of *every* individual as one who is just as beloved of God as we are. His Holy Spirit is in all human souls and that truth we must duly reverence. In other words we are to strive to be like our Heavenly Father in our manner of impartially loving, even as we see this perfectly mirrored in the life and teaching of His Unique Son, Jesus of Nazareth.

(3) We must be on our guard about the kind of mental picture we form of another person. Whenever we allow that image to become sour, to deteriorate through unreconciled bitterness or disagreement, we must seek to cleanse and restore it to former harmony by every means we can and by earnestly desiring that person's good — and only his good.

(4) In the Sermon on the Mount Jesus likened our actions and attitudes to light and salt.

Light has no real significance unless it grants us not only the ability to see but to do so clearly. Salt preserves and also draws out flavour but can perform neither of these functions when it has become stale.

In other words light and salt have the capacity to endow things with their best aspects and qualities.

So when Jesus bade us to be as light and salt He meant our lives should lift from the world, as opportunity gives us to do, any darkness or evil. This we achieve by untiring compassionate regard for others and by our unselfishness.

It is through such loving we become endued with that quality of life which Jesus called eternal life.

Thus we are assured that, even here and now, eternal life is abiding in us. Then becomes clear St Paul's own conviction that *already* we have passed out of death (i.e. out of the self-centred and therefore decaying life) into the life eternal.